THE

FEMINIST

and

THE COWBOY

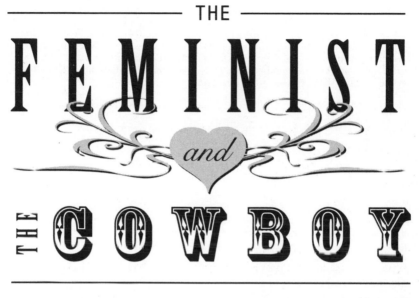

THE FEMINIST *and* THE COWBOY

AN UNLIKELY LOVE STORY

Alisa Valdes

Gotham Books

GOTHAM BOOKS
Published by the Penguin Group
Penguin Group (USA) Inc., 375 Hudson Street, New York, New York 10014, USA; Penguin Group (Canada), 90 Eglinton Avenue East, Suite 700, Toronto, Ontario M4P 2Y3, Canada (a division of Pearson Penguin Canada Inc.); Penguin Books Ltd, 80 Strand, London WC2R 0RL, England; Penguin Ireland, 25 St Stephen's Green, Dublin 2, Ireland (a division of Penguin Books Ltd); Penguin Group (Australia), 707 Collins Street, Melbourne, Victoria 3008, Australia (a division of Pearson Australia Group Pty Ltd); Penguin Books India Pvt Ltd, 11 Community Centre, Panchsheel Park, New Delhi–110 017, India; Penguin Group (NZ), 67 Apollo Drive, Rosedale, Auckland 0632, New Zealand (a division of Pearson New Zealand Ltd); Penguin Books, Rosebank Office Park, 181 Jan Smuts Avenue, Parktown North 2193, South Africa; Penguin China, B7 Jaiming Center, 27 East Third Ring Road North, Chaoyang District, Beijing 100020, China

Penguin Books Ltd, Registered Offices: 80 Strand, London WC2R 0RL, England

Published by Gotham Books, a member of Penguin Group (USA) Inc.

First printing, January 2013
10 9 8 7 6 5 4 3 2 1

LIBRARY OF CONGRESS CATALOGING-IN-PUBLICATION DATA
Valdes, Alisa.
    The feminist and the cowboy : an unlikely love story / by Alisa Valdes.
        p. cm.
    ISBN 978-1-592-40790-3 (hardcover)
    1. Valdes, Alisa. 2. Women novelists, American—Biography. I. Title.
    PS3622.A425Z46 2013
    813'.6—dc23
    [B]
                                    2012017538

Printed in the United States of America
Set in Janson Text
Designed by Spring Hoteling

While the author has made every effort to provide accurate telephone numbers, Internet addresses, and other contact information at the time of publication, neither the publisher nor the author assumes any responsibility for errors, or for changes that occur after publication. Further, publisher does not have any control over and does not assume any responsibility for author or third-party websites or their content.

Penguin is committed to publishing works of quality and integrity.
In that spirit, we are proud to offer this book to our readers;
however, the story, the experiences, and the words
are the author's alone.

ALWAYS LEARNING   PEARSON

THE

FEMINIST

and

COWBOY

A COWBOY REACHES OUT

The story of my awakening begins as so many do, with a disagree-ment. A conservative rural cowboy wanted to meet me. He thought he might be exactly what I needed. I, a progressive feminist from the city, disagreed, as vehemently as my bleeding heart allowed.

It was 2010. I was forty-one years old and a single mom to a preteen boy. I was a (recovering) journalist and reformed Ivy Leaguer, happily making a living as a writer of commercial fiction, but with no personal life to speak of unless you counted fantasizing about which of the Jonas Brothers might be the best lover, which was not only creepy but probably also illegal in most states. I worked from home, often in my (stained) pajamas, which I didn't wash often enough because, frankly, who would care if I had coffee dribbled down the front of my shirt? I didn't meet many new people, and my social sphere was limited to extended family, female friends, and the women who showed up at my book signings, more than a few of them armed with glitter pens.

I mention all of this to somewhat lessen the blow to my ego of admitting that I, hoping to meet a real-live man-person, had joined an online dating site. Okay? I admit it. Let's move on.

I had been divorced for five years by then, with no noteworthy relationships in the interim. I'd learned to live single but wasn't sure I wanted to do so forever. I had actually liked being married as a concept; I just hadn't liked, you know, my husband. I was starting to secretly fantasize about unspeakable sins of domestic bliss once again—cooking for someone who might like wild-caught salmon better than SpongeBob-shaped macaroni, for example, or one day sharing a bed with something other than . . . well, let's just say something that wasn't battery operated.

Thusly inspired, I signed up for the site. I filled out my profile, checking all the appropriate boxes that I hoped would draw a like-minded man to me. You know, a politically progressive man. A man who lived in the city and recycled. A professional man who might have nice ties and belong to an expensive gym, or, better yet, ride a recumbent bike to his job at, say, the university, where he'd know history or art or be working on a vaccine. A man with a flurry of liberal bumper stickers on his Subaru, perhaps. A man who might read *The New York Times* on Sunday mornings and comment intelligently through his stylish eyeglasses about things like gender bias in the news media's word choices. Swoon! Oh! Or a man who could follow me if I spoke of Kant or Hegel—or their cheery combination, Kegels. A man who would not be threatened by me, my success, or my mind. In short, I wanted a guy who belonged to a food co-op yet understood snark and appreciated sushi. I was quite specific in letting everyone know that Larry David's HBO series *Curb Your Enthusiasm* was my dating litmus test. If a guy understood that Larry wasn't actually a jerk, then we were golden. If a guy thought Larry was rude and obnoxious, I advised him to keep moving and alight upon some more humorless sap than me. Yes, sir. I wanted a cynical, funny, sarcastic, educated, hip, insightful guy, and I wasn't about to settle for anything less. I wanted Larry David, truth be told. Well, maybe a slightly better-looking Larry David. A less reedy Larry David. With more biceps, and fewer corduroy pants, and better sweaters—or, God willing, no sweaters at all.

I went on many first dates, with men who met all my criteria. They were, every single one of them, smart, educated, well-to-do, decent looking, and moderately interesting. And, of course, liberal. Had to be liberal. Progressive, feminist men—latter-day Alan Aldas for whom I could also open doors, men who could cry into their tapas and sangria if they needed to, just as I'd been raised by my parents and community to seek. Yet they all, to a man, bored me, scared me, or just did nothing for me below the waist (in spite of my exuberant Kegels), and I was not generally interested in a second date. Forget a third. Perhaps, I began to think, that part of me that existed below the waist had simply up and died from the misuse and neglect that is a bad marriage.

Let me pull back the curtain on my online dating memories and show you what I mean. Indulge me as I list the ways in which I was disappointed.

There was the mechanical engineer who resented his ex-wife out loud every five minutes or so and who whipped out a calculator at the end of our first date to make sure we paid exactly half each, to the stinkin' penny. He had white crust in the corners of his mouth and did not drink water. At all.

There was the Green Party environmental biologist who admitted early on to having snorted coke and cheated on his frigid veterinarian wife with a pliant and flexible stripper on a trip to Miami "with the boys."

There was the programmer who talked nonstop about how much he'd enjoyed decorating his house, sewing, and playing dolls with his daughter. I suspected one day he'd open the closet and find himself standing there in a George Michael sweatshirt and leg warmers, and I wasn't about to court that brand of disappointment.

There was the revolutionary graduate student who dressed and shaved (or didn't, I guess) like Che Guevara but still believed in "free love" and did not seem to believe in shampoo.

There was the engineer who'd nobly outfitted his Volkswagen to run on French fry drippings but who told me I could never compare to his drug-addicted ex-wife because she was rail thin.

There was the well-known blogger for the Democratic Party who tweeted about women's rights but was addicted to hard-core pornography and wanted nothing more than to spray his man-juice on a woman's face as she knelt before him in a suit.

There was even, once, the state government official (a Democrat) whom I was going to meet for coffee but decided against after he began to call me every half hour to ask my voice mail why I hadn't returned his twenty-seven other calls yet. "You better not have met anyone else," he threatened, before having met me at all. After I played his messages for my friends Esther, Kristy, and Bonnie, we agreed I would have to be half-stupid to meet that guy. Oh, how right we were. This man ended up on the front page of the paper a couple of months later for shooting his two sons dead before turning the gun on himself, all to spite his ex-wife. He now resides in hell.

There was, in short, an endless parade of icky "liberal" men, each icky in his own unique and decidedly hypocritical or terrifying way. I became the queen of the first date, so picky that even my own mother, who had groomed me to be independent and need no man, took me aside and suggested that I wasn't giving any of these men a chance and might therefore end up alone forever. I was cool with that. Well, not really. But it was what it was, because they were what they were. I pretty much gave up.

Then, one day, a different sort of message came to me through the site.

"I'm not quite what you're looking for," it said, "but I was impressed by your profile and wanted to let you know how interesting I think you are." He told me that he was a ranch manager on a ten-thousand-acre ranch in southern New Mexico and that he liked my

profile, my eyes, and my sense of humor. Out of curiosity and bore-
dom, I clicked on the profile of the man who'd sent it.

Indeed, he was exactly not what I was looking for. At all. He
was "conservative," for one. That was an instant deal breaker for
me. I couldn't imagine for the life of me ever sitting across a dinner
table from a conservative, much less doing so for, like, all eternity.
I could not fathom in any way, shape, or form ever bringing a conservative man home to meet my extremely liberal parents, much
less a yee-haw cowboy from the middle of no-freakin'-where.
They'd disown me, surely. To top that off, he was eleven years
older than I was. I'd almost always dated men my own age or significantly younger than I was (though not quite as young as the
Jonas Brothers, don't worry). Never older. And now that I was in
my forties, older than me meant . . . what? Viagra prescriptions?
Prostate problems? God knew I had enough problems all by myself. The last thing I needed was someone I'd have to push around
in a wheelchair—much less someone raised before the women's
movement. In a cowboy hat.

I almost closed the profile and ignored the email altogether,
except that this man was uncommonly good-looking, in a manlier,
hotter Kevin Costner sort of way. I am ashamed to admit this, but
the truth is, I am a shallow animal at times, and this man's unusual hotness held my attention longer than it probably should
have. In short, he was stunning. Evolution kicked in, and mama
said meow.

He was quite masculine, in the way I'd been conditioned to
mock (even as it scrambled my belly with butterfly jelly). He had a
cleft chin, strong jaw, and powerful neck. He had full, well-formed
lips and sparkly blue eyes. He looked cocky, confident, and hot in a
bad-boy way that I could never admit to any self-respecting intellectual I knew actually . . . excited me. His photos were so attractive,
in fact, that I wondered for a moment if it were a hoax. Perhaps, I
thought, our next email exchange would involve a cable from Nige-

ria, promising me a grand inheritance and a bigger penis. Oh, the possibilities.

I read his email again, more closely. He told me that he lived near a town that, I discovered when I Googled it, was almost five hours away by car from my city of Albuquerque. Another deal breaker. I wasn't about to go driving around the state for some guy. Even a guy who looked like that. I was busy. Didn't he realize that I had a life of my own? Perhaps Mr. Conservative Pants missed the memo, the one that said women didn't need men; we chose them only if we wanted them and if they were easy to deal with and put our needs on par with their own. If there was going to be a guy at all, he was going to have to be convenient, because I had been raised to believe that a woman sacrificing for a man was the equivalent of Kryptonite for the Woman's Soul—which, last time I checked, was not nearly as successful a book series as the Chicken Soup one. The nerve of some men, to think you might be bothered to travel for them, especially when they did not meet any of your requested qualifications. *Forget this dude*, I thought. *Damn.*

And then my eye got caught on his dimples. Again. And my gaze became stuck on the cock of his brow. And I got a bit of a tingle from the way his mouth rose halfway in a grin that any woman in her right mind would want to taste. And something visceral and ancient deep inside my lower belly just sort of sat up and started to wag her tail.

I decided to read what he'd written in his profile.

He wrote well, this man. And he was clever. He even seemed to be honest when he described himself as "challenging." You'd be surprised how rare these qualities are on dating sites, where most men type in ALL CAPS when they're not posing shirtless in the low-rent bathroom for the smudgy camera phones at the end of their outstretched arms, and promising they are "LAYD BAK." Most men on dating sites don't know the difference between *your* and *you're* either, and I had begun, in fact, to wonder if that particular ignorance was a requirement of signing up for such things.

This distant older conservative cowboy was chock-full of grammatically intact wiseassery. It made no sense. There weren't any smart conservatives, right? Everyone I'd ever gone to Columbia University with or worked with in newspapers back east knew the hard-and-fast rule: Conservatives were stupid! Or evil! There was no other kind. Period.

I came to my senses. This type of man could never make a woman like me happy, and I knew it. I wrote back, a quick note to say that while I was flattered he'd reached out, and while his pictures were (cough) very pleasant to behold, I felt that our political and geographical differences would be too difficult to overcome. I thanked him and wished him luck. He accepted what I said but gave me his personal email and said that if I changed my mind or wanted to talk he would be happy to get to know me. This impressed me, and we wrote back and forth a couple of times. Then I got busy and, being spacey and not terribly interested in him, forgot about him.

We lost touch.

On I went with my search.

There was the soft and squishy computer guy who couldn't quite admit he was fat in spite of having lost his chin somewhere among the detritus of fast-food bags that littered his car and who liked comic books too much for a grown man. Next!

There was the Princeton-educated, prizewinning architect who crossed his legs and flopped his wrists with the gayest of glee and who, I discovered when he picked me up for a date, had a court-ordered Breathalyzer installed in his car because of a drunk-driving arrest. Next!

There was the touchy-feely psychologist guy, a therapist who, after a few beers on our first (and last) date, admitted to having gone into his field to try to figure out why he personally hated women so much, even though he really liked to have sex with them, especially when they gave him blow jobs, and what the hell, he figured men would probably give good blow jobs too, and he might want to try that one of these days. He wanted me to know he really liked blow jobs but couldn't respect any woman who'd actually give him one. And, by the way, would I blow him? Next!

On it went. A parade of highly accomplished, talented, intelligent, progressive, freakin' weird, metrosexual . . . losers.

I began to give up again.

I invested in batteries.

I took up knitting because that's what cat ladies do when the batteries run out.

Several months later, I got another email from the same conservative guy on the ranch. The guy I'd blown off once already. He wanted to let me know that his membership on the site was about to expire, and he wanted to reach out one last time to say I was someone he'd like to know, even if we weren't romantically involved. "I just once again wanted to tell you that I find you very impressive," he wrote. I responded by saying I wondered where he'd gone, even though, as he reminded me, it was I who had disappeared. We exchanged a couple of emails, and then he told me he was coming up to my city to meet a couple of guy friends for a weekend of golf. He suggested we have lunch the Friday of that weekend.

Figuring he couldn't possibly be any worse than the bearded, tree-hugging forest ranger whose poetry rhymed and who'd shown up two hours late for a dinner party at my house stoned and in cycling shorts, I agreed. It was just lunch, right?

"Good girl," he wrote back.

He might as well have patted me on the head and given me a dog biscuit. His patronizing attitude offended me, because, you know, it was supposed to. After all, my first foray into the world of published writing was when I, at twenty-two, was included in an anthology of essays edited by Barbara Findlen, then the editor of *Ms.* magazine. The book was called *Listen Up: Voices from the Next Feminist Generation,* and featured some of the top feminist writers under thirty years of age in the United States. Robin Morgan blurbed us. Gloria Steinem attended our book launch. I sat next to Alice Walker's daughter, Rebecca. See, I wasn't just an armchair feminist; I was one of the demanding ones, combating injustice and inequality on the front lines. The feminist mantra about no woman being a girl after puberty chimed in: I was no girl, damn it. I was, as Sinéad sang, "no man's woman," or, as Helen sang, "woman, hear me roar," yadda yadda yadda. Amen, and pass the tofurkey.

"Where would you like to meet?" he asked me on the phone. "Since you know the town better."

"Meet me at Kelley's," I ordered.

"What's Kelley's?" he asked, in a smooth, deep voice with a sexy Western accent I couldn't quite place. "Remember, darlin', I'm not from the city."

"Yes, how could I forget," I deadpanned, certain already that he would turn out to be a narcissist.

He chuckled a little and said nothing.

"It's a deco kind of indie brew pub in Nob Hill," I said. "Used to be a gas station. Route 66, Central Avenue. Very hip joint now."

"Bet it's by the university," he said with bemusement.

"Yeah."

"Great," came the sarcastic reply.

"Something wrong?" I asked, annoyed with his apparent distaste for my beloved neighborhood.

He took a deep breath before answering, all cockiness. "Let me warn you, darlin', I'm probably going to show up in a real pickup truck, not the little scoot-arounds you find in Albuquerque, and I'll probably be the only guy in a cowboy hat and Wranglers."

"Yeah. Well, this is the same neighborhood where they have giant leather teddy bears with clitoral piercings on display in the tattoo parlor windows. Pretty sure I can handle whatever costume you decide to wear."

He paused before answering, and then did so coolly. "You strike me as a woman who might be able to handle lots of things." I could almost hear his eyebrow arching up naughtily.

"We done?" I asked, growing more offended by this wannabe

John Wayne by the second. I'd never been very comfortable with flirting, as it made me feel too, I don't know, vulnerable or something. Girly. God forbid.

He chuckled again, totally nonthreatened and unfazed by my show of hostility. Indeed, he seemed challenged by it.

"Wow," he said brightly. "I knew I'd like you. Just somethin' about you." He paused. "Yeah, I suppose we're done, for now. See you soon, dear."

I hung up and fumed. Dear? Who did he think he was, calling me darlin' and dear? Didn't he know who I was? How many prizes I'd won because of my brain? The movie deals I had? You didn't get things like that by being any man's dear or darling! Who the hell was he to call me things like that? How patronizing!

I looked around my room and sighed. It was quite likely I'd just agreed to another first-and-last date with a random jerk I'd met online. And a conservative one at that. Who called me darlin'. Which, truth be told (and only to myself!), I kind of liked.

Wait. What?

I knew better. I should have hated being called dear. And yet, what was this strange, warm, electric feeling in my belly? Something I hadn't felt in, what?

Decades.

Maybe ever.

Suddenly, I understood.

To my abject horror, I understood.

With just a few well-chosen, well-placed, confident words, with a handful of amused chuffs at my expense, the cowboy—this conservative caveman—had succeeded, against my better judgment and rational mind, in doing something no other man in recent history had managed to do to me, even in person.

He'd turned me on.

THE FIRST DATE

There was a gay pride thing going on at Kelley's Brew Pub the day I met the cowboy for our first date. This was not unusual, of course. At Kelley's, it's either wannabe weekend badass bikers who are actually lawyers (and by *badass* I mean literally a bad ass, all flat and wide from hours in the office), or flamboyant gayboys channeling Mommie Dearest. Sometimes, if you were lucky, it was both all wrapped up in one stellar human being who has downed one too many pale ales and decided to sing something by Depeche Mode for all the world to enjoy, much in the same way you might enjoy being hit on the head with a tub of marbles. I'm not sure why I picked the place, except to say that they have a killer quinoa salad and, barring any other pleasant thing that might come to pass that day, at least I was assured a good and guiltless meal.

Kelley's is in the heart of the Nob Hill district in Albuquerque, a deco college and hipster hangout that makes its own (very good) beer. Until I met the cowboy, it was also just the most natural sort of place to suggest for a first-date lunch. Then again, until the cowboy I'd only dated people just like me—well, that is to say "like me" if I were a psycho-killer porn addict. Whose poetry rhymed. Anyway.

I arrived at Kelley's a little before the cowboy did, and parked by the curb in front of the restaurant. I should tell you here that I owned at the time a gold Hyundai Elantra with an anti–Fox News bumper sticker on the back. It was a car that did not draw much attention in that neighborhood, fitting in there the way Lady Gaga might fit in at a drag queen convention. I put a few coins in the meter and then stood there in the sun waiting nervously. I tuned my ear to an internal dialogue that went something like this: *What are you, stupid? Yes, why do you ask? Shut up and let me do the questioning here. Fine, bitch. That's better. Now, why would you actually agree to meet someone like this? He's bound to annoy you. You're probably going to storm out in the middle of the meal like you did with that one loser who got all up in your face about how "illegals" shouldn't be allowed to go to school. Yeah, I hated that bigot. Well, so why are you agreeing to meet another one just like him? I don't know. Bored? You know better. Are you really this desperate? Of course I am. You've seen our battery bill.*

And so on.

The cowboy called to say he was close but couldn't find parking. I texted to say I was standing on the sidewalk and that there was a spot next to Kelley's, at the Korean barbecue place. He asked if it was large enough to accommodate his pickup.

Dude, this is Albuquerque, not Manhattan. You're not the only guy compensating for something with a big truck, I thought unkindly.

Then there he was, roaring up to the curb behind my car in a black Ford F-250 with a diesel engine only slightly less noisy than a fighter jet. It stood out in a town where pickups were common but nowhere near as utilitarian. Heads turned to see what all the ruckus was. The pickup, it turned out, fit in like Lady Gaga at a Daughters of the American Revolution convention.

I pursed my lips, disliking him already, and realized just how far I'd fallen to have to meet him.

"Nice shoes, Miz Valdes," he purred into the phone, ignoring my snide attitude. "Be right there."

I wore a black skirt from Banana Republic, with a black long-sleeve T-shirt and red strappy heels. I had made an effort to look my best because, one assumes, hope springs eternal, especially in the pathetic but not yet entirely jaded dating-after-forty crowd. I tried to see his face in the pickup, but he wore a black cowboy hat and dark glasses. All I could see was his jaw. And Holy Mother of God, what a freakin' jaw. Wow. Strong, square, chiseled. The perfect stage for his perfectly cleft chin.

As he unfolded himself from the pickup, I gaped at all six foot two of him, six-four with the added height from his ranchman's footwear. He was quite fit, wore dark, tight jeans with cowboy boots, a crisp white shirt with a black vest, and the hat, and was by far the handsomest man I had ever seen in person—or anywhere, really. There was no movie star, even, who could compare. No model. Nothing. He was exquisite. So handsome it made you ache. So handsome you forgot to breathe. I gulped and sucked in my gut, hoping I'd measure up somehow. I mean, I knew he was ideologically my opposite and lived far away, etcetera, but in that moment I just sort of forgot all that and felt for a moment something like a girl on a date with a very pretty boy. A boy all out of my league.

"Hello, Miz Valdes," he said with a smile, walking up to me and extending his hand. I shook it. What a hand. It was large, rough, tanned, and strong—nothing like the squishy computer-keyboarding hamster hands of the men I usually dated.

"Any trouble finding the place?" I asked him, trying to sound like the kind of woman who met conservative cowboys every day and didn't much care one way or the other for rock-hard monumental handsomeness.

"Nope. I'm pretty good at finding things I want." He peeked up over the tops of the dark glasses and gave me a teasing, significant look, clearly meaning me. He'd wanted to find me. My belly fluttered a bit, but I stopped it by remembering that guys like this were smooth because they generally cared about only one thing—sex. Okay, two things: sex and, like, Fox News.

He gestured with one hand for me to walk toward the door of the restaurant, taking charge of the situation. He quickly positioned himself on the curb side of the street. I found this display of caretaking awkward and controlling, of course. The men I'd dated never did such things; usually, they waited for me to tell them what to do and how to do it, and then simmered for years in unspoken emasculated resentment because of it. I laughed about the cowboy's chivalry, and he ignored me. I was far too egalitarian-minded to find anything remotely charming about his gentlemanly behavior, except that, truth be told (and only to myself, naturally), I actually sort of really, um, liked it.

Wait. What?

As we walked across the outdoor patio I noticed the group of young and decidedly flamboyant gay men at one of the tables. I wondered how the cowboy would react to them. I snuck a look at him as he removed his dark glasses to reveal the most beautiful blue eyes I had ever seen. I thought I saw that he'd registered the gayboys in his peripheral vision and I was surprised that he not only seemed unfazed, he didn't really care.

They, however, had abso-posilutely noticed *him*.

They stared, openmouthed, because he looked like he'd just stepped out of a Ralph Lauren advertisement. He had movie-star looks and charisma, a sort of importance just radiating out from him in every direction like the rays of the sun, and they wanted him. Why wouldn't they? He was perfect looking. But that, I reminded myself, didn't mean much if he was morally disgusting, as I was absolutely convinced most, if not all, conservatives were. *Do not*, I told myself, *fall for the illusion that just because this man is handsome, confident, gentlemanly, and possibly intelligent he might be a good match for you.*

He walked after me now, toward the hostess podium, and stood protectively behind me when we got there. I felt him close, big, and powerful. It bothered me, just as the thin, pretty young hostesses with their perfect blond hair and perky boobs bothered me. How could I compete with them? Would he find them attractive? Would he, like my ex-husband, stare with wolfish hunger at other women in my presence and then deny it if I complained?

"Hi," said one of the hostesses, her cleavage lifted just a bit higher at the sight of him. *Bitch.*

"Hello," he said warmly, all Westerny and cowboy. "Table for two, please."

I watched in dismay as the hostess fumbled for menus, distracted by his comely face. I looked to see if he noticed; it seemed that he did but that he was both used to being ogled and also no longer interested in it, if ever he had been. Odd. Most people craved his sort of looks and the attention they might bring, but this man seemed dissociated from all that. He also seemed to figure out pretty quickly that I was looking to see if he noticed that the girl noticed him, and he set me at ease by pretending not to. All of this information was passed back and forth between us in nothing but body language, in mere seconds. It conveyed to me an emotional intelligence and almost unfathomably quick and observant mind in him.

"Right this way," said the hostess.

The cowboy waited for me to walk ahead of him, and followed close behind.

"Is this okay?" the hostess asked of a booth near the windows. The cowboy looked to me questioningly. I nodded approval.

"Perfect," he told the hostess.

He stood back, waiting for me to take my seat. Then he lowered himself into the booth, wincing just a bit as his knees bent.

"You okay?" I asked, pleased to see weakness—and proof that he wasn't perfect.

He smirked. "You make choices in life, dear, and you live with the consequences."

"What do you mean?"

"Oh, you know." He removed his hat now, ran his fingers through his salt-and-pepper hair to get rid of the indentations. "You play football in high school and college, let your coaches tell you to take steroids, you destroy your knees, it's something you have to live with."

"Steroids?"

"We didn't know better back then, darlin'. This was a different time and place. You did what your coach told you to do, no questions asked."

"That's terrible," I said, instantly noticing that my sympathy and judgment inspired annoyance in him, rather than the usual liberal nods of agreement when power is abused and underlings injured as a result.

"It's not *terrible*," he said with irritation. "Jesus. It was my *choice*. No one to blame but myself." He narrowed his eyes, as though measuring me with his gaze, and then grinned and said, "That's the problem with liberals. You all think everything is someone else's fault or responsibility. No accountability, just a sense of entitlement."

I blinked at him and held my face in check. Great. We were fighting already. I wasn't surprised. My adrenaline surged, but I decided not to give this caveman the pleasure of debating something about which he was so clearly in the wrong.

"So," I said, looking at my menu so that I wouldn't look at him anymore. I didn't want to take his bait. I wasn't here to argue.

"So," he echoed, slipping a friendly glance at me, letting me know he'd been teasing, a little. "What's good here?"

"I like the quinoa salad," I told him.

"The *what*, now?"

I spoke slowly. "Quinoa. Salad."

He laughed as though this were monumentally amusing. "Of course you do."

"What is that supposed to mean?" I asked, defensively, before inadvertently quoting the back of a box of something-or-other I'd once purchased at Whole Foods. "It's an ancient grain, with tons of protein, very good for you."

"Think they might have a steak or somethin' crazy like that around here?" he asked in a teasing sort of way that I knew was both serious but also designed to annoy me. I realized he knew what quinoa was and had just been playing the ignorant yahoo because that's what I expected. He was toying with my low expectations of him, having picked up on them as well from my body language and facial expressions.

"Steak?" I volleyed back. "Right, because you don't get enough cow during the day, I bet, being a cowboy with cows and all."

He lifted one eyebrow just a bit, surprised by and seeming to enjoy my repartee. Pleased to have met a woman who could be pushed a little, and push back in kind.

"I knew I'd like you," he mused, glancing once again at the menu, the grin still playing on his face.

Lunch went on.

We talked. He smiled in a way that made me think he found me attractive. This stunned me. How could he? I wondered. Then I berated myself silently for being so insecure. Then I got back to the conversation, in which we appeared to be debating illegal immigration, bilingual education, and Ayn Rand's "virtue" of selfishness. I will let you decide which side of those I was on. We disagreed. None of that surprised me. All of it gave me a headache.

Then he did surprise me. It turned out that he believed Sarah Palin was, um, let's just say, less than bright. We agreed on something. Huh. As we continued to talk, it turned out that we also both agreed that while there might be a God, it was far too grand for human beings to even begin to try to understand, much less speak for; we agreed that organized religion was problematic and prone to human corruption. We also agreed that our country needed to stop spending so much money in foreign wars, and that a better use of those funds might be to take care of our own people and rebuild America's decaying infrastructure. Most shocking? This self-described conservative man disliked neocons almost as much as I did.

"Liberals have this idea that all conservatives are crazy, on the fringe," he said. "That's why I prefer the term *traditionalist* to conservative, because most of us aren't neocons; we're just people who like traditional values. I also don't want to see liberals disappear off the face of the earth, because you guys are the conscience of humanity. We make the hard decisions that you guys won't, but we need you there to remind us to be human."

Huh.

There was some common ground. Not much. But more than I'd expected.

What surprised me most that day, however, was that there was an intellectual depth to his eyes and an intense capacity for empathy. He had a certain calm patience, a worldliness that caught me all off guard. He spoke beautifully. Poetically at times. With wisdom. He was quick-witted and followed my mind wherever it wandered, effortlessly insightful. He kept my gaze, with confidence. He watched, and from the glint in his eyes I knew he liked what he saw across the table just as much as I did.

He reached across the table after our plates were cleared and touched my hand. It sent shivers through me. My world was starting to be tipped on its side, and I didn't know how to handle it.

"I do, I like you," he said, matter-of-fact, his sparkling blue eyes so very, very confident and competent. His voice trailed off as he looked at me, and I, unable to bear the thrill he gave me, looked away and pulled back my hand.

"Sorry," he said.

"For what?" I played stupid.

"I didn't mean to make you uncomfortable."

"I'm fine."

"What are you doing later?" he asked.

I told him that I had to attend a dinner gala at the Sandia Casino and Resort, organized by my friend Lorena at the University of New Mexico's office of diversity inclusion. I did not tell the cowboy that the event featured a keynote talk by a radical hipster self-described "Chicano" cartoonist in town from Los Angeles, someone I'd long had a massive crush on and with whom I had plans to spend the evening afterwards, in spite of said person being married. I'm never proud of my shortcomings.

"How about you?" I asked him.

He told me he was hitting the bars with his golfing buddies. "I think I'd much rather spend the evening with you," he said. "But, hell, I already made plans."

Lunch came to an end. He walked me to my car. I wondered if he would try to kiss me, as so many of the liberal men had after just one date—or, in some cases, within minutes of meeting me. I wanted to taste that spectacular mouth of his, but I also suspected that a guy like this might like me better if I didn't *let* him. I'd read the dating book *The Rules* as research for one of my novels (*The Three Kings: A Christmas Dating Story*), and instinctively I knew that the advice in it, while often made fun of by the ambitious women in my feminist social circles, was probably pretty effective in reality.

I backed up, away from him.

He opened my car door for me, and as I stepped carefully around him to get in, he asked me, "Think you might like to do this again sometime?"

"Sure," I said, trying to sound calm even though my heart was knocking against my sternum as though it wanted to get out. I craved this man. Badly. This embarrassed me.

"Good. I'll be in touch, Miz Valdes."

He shut the door and put the dark glasses back on and walked to his truck. I watched him go, in the side mirror of my car. He was graceful, confident, and abso-freakin'-lutely beautiful.

Moments later, I pulled up next to the cowboy at a red light, on his left. I looked over and saw that his window was down, his dark glasses lowered, and his blue eyes lasering in on mine, filled with mischief. I rolled my passenger window down and asked him what music he was listening to. I expected Toby Keith.

"Robert Plant duet with Alison Krauss," he told me. "How 'bout you?"

I held up my iPod Touch, which had been baking, almost melting, in the car while we lunched, and showed him the "temperature" warning.

"Nothing," I said, frowning. "Too hot."

The cowboy's brow twitched devilishly as he took bait I had not intended to lay for him, but which I realized only too late I'd given.

"I'd say there are a lot of things about you that are too hot." His gaze was focused on me.

I was speechless. His answer had been so quick, and only mildly sarcastic. So unlike anything any of my progressive male friends would have said to a woman. Ever. No, they would have wanted me to know that any move they ever made on me would have been because I'd asked them to, or in response to my having made the first move all on my own.

I blushed and looked down. I loved it. I hated that I loved it. I was . . . confused.

"Um, Miz Valdes?" he called as the light turned green.

I looked up, still red faced. "Yes?"

"I don't think I'm quite ready to be done with you yet."

I pushed down the butterflies. I tried not to think about all the delicious things this comment of his might portend. I tried not to imagine him pushing me up against a dark wall in a nightclub somewhere and just . . . doing whatever he felt like with me. Because he was the kind of guy, I realized, who'd probably be very good at that sort of thing. Taking charge. Taking control. Taking . . . me.

No, no. I could not, would not go there. I forced myself to answer as a good feminist woman should. "With all due respect, sir, that isn't up to you."

The cowboy gave me a look whose meaning was very clear before speeding noisily away with the most self-assured grin I had ever seen.

It said, *We'll just see about that.*

WHAT THE COWBOY
WAS UP AGAINST

Before I take you with me on my second date with the cowboy, I want to yank you back in time so that you can get a sense of what sort of soggy city mess, exactly, this traditional rural American man was up against. While I might have looked like any other fortysome-thing single mom in a Banana Republic skirt to him, there was a lot more going on inside my soul that he would eventually have to wrestle with if he hoped to get close to me.

I was born in Albuquerque in 1969, the second year a handful of feminists protested the Miss America pageant and the media went nuts over a few burned bras, forever changing American culture between the sexes.

My Marxist father, twenty-four at my birth, was a pugnacious PhD candidate at the University of New Mexico, specializing in Chinese history and classical European sociology. Five foot six, he wore his dark hair over his ears, sported a Freddy Fender mustache, and, in those days, wore pink-tinted eyeglasses (à la Father Guido Sarducci) and thick-heeled clogs or cowboy boots for height.

For my dad, the political divisions of left and right were more than academic or theoretical; they were the entire reason he was an exile from his native country, a stranger in a strange land, because the communist revolution in Cuba had been the reason my dad's stepfather had sent him away to Miami at the age of fifteen, by himself. Left and right were personal for my father because his biological father had been a young man from a "ruling class" family in Santa Clara, Cuba, while his mother had been the young maid in this man's house; the product of that unhappy union had been my father. His mother had been banished not just from the house but from the entire town when it was discovered she was pregnant, and she moved alone to Havana to pretend to be a widow and work as a domestic servant.

For my dad, as for most of us, really, the political had always been personal, whether he realized it or not, and for the rest of his life he would play out his psychic wounds through the puppetry of politics, with the capitalist/fascists being the patriarchal oppressors (wealthy biological fathers) who didn't love the people (their kids), and socialist and communist leaders (loan-shark stepfathers from the working class) being the ones who took the oppressed (mothers) in and cared for them and their communities (children).

It should be noted here, too, that my father, now an avowed feminist who supports equal pay for women and believes women should be allowed to participate in all sectors of society, took a long journey to get to that point of view. Cuba in the 1940s and 1950s was a very sexist place, and my father grew up with many sexist ideas that he has struggled to overcome—and some that he might only pretend to overcome in my presence.

So when I say I was raised by feminist parents, it is actually a little more complicated than that. My father was both a sexist and a feminist, his upbringing intermingling with political theory, and his stated public positions on such issues not always lining up neatly with the way he conducted his personal life. As my mother would later put it, "Your dad's feminism stopped at the door of our home." This is because people, all people, are complicated and tend not to fall neatly into boxes. So it is that I am able to say that my dad was a feminist in theory, and that he never outwardly told me I couldn't do certain things because of my sex; nonetheless, he often behaved in sexist, controlling, and domineering ways toward my mother, and I witnessed it. I hope that makes sense, though I suspect it sounds confusing. If you think it's confusing to read here in this book, imagine what it was like to live it. That's all I'm saying.

My mother, twenty-five at my birth, was a college graduate, a writer and aspiring actress, five foot eleven, a light-haired, blue-eyed former beauty queen who looked like Jayne Mansfield but favored Jane Fonda in politics. She liked heels but never wore them because my father was five inches shorter than she was and he didn't want her to tower over him. Like my dad, my mom was a mix of feminist and sexist. Rural New Mexico in the 1940s and 1950s was not much better than Cuba for women, and though my mom had a strong career woman for a mother, she was blessed and cursed with extreme physical beauty, which set her up to be objectified and underestimated at the time, but also set her up for getting attention. My mom was very attached to her beauty as a weapon and tool, but she also resented men who noticed nothing more about her. She was subjected to certain trauma and abuse as a child that I will not detail here out of respect for her wishes that such information remain private. I can say that such experiences only further confused my mother when she was a child and led to a complicated struggle inside her surrounding issues of beauty, power, sexuality, victimhood, and a woman's place in the world. Naturally, she passed all of this complexity and pain on to me indirectly, through her very person and actions in the world.

By the time I began to toddle, my father was a professor. My mother had long since traded her pageant sashes for exotic shawls and was in the process of exchanging her *Betty Crocker's Picture Cook Book* for Erica Jong's *Fear of Flying*, a book she would give me, in a huge cardboard box of other such feminist tomes (and an ERA T-shirt) for my twelfth birthday, along with a handwritten note begging me to not be like her. This meant, as far as I could tell, that she hoped I'd not gravitate, as she did, toward narcissistic, domineering men, or that I'd not be too insecure to live a dream (her dream, it turns out) of total independence. I remember reading *The Feminine Mystique*, by Betty Friedan, and being shocked by what I found there. My mother had given me a book that was all about how nuclear families like ours, with working fathers and stay-at-home mothers, were the reason women like her were so unhappy. I'd loved our intact nuclear family and had felt nurtured in that environment as a child, but here was my mom telling me that it was all a lie predicated on her own misery. The book also talked about how terrible it was for women to have to be beautiful all the time, and yet it had been given to me by my mother, a woman who refused to leave the house without makeup on and who had once told me, when I was nine or ten, that the moment she got wrinkles she intended to kill herself. I felt, quite strongly, that my mother's obvious discontent was my fault, that I had not actually been wanted by her, that if not for me, and having to care for me, she could have been the free woman these books described.

Anyway, my parents—like so many rebellious young American "radicals" in the 1970s—hated, aggressively. This they did in the name of love, of course, and the list of things they hated was quite long and occupied most of our family dinnertime conversation. It included the Vietnam War, Richard Nixon, Capitalist Pigs, Phyllis Schlafly, Fascist Pigs, John Wayne, Conservative Pigs, Imperialist Pigs, Colonialist Pigs, The Rich, Racists, Religion, Sexist Pigs, Lawrence Welk, and Displays of Patriotism Anywhere but Communist Countries and Indian Reservations.

Happily, they still enjoyed pig itself, and especially bacon, which my mother, born to ranching stock in New Mexico, could not shake in spite of growing pressure among her peers to go vegetarian. For this same reason, we also regularly enjoyed such small-town New Mexico delicacies as chicken-fried steak, Frito pie, pork chops, homemade biscuits, peach cobbler, and calf liver fried with onions.

In spite of her own quiet feminist awakening during my early childhood, and her constant whispered insistence that I grow up to "be somebody important," my mother continued her role as a housewife, a role she seemed to think she had been groomed for even though her own mother had always held a job as a bank teller. My mother was a bundle of resentments, with a palpable rage simmering just below the surface of everything she did. In retrospect, I get it. I cannot blame her. After all, when I was an infant and my mother got the flu badly enough to actually faint from it, she says my father didn't even notice, being too wrapped up in his own importance. He'd gone to work that day and left her ailing with two children to care for. My mother had called her own mom to come and help her, and my father, unconscious more than hateful, simply carried on as though nothing were amiss. "He not only never did any housework," she tells me now. "He didn't even notice that it was ever being done. He just assumed things kept themselves clean, I think, and meals presented themselves to him upon the table."

In retrospect, my mother being a housewife was very good for me in my formative years—there was always someone home, she walked me to school every day, she took me to my dance and music classes, dinner was hot and on the table every night, and she made my recital costumes by hand; I felt, as a result, very loved. But I don't think *she* saw it that way then. She saw it as a form of slavery. Back then, my mother, enamored of the countercultural movements of the time, wrote poems about not wanting to have sex with my dad but doing it anyway, and short stories about miserable housewives who had to cook chicken on Sundays for their families and hated every minute of it. She got these works published in secret, in feminist magazines. She showed them to me, but not to my father. He found out about them and was furious and hurt, and they fought a lot. Though my dad was, on the surface, a leftist and a feminist in theory, he was still . . . Cuban, and male. He'd been raised in a very sexist culture that coddled boys and men and never really required them to do much of anything except get waited on and doted on by women. My father tells me now that he never had to do a single chore as a boy growing up in Havana, that he had his mother for that until her death when he was nine years old, and a maid and nanny for that until he was fifteen and moved to the United States. Like so many liberals, he had all the right compassion at a macro scale, wanting to free the women of the world from oppression, but in microcosm, he ruled his own little family, and my mother in particular, with a bit of an iron fist at that time. He is a very different and much mellowed person now, and I consider him among my closest friends.

I internalized my mother's anger and resentments. Her writings and misery made me feel very guilty for existing. But my father's naive disregard of her needs made me think she might have had a point. In short, I was mightily confused by the mixed messages and uneasy roles my parents were giving and taking, and being an extremely ambitious and responsible child, I felt it was my job to fix it all and please everybody along the way.

My formative years, of course, coincided with the 1970s, a decade when my parents busied themselves growing marijuana plants in the backyard and dumping heaps of wheat germ onto almost everything we ate because someone named Adelle Davis said it was good for us. My mother was my father's editor on many of his academic papers, including his dissertation and his first published book, but she never got credit for it. He took the glory, and she let him. It angered her. I could see it in her face. She never spoke of it, but I knew it was there; it pinched the corners of her pretty mouth; it deadened her eyes. My father never seemed to notice her feelings at all, and she never spoke of them. So, in a sense, the budding feminism of my parents was mostly theory, for a time, and I was witness to my mother's angry-housewife desperation and my father's simple expectations of service on a daily basis. I vowed as a young girl to do everything I could to make this woman happy, and proud of me, to make good on the promise she pulled out of me, that I would not be like her when I grew up. It was too late for her, she told me with tears in her eyes, but not for me. She played Helen Reddy songs for me. She propped me up enormously, told me daily how wonderful and capable I was. She armed me for battle with an unflagging self-esteem that was rooted in her own self-loathing.

We lived in a modest adobe house filled with macramé, roach clips, red-eyed graduate students, and the dusky smoke of incense. This same house was notable for its lack of boundaries, consequences, and sugary cereal—the latter being laden, my mother said, with carcinogenic additives. The house sat on a busy corner, at the northeastern periphery of the university where my dad taught. Sometimes our family walked across campus on warm summer evenings as cicadas droned in the poplar trees, to the student union building to watch Woody Allen movies that I didn't understand and was sure I never would. (I was mercifully correct.) I sometimes sat with my coloring books in coffeehouses while my parents and their radical friends nodded bohemian approval for folksingers who railed against the evils of our nation and its barbaric antiworker, antiwoman customs. It was tricky, managing the public persona of my parents as they wished to be seen while knowing that these ideals were not much lived up to in our own family and home. I guess an apt comparison might be made to living in a family where the father is a passionate and popular Christian preacher who says all the right things on Sunday morning but who maybe sinned an awful lot during the rest of the week. It wasn't that my parents didn't believe in what they said, or read, or stood for; rather, it was that they, like so many people who are evolving and self-aware, hadn't quite gotten there yet and weren't quite sure how to. As with most such situations, there was a lot of denial, and a lot of silence, and a lot of building resentment. I tried to figure it out. The best I could manage, when I was quite young, was that many of our social ills, I understood then, owed to something mysterious called a June Cleaver, which I imagined being a blade that hacked through happy summertime.

My childhood living room was often filled in the evenings with long-haired, bearded men and hairy-legged women in gauzy sundresses, all of them talking urgently about equality and justice, even as the women did the dishes and served the men, all of them wearing sensible ugly sandals, which never seemed to deter any of them from

pawing one another with uncensored abandon. My mother watched
the discussions but seemed too shy to join in. My father, on the
other hand, was extremely comfortable in the spotlight, always
thinking himself to be behind the professor's podium, always regal-
ing the group with his stories, facts, theories, and brilliance. In
truth, *both* of my parents were brilliant, but only one allowed himself to shine. My father seemed quite content to let my mother be
the drop-dead gorgeous trophy (albeit a hippie trophy) wife in public, and his savvy editor and intellectual equal *in private*. I couldn't
understand how he could so easily reconcile the "equality" of the
teachings he spouted daily with the sometimes domineering manner in which he treated her. I'd learn over the years just how brutal
his own upbringing had been, and just how far he'd actually come
from the very sexist culture he'd been raised with in Cuba, but back
when I was a kid, I just knew that I hated watching my mother get
pushed around by my dad. This blatant hypocrisy angered me a lot.
I knew one thing for certain: I would never be like her. Ever. I didn't
want to be like him either, but sometimes you don't get what you
want.

As her resentment grew, so did my determination to be more
like him than like her, for her sake. In retrospect, I understand now
that it was every bit as much up to her to stand up for herself as it
was up to my father to include her, but as a child the only thing I
really understood was that my mother was being oppressed and my
father at best didn't see it and at worst was the perpetrator.

Our family was not religious. We never went to church, because
fairness at the macro level, and science, were our faiths, and we, being wholly superior to those sheep that lived and died by fairy tales
about honor and duty, did not need any others. I was, in fact, taught
through example to mock and pity the religious, and did so at my
school with abandon. I remember one girl in particular, Jenny, who
wore a pin every day on her sweaters that said, I AM JESUS' LITTLE
LAMB. I wasted no time in setting her straight, telling her God was

a lie and her religion made her stupid. Jenny cried and ran away, terrified.

In spite of my tendency to preach intolerance in the name of progress, I astoundingly managed to make (and keep!) some friends. Many of them had a game called Monopoly at their homes, it being quite popular in those days, along with Twister, Slip'N Slide, Pet Rocks, and Big Wheels. My older brother and I one day told our parents we'd like to play Monopoly, "like everyone else." My mother bit her lip as she does when she is distressed and controlling her temper, and her pretty blue eyes strayed to my father's angry hazel eyes on the other side of the dinner table. My father scowled and announced, "Absolutely not. Not in this house." When we began to whine, as children without boundaries so often do, he calmly explained to us that Monopoly the board game was a propaganda tool designed to create ignorant capitalist pigs out of unsuspecting children. Then we got a lecture on the greed inherent in the capitalist system. I cried because I didn't understand what he was saying, or why it was a big deal, and he assured me that when I was an adult I'd not only understand; I'd thank him.

Soon thereafter, my father came excitedly home one day with a board game for us. It wasn't Monopoly. It was something called Class Struggle and featured a scowling Karl Marx on the dark and dreary cover. The object of the game was to redistribute one's wealth, which was accumulated simply by, you know, breathing. Winning was never very hard. Competition was never fierce. By game's end, we all wore Karl's frown.

Speaking of my brother, let me say this. He was tall and skinny, asthmatic and smart. He played the clarinet, loved to read J. R. R. Tolkien, and tried to play football, a sport whose coaches thought it best for him to sit on a bench. Because we lived on a state university professor's salary, we recycled my brother's clothes, meaning I wore his hand-me-down bell-bottomed pants to school. I had some of my own clothes, mostly itchy affairs my mother got for me at Kmart.

Though my beautiful mother had her own hair long and styled as she was accustomed, she cut mine in a short, androgynous shag that she assured me was fashionable. More than once, old ladies on the street mistook me for a boy. One horrible Halloween everyone mistook me for a boy because my mother had dressed me as a "gypsy," but really I looked like a pirate without an eye patch.

I don't suppose it will surprise anyone to know that I was not allowed to own or play with Barbie dolls, because they, too, were tools of an evil American propaganda machine—this one designed to keep women oppressed and miserable. Instead, I got toy cars, stuffed animals, and a strange set of ugly dolls called the Sunshine Family, whose mom was nowhere near as curvy as a Barbie doll and, in fact, somewhat resembled the sexless dad. They'd had a baby sometime before I removed them from the box. I'm not sure how.

Whenever I went to my friend Chrissy's house, I went straight to the pink toy chest that was her treasure trove of Barbies. She had them all, and oodles of clothes and accessories for them. I was mesmerized by the obvious sexuality of the voluptuous dolls, and fascinated by Ken's sturdy inverted-triangle torso. We made them kiss—and more—and we'd giggle about it and feel strange stirrings of things to come for us one day. It was all a delicious, forbidden mystery. I loved Barbies, secretly, desperately. Walking home from Chrissy's house, I'd be consumed with guilt so intense I could hardly look at my parents when I got home. I knew I'd betrayed them.

When I was in the second grade, my best friend, Stacy, joined the Girl Scouts and couldn't stop raving about it. All those patches! All those songs! All that fun! And camp! I wanted to join too, but my parents refused, telling me over dinner that such institutions were designed to teach American girls to be docile patriotic slaves. You, they told me, were meant for greater things than selling cookies to potential perverts. They enrolled me in karate, track and field, and basketball instead. I took piano and saxophone lessons. They cheered at my track meets and band concerts, pointing me in the direction of my future self the way adults point dizzy blindfolded children toward the piñata.

In the evenings, my mother sat cross-legged and played guitar on her bed with me, and we sang Woody Guthrie songs. I have never forgotten the lyrics to one of them. It was about a union maid. I didn't know what unions were. I didn't really even know what a maid was. All I knew was that this song made my dad proud of me and my mom. As we sang, my father would stand in the doorway, arms folded across his puffed-up chest, his face beaming with pride. His look said it all: He thought we were perfect, absolutely perfect. I didn't know what a goon or a gink was, or a legion boy, but I felt successful, and important, and good. I thought all families did this sort of thing after dinner.

My parents took me to rallies, and I marched, my fist raised in solidarity for all their causes, always drawing adoring looks and hugs from Mom and Dad and all the other flower-powered adults around. They took me to grown-up parties where college students and professors danced to my dad's collection of albums from his native Cuba, plastic cups of beer sloshing onto the hardwood floors and lending them a damp, acrid smell. I'd dance, too, on my father's feet, looking around for approval. Everyone would smile at the bright and enlightened young woman with cropped hair and in boy's bell-bottoms, the girl my parents were raising with all the right values.

My folks took me to lectures by famous thinkers, about justice, fairness, oppression, and resistance. It was all about resistance, everything about my upbringing. It was all about the fight. From day one I was groomed to live in reaction to crimes committed against others, years before I was even born. Like a Spartan, I donned my battle gear early and pledged allegiance to the cause.

Like so many children of second-wave feminism, I began to subconsciously equate being the dominator with being free; it was a flawed fix to a broken paradigm, and one that would take me four decades of life to figure out was wrong and crippling to me and those I loved. If sexism's legacy was my mother cowering as my father threw a full wineglass at her head, then the fix, to a child, was for the woman to throw the glass next time.

By the fourth grade, I was so completely indoctrinated in the struggle, so passionate about the Equal Rights Amendment, whose slogan T-shirts I wore nearly every day, that I spent an entire week of recesses forcing Stacy and my other female friends to literally carve a giant women's lib symbol into the hard beige dirt of our New Mexico playground, with rocks. My object was to make the sign large enough for people to see it from airplanes. My friends whined and cried because they wanted to play hopscotch or tetherball, but I was a relentless taskmaster and overlord, a chubby girl with fearsome dark eyes. *Do it*, I demanded, *or else*. The revolution was going to be won. I would see to it. The girls complied, though they weren't sure what I was doing or why. I will never forget the resentful, fearful looks they gave me, or how powerful that made me feel. I made them dig until their knuckles bled. The day we finished our masterpiece I ran all the way home to share the good news with my parents. They were proud of me, their little freedom fighter, and certain they were "doing something right."

When I was eleven years old, my mother finally snapped. She'd had enough. She had something of a breakdown and left us in search of the soul and self she'd lost somewhere along the way to making dinner for my dad. My parents divorced and my "emancipated" mother abandoned me and my brother altogether, leaving me in the care of my father while she chased men with Harley-Davidson motorcycles, tattoos, Aryan Nation associations, and prison records because, I assume, women were no longer beholden in her mind to ridiculously traditional roles such as raising their own kids. Children were like bras, to be burned. She'd had enough of being the good wife, and now it was her time to be the bad girl, with bad men who made my dad look like a saint. There was no room in her life anymore for me, and given where her life took her for a time, this was probably a blessing in disguise.

My father cared for me the best he could but in many ways just expected me to pick up the role my mother had held in the house, cooking and cleaning and listening to his monologues and diatribes about politics and society. I'd not wanted to be like her, and yet she left me in his care *and he expected me* to be like her. Not only did I resent my father and men in general for what they'd "done" to my "poor" mother, I began to think that no one who loved me would ever be reliable. They'd always leave, or hurt me, or expect me to take care of them while ignoring things like the fact that I needed lunch money *every* day at school, not just some days. In short, I learned, at a subconscious and emotionally reactive level that still haunts me to this day, that I could trust no one except myself.

My mother happened to be in town the day I got my first period, when I was twelve. I was terrified and called her because I didn't really want to call my dad at work to ask him about it. My mother left a brown paper grocery bag full of pads and tampons on the front porch of the house I shared with my dad. She rang the doorbell and left before I had time to answer it. I opened the door to find the bag of complicated and incomprehensible paper products rumpled there. I was doubled over with cramps, and scared. I knew what a period was, sort of (for all their "openness," my parents rarely spoke of sexuality with us), but I did not have a clue how to staunch the flow of blood. Apparently, my womanhood was not something anyone wanted to be much concerned about; it was something secret and unspeakable that I would have to negotiate entirely on my own.

Later that day, my father (informed by my mother by phone of my period) asked his girlfriend at the time to take me out for ice cream to "celebrate." I didn't know her very well, and surely not well enough to talk about my new bodily function with her. It was awkward, sitting there at Baskin-Robbins, halfheartedly licking a mint chocolate chip cone with her knowing I was bleeding between my legs. When I got home, my father, choking back tears and holding me dramatically by the shoulders, told me he was proud of me for becoming a woman. I was mortified. Proud? My period wasn't something I'd chosen to do, and now here he was, crying. I felt humiliated for him and sorry for having put my mother out that morning.

Now, please allow me to note the following: My mother is a good person who has had a troubled journey through life. As an adult, I can understand her difficulties. I can also have forgiving compassion for her for any of the harm she might have inadvertently done to me while she was in the throes of her own personal hell and despair.

Without sharing too much detail, I'll just say she slipped off course for a time after the divorce, and it was extremely hard on me. She fell into bad company and effectively abandoned her children. She fled Albuquerque for New Orleans when I was thirteen, and I was left in the care of my father.

Still, the feminist indoctrination continued, by my father, who was more determined than ever, watching my mother self-destruct, to arm me to take on a world that reveled in destroying and objectifying women. The best way he could think of to do that, unfortunately, was to make me as little like a girl as possible.

For example, I loved to dance and had a talent for it, and though my dad let me take ballet, jazz, and tap, he would not let me be a cheerleader. When I made the cheerleading squad my freshman year in high school, along with my two best friends—and was in fact offered the position of captain of the team—he discouraged me from joining.

"No daughter of mine should waste her life cheering for the accomplishments of boys," he said, compassion and fury burning in his eyes. "We raised you for bigger and better things. You should seek your own accomplishments, to be cheered for by men for it."

And so it went. It wasn't an outright no, but it was pressure enough to know that it would disappoint my father so greatly if I did anything so traditionally female; what I didn't understand then was that his lack of respect for those things traditionally considered to be the domain of females was probably due to his own conflicted emotions about women in general. Like so many men from Latin America, my father was mightily drawn to feminine women; he just didn't want his daughter to be one of them.

By the time I graduated from high school—where I'd been impeached as freshman class president for refusing to hold a traditional bake sale, saying it was too "girly" and opting instead to host a nuclear sit-in at the Coronado Mall (to my great surprise, no one but me and my dad showed up)—I had a reputation for being mean, weird, combative, and angry. I had never been invited by a boy to a single dance in spite of being regarded as physically attractive. The longest relationship I had in high school was with Josh, a boy who would grow up to be a famous flute player for the Cleveland Symphony, and gay. More than once, boys told me things like, "You know, you'd be beautiful if you'd smile," to which I often replied with something gracious and ladylike, such as "Fuck off."

I was scary to people, boys and girls alike, a girl who took issue with her teachers and their rendering of history, a girl outspoken and bold, with a chip the size of a Western state on her shoulder. I'd watched my mother fail to live up to the feminist movement's expectations of a free and happy life for women. I'd heard her tell me not to do the same as she. I'd seen her sink, and nearly die at the hands of ex-con neo-Nazi types.

I wasn't about to do the same.

I picked up the sword she'd dropped, and I brandished it at everyone. I was another well-intentioned, tragic social creation, born of the confusing 1970s. I had been, for my parents, less a daughter than I was a chance to create a brave new desexualized female citizen immune to discrimination. I was not alone; there were millions like me. I was one in a confused, skirtless army of girl Frankensteins, the first postfeminist prototypes of the All-American un-Girl.

All of this led to a spectacularly combative life as a young woman, and a spectacularly miserable love life, long past the time when youth had flown. I'll get to that in a minute. I just wanted you to have a snapshot of the tangled mess of contradictions that went into making me a combative "feminist" as an adult, so that the second date with the cowboy might make more sense.

Onward.

SECOND DATE WITH THE COWBOY

A couple of weeks went by. I heard from the cowboy, mostly in flirty yet still clean and respectful little text messages. He wanted to see me again. I wanted to see him again. We tried to figure out a way to do that, but it proved trickier than your average second date, given that he lived a four-hour drive from me, in the middle of absolutely nowhere. I Googled the town he lived closest to. It was a speck on the map, with an official population of thirty-seven. That's right.

Thirty-seven.

And it took an hour to get from that speck on the map to the cowboy's actual ranch, or, I should say, the ranch he managed.

It made more sense, I thought, for him to come see me again, in Albuquerque. You know, in a place with, like, restaurants. And, oh, I dunno, *roads.* And people. Lots and lots of people, in case this guy turned out to have a temper like Yosemite Sam's.

But the cowboy couldn't swing another trip to Albuquerque for quite some time, for whatever reason. He gave me reasons. I'm sure they were valid, something involving water lines and wells, and phone lines and dogs, and God knows what else, and so there we were. At a bit of an impasse.

I knew that the books on rules for dating men were very specific about how a woman was not supposed to rush right out to meet the guy, not at the start. She was supposed to make him work for it. Make him come to you. Make him prove that he was going to make an effort. I knew all that, but I also knew I wanted to see this man again, as soon as humanly possible. I was almost afraid he wasn't real. So I was willing to break a rule or two. And it wasn't like I hadn't broken one already.

Cough.

I should note here—and mostly only because it's somewhat humiliating and I find self-flagellation to be occasionally amusing, particularly in a memoir (seriously, why else would you read this stuff?)—that I *did* text him first, after the first lunch date. Yes, I was aware this broke "the rules." Yes, it was stupid. No, I'm not proud. Yes, I have an excuse. No, it's not a pretty one. Yes, I'm gonna share it anyway. Here goes.

I texted the night of our first lunch date, after attending that formal function in the ballroom of a luxury hotel. Remember? The one my friend at the university had organized, with the famous Chicano cartoonist keynoting? Right. The point is, I'd sat around in the fancy hotel bar after the event with the cartoonist and some other friends, drinking cranberry vodkas. Okay, fine. I admit it. I probably drank just a few too many cranberry vodkas. This excess, of course, made me bold in all the wrong ways. For instance, there I sat, gushing to my hipster academic city-type friends all about the tall, slick, handsome gringo cowboy I'd met, and how I couldn't stop thinking about his pretty eyes and tight jeans. They all just kind of shook their heads in confusion, especially the cartoonist. It made no sense to them, or to anyone else who knew me at the time. Why would an outspoken feminist and progressive, and one of the top "Latina" writers in the nation, be obsessing over some white cowboy who openly said he was conservative?

"He's *so* hot," I told my friend Lorena by way of explanation. "You have no idea."

Mercifully, Lorena had grown up in Roswell and knew all about cowboys, of all ethnic backgrounds. She understood completely. Her own husband, Aaron, was Mexican American *and* a former bull rider. That sort of thing happens a lot out west, apparently, and they reminded me that the entire occupation of "cowboy" began in Spain and was refined in Mexico (including those parts of the United States that used to be part of Mexico).

"Where do you think the word *rodeo* comes from?" asked Aaron. "Don't say English, because that's wrong."

Lorena's best friend, Clarissa, was married to a gringo cowboy. Cowboys, they assured me, came in all shades and sizes, and all made good, stoic, hardworking, reliable man-stock.

"You should see him again," she told me, quickly winning my heart as one of my most open-minded friends.

So I texted him. That's the point.

I'm not *blaming* Lorena for this, okay? I take full responsibility. She is just the awesomely open-minded friend who said I should *see* him again, to which I replied something humid and inebriated about how I knew my dad would disown me, to which she replied with a surprised and very grown-up pursing of her lips that reminded me that most women our age didn't really much worry about making their dads happy with their dating choices. *Right*, I thought. *Right. I was old. I made my own decisions.*

I don't remember exactly what I typed. Just that I was in my car in the parking lot of the hotel, sipping hot coffee and waiting to sober up a little before driving home. There were stray cats in the parking lot, darting in and out between the parked cars as a cold wind wailed down off the Sandia Mountains. I felt sorry for them. The cats, not the mountains. This pity somehow amplified my amorousness. I felt like hugging something. Someone. I felt like spreading love around. Or something. My amorousness made me want to touch the cowboy. In retrospect, I wonder if there is some deep-seated ancient visceral connection between cats and lonely women, because at that point in my journey through this life it did seem that I might have settled for either cats or the cowboy. This scared me. I did not want to be a cat lady. I wanted to be in bed with the cowboy.

So I texted away, knowing vaguely as I did so that I probably should not be doing it, but being just a wee bit too vodka-fuzzy and cat-frightened to care. Something about where are you, or are you having fun, or where are you guys at so maybe me and my friends could join you, or hey, cowboy, let's dance. Something. Something stupid. I don't know.

I was *drunkish*, remember? And, no, I do not make a habit of drinking. I'm of that group of people who get drunk four or five times a year. And I *never* drive drunk.

Anyway, it was probably a bit too forward and a bit too scary, because he gallantly did *not* text back for a couple of days. Or at least that was how I interpreted his silence at the *time*. In truth there was another reason, but I would not know what this reason was (or shall I say *who* this reason was) for a couple more months. I'm getting ahead of myself. And I'm not even drunk. I guess the memory of being drunk, in the head of one with imaginational overexcitabilities as often is the case with novelists, can almost replicate that unbalanced state.

Hiccup.

Hang on a second.

I feel a sudden urge to blast Rihanna and dance. That only happens when I drink.

My apologies.

Back to his silence.

He was silent in the face of my boldly seductive text message. This worried me at first, but I decided to play it cool and pretend like it wasn't me who'd texted him about meeting up at, like, one in the morning. That wasn't something a decent girl *did*, see. Not that I was a decent girl, exactly. In fact, I was writing a memoir at the time, called *Puta: My Life in Sex*. It was well-written but poorly considered and, frankly, in very bad taste. It was meant, like so many of my book titles, to be ironic, in a world filled with nonironic people who take all at face value and would literally think I was a slut just like they literally think *The Dirty Girls Social Club* is about sluts instead of what it was actually about, which was empowered, college-educated, professional women. Irony in the wasteland that is humorless America is unwise. I see that now. I did not see it then. Then, I thought, as so many knee-jerk liberals think, that if only people could hear what I had to say, and the hilarious ironic tone with which I said it, then they'd come around to my side and think me a genius. I thought the world was hard on women, and that was the point.

Anyway.

I wanted to come across as the decent woman I was, for the sake of this seemingly decent man, so I pretended I hadn't sent that ridiculous late-night text, and he, ever the gentleman, never brought it up. I stopped contacting him, like a good rules girl, and waited to see if he contacted me.

Which he did. Because that's what the good ones do when you stop paying attention to them.

What did he do?

Flirt.

He flirted mildly, and tastefully, in email and on text. He had an amazing way with words. And I guess if there's a subtextual moral to this tale, it would be that the fastest way to a writer's heart is through writing well. He wrote so well it sometimes took my breath away. "How are you not a writer?" I asked him. "That's *your* job," he told me. "And what's your job, as far as I'm concerned?" I asked. "That all depends on how well you get to know me," he replied.

Etcetera.

All via text.

At any rate, somewhere along the way in those next two weeks of us both being very busy with whatever it was we were doing—in my case, taking care of my son, mostly—we arranged for me to go down to his place for our second date.

Let me repeat this. I agreed to go to his place. For a second date.

His *place*.

Which was a ranch.

In the middle of . . . nowhere.

Ugh.

I knew it was stupid to agree to something like that. You didn't go *home* with a man on the second date, ever. And you certainly didn't go home with him *as* your second date. Just ask the Millionaire Matchmaker, Patti Stanger. You don't go home with him until there's an agreement of monogamy. You make him wine you and dine you. You make him work. His place? Patti would be ashamed of me. My God, what was I, a moron? Don't answer that. I know the answer already. I don't need to hear it from *you*.

But given his remoteness, and something to do with water lines and whatever, he needed to stay out there. And given my being somewhere in my sexual peak, and being somewhere in the middle of really stinkin' lonely, and being a little too close for comfort to becoming a cat lady, and craving to see him again, I decided I needed to drive to wherever he was, ASAP. Even if it meant I was an idiot.

I tried to save face a little by acting like I wasn't sure I should be doing this. I assured him that just because I was coming down there did not mean I was going to sleep with him or anything like that, because I wasn't that kind of girl. Part of me realized that most of the girls who said this sort of thing usually didn't actually turn out to be that kind of girl, because the girls who did this stuff right would not put themselves in a position to have to say something like this.

Anyway.

He reassured me by telling me there were three houses on the ranch, and that I was welcome to stay in one house while he stayed far away in the other. He promised to be a gentleman, and we agreed that we'd simply have dinner, talk, and get to know each other before retreating to our separate domiciles. He promised that it was fine and safe and that he was a nice guy. He said he was used to having people come out to stay at the ranch because he ran a hunting operation there and several times a year people came through with guns and arrows in search of deer and sheep.

Naturally, this comforting treatise on, oh, you know, *killing stuff,* did nothing to reassure me, because in those days, thanks to my upbringing and sheltered East Coast Ivy League existence, guns and arrows and hunting and basically anything involving camouflage ranked somewhere alongside, well, like, *Hitler* on my list of things that were wrong with humanity.

He then sent me detailed directions to find the ranch, ending them at the intersection of a county dirt road and a rural highway, saying that we'd have to meet there and that the last hour of the drive from that point to the ranch would be done in his pickup because the road was far too rough for my delicate, girly Hyundai.

The sensible part of me stood there in tight Spanish pants, waving a red matador's cape at the bull of my fears. *Hello? You're about to drive two hundred miles to leave your car somewhere and get in a pickup truck with a man you don't know at* all, *in order to have him drive you an hour into the remotest of places, to the ranch he manages in the middle of literally nowhere?*

Right, said the stupid part of me. *Did you not notice how hot he was? C'mon, now. When's the last time anything that hot wanted to make dinner for you? Ever? Never! That's when.*

The sensible part started to chuck stones at the stupid part's window to get her attention. *Hello? What part of "stupid" did I not understand?* It was *so* stupid, this thing I was planning, as to have seemed nearly suicidal, and yet . . . I agreed to do it. Enthusiastically. The part of me that had shivered and trembled at his touch, and swooned at his lips and swagger, pretty much won out over the part of me that, you know, made sure I did stuff that would keep me out of danger and alive.

Not one of my most shining moments.

I suppose I rationalized my bad decision making by reassuring myself about how strong and capable I was, how I was Helen Reddy, "hear me roar" and all that jive. I told myself I'd surely be able to get away if something went wrong. I had strong legs, like Shakira and her mother. I could run like Forrest Gump. I'd be fine.

But in reality, both sides of me knew exactly what was going on. I was lusting after a conservative cowboy, partly because he was so exotic in my world, mostly because his jeans fit him the way they fit him, and I had a chance to go hang out with him on a ranch. And I was quite likely ovulating.

Like I said, I'm not proud. But I'm also not going to lie. At least not to you. I might tell my son there's a Santa Claus, but that's different.

Kind of.

So. (Cough.)

We set the date, and I packed my bags, and away I went, into the manly, leathery, empty unknown.

Yee-haw.

THE DRIVE

It was early April 2011. I was a chunky old thing, probably about a size sixteen. Okay, a size sixteen. Sometimes an eighteen. At five foot six. I was among that legion of girthy women who avoid mirrors. In spite of my being fifty or sixty pounds overweight and forty-two years old, I managed to carry myself with some confidence and was pretty enough to occasionally turn a head or two in the right light and as long as my shirt wasn't tucked in. With my shirt tucked in, I looked like Pat from the "It's Pat" skits on *Saturday Night Live* a while back. My hair was cut in a stylish boblike thing that hovered somewhere just above my shoulders, and I had it colored mostly blond and light brown, while in fact beneath all that it was pretty much half dark brown and half gray. I'd been told my eyes were the best thing about me, so I played them up with expertly applied makeup. I tended toward the flashy in my dress and fancied myself something like a slightly more intellectual JLo. Well, okay, a *lot* more intellectual. Also a lot fatter, with less perfect eyebrows. But still *kind* of from the block, right, though I liked to think that *my* block was located somewhere near the university and contained a rare-books shop filled with original Charles Dickens manuscripts. I was less "from the 'hood," and more "Malamud." I wasn't so much an "around the way girl" as I was a "St. Vincent Mil*lay*" girl. Where JLo was all about the *bling* theory, I was all about the *string* theory, yo yo yo, whatup whatup whatup, *homie*.

That's about right.

That day, the day of my *second* date with the cowboy, I did the usual things I did before dates. I showered carefully. I moisturized. I deodorized. I spritzed. I round-brushed my naturally wavy hair into submission with the verve and muscle of a lion tamer, and then I flat ironed it like a German laundress with a linen shirt, just to prove my point. I applied makeup, rather fabulously if I might say so myself, thanks to my days as a cosmetics counter girl at the Watertown Mall outside of Boston, back when I was in college. It had been there, in the bus-accessed, frosty, far-flung suburbs of Beantown, that I'd learned about things like my color wheel (I'm a winter, in case you were wondering) and eye shadow primer. Important things that, as you might recall, I had never had the opportunity to learn in the home where I grew up because we were too busy discussing Karl Marx and making sure I was nothing like an actual *girl*.

It was warm that Friday. Warm even for that time of year. Then again, if the Weather Channel is to be believed, we should pretty much dispense with this whole idea that winter is supposed to be cold in North America anymore, thanks to global climate change, a phenomenon that I was quite sure someone like the cowboy would not believe was true, and seriously, wasn't that reason enough for me to stay home and not go racing down to the bottom of the state to meet my disappointment and doom on the ranch? I should take a moment to tell you here that in spite of its many cartoonish stereotypes, New Mexico is not a flat, barren, hot desert drawn by Hanna-Barbera. At least not everywhere, and not all the time. So don't start going all, *What does she mean it was warm in New Mexico, the Bugs Bunny cartoons say it's always warm in New Mexico, which is just the same as stereotypical Arizona for that minority of Americans who even know that New Mexico is an actual state and not a foreign country.* We New Mexicans are really sick of that kind of diatribe.

Fact: Albuquerque itself sits higher than Denver, in the Rocky Mountains, and we have four well-defined though not extreme seasons. There is snow in the winter. There is spring. And there is summer. Trees shed their leaves with colorful drama in the fall just like they do in other places. The day I set out for the ranch was somewhere in the spring but felt an awful lot like flirting with summer. The kind of day a girl might get burned.

Aware of all this, I chose to wear an outfit that to me screamed "weekend at the ranch" back then. This was because my idea of a "ranch" was gleaned entirely from having been to the Sundance Film Festival in Utah a couple of months before, with my big-shot Hollywood manager, who had a film he'd produced showing there. Movie-type people who reminded me of Robert Redford and Jane Fonda had slunk around the place and worn cowboy hats, just like, I thought, the cowboy. And they'd worn Uggs, because that's what glamorous Hollywood ranchy types did on the weekends in the country. They were PETA activists who wore dead sheep on their feet so that their skinny legs looked like pencils with big erasers on the bottoms. I was a glamorous, bestselling author with some film deals in the works, so it was only fitting that I, therefore, wear short jean shorts with a formfitting black shirt from Bebe (the logo sparkly in rhinestones across the front) with a zippered black hoodie, big silver hoop earrings, and black Uggs. You know, a ranch outfit. My legs have long been the best thing about my physical self from the neck down, being defiantly muscular and pretty, regardless of what the rest of me was up to, so I chose to show them off a little, while, I thought, not looking like I was trying too hard.

I'm not sure what I told my father I was up to that weekend, but I know for sure it was *not* the truth. Something about maybe going to visit my mother, or getting out of town to do some writing while my son spent the weekend with his father. I hate to lie to my dad. But I hate to face his anticonservative wrath even more. At any rate, I do remember being absolutely terrified that my dad would literally disown me if he knew I was so much as talking to a member of the enemy's ranks, much less one who was so John Wayne–ish. My father has never been a big fan of a certain kind of man—that kind being taller than he and owning guns and driving trucks, etcetera.

I left in the morning, around ten A.M., and the day was clear and sunny. I connected my iPod to the stereo—which was an astonishingly good stereo considering that the car was a Hyundai Elantra—and I drove many, many miles. About two hundred miles, in fact. I take it back. The Hyundai Elantra does not deserve to be maligned thusly. It has been a good car, and well worth the money. This does not negate my longing for an Infiniti, but at that point in time I was in a famine swing and had replaced my feast-era luxury car with said bland, reliable Korean import.

The city gave way to the farmy southern suburbs, and eventually those gave way to vast expanses of desert that were home to things like the Very Large Array—aka the world's largest radio telescope, located somewhere desolate outside of Socorro, New Mexico. Incidentally, *socorro* means *help* in Spanish. I noted this with a flinch as I drove past. I needed Socorro. No doubt about it. Oh, and I should mention, you might remember the Very Large Array from that Jodie Foster movie *Contact* that was based on a Carl Sagan novel. You might be stunned that Carl Sagan wrote novels. Then again, you might not know who Carl Sagan was, like most people who don't live in the Malamud 'hood like I do. It doesn't matter either way, because it's all just a tangent to help express the frenetic unfortunate energy that permeated my being as I drove to the ranch and made my thoughts bounce from one thing to another like a rubber ball in a rubber room.

The ranch. I was going to the ranch. I was insane, and not in the good, obsessive-genius way like Carl Sagan. I was the bad insane of women who end up on the evening news because no one can find them.

I kept going south, like a wintering goose, until I was to go east, and then I did *that*. The mountainous desert became flat and very yellow, grassy plains, and I watched it all unfold before me out the window, pleased with myself. I'd never visited this part of New Mexico, mostly because in the circles I ran around in we tended to think that *road trip* meant Points North, such as Santa Fe and Taos—you know, the glamorous places. No one I knew in the city actually went to cow country by choice. It was a place you sort of knew was there but avoided because it reminded you of West Texas. I knew I'd strayed from my comfort zone when a gas station in San Antonio, New Mexico, had a sign above the door that read COWBOYS KICK THE SHIT OFF THEM BOOTS BEFORE COMING IN HERE.

I played Tito Rojas and Grupo Niche and sang along at top volume, Facebooked on my BlackBerry about how cool it was to be blasting Nuyorican salsa in New Mexico cattle country, and took in the sights through my stupidly oversize glamour shades.

I was struck most of all by the color of yellow of the grasses that stretched for as far as you could see. It was familiar, that color, but not for a reason that will likely score any points in making me a reliable narrator. In fact, I hesitate here to tell you what I'm talking about, because it sounds like something Shirley MacLaine might say. Oh, what the hell. Here goes.

Like Daphne on the excellent old sitcom *Frasier*, I've always been what you might call just a little bit psychic. I have not wanted to be thus. I don't particularly love sharing this information with you either, because chances are you will suddenly decide it might be a better use of your time to close this book and hit the Sudoku. Be patient. Trust me. I'm as skeptical as you are. Really. I have not courted it or even thought much of it. Stuff has just sort of happened and I've just sort of had to accept it. For instance, when I was nine years old I had a dream that a doll of mine, which I'd named after the aunt in Cuba who'd sent it to me, was lying in a coffin. I woke and told my dad about it. That afternoon we got a call from Cuba, letting us know that the evening before, said aunt had been badly beaten and was in the hospital. She wasn't dead. So I'm not an accurate psychic, necessarily. Just a badly drawn one who colors outside the lines. I'm kind of like a radio with a homemade aluminum foil antenna. I suppose I could develop it if I wanted to, but I don't want to. I'd rather make people laugh. But the point is, and I assure you I will always meander back to the point eventually if you just hang in there with me, the yellow grass had been part of a premonition I'd been given by the universe when I was fourteen years old.

I had been in the eighth grade. It was a spring day, much like the one when I went to the ranch. I'd been walking home from Jefferson Middle School, thinking about my life and my future, and connecting to this very powerful force I had always felt with me. Something like a guardian angel, really, though I suspected and continue to suspect that it is and was my father's mother, Eugenia Leyba. My Cuban grandmother, who'd died when my dad was nine years old. I know I've probably lost a few of you now, but I beg you to indulge me. At any rate, there I was, walking home from school, looking at the beautiful blue New Mexico sky, and wondering about my future. I asked this thing, this guardian, or whatever it was, God, the universe, the energy I felt around me, what the future held for me. Specifically I asked two questions: What was I going to be when I grew up, and who was the love of my life going to be?

I got answers.

I didn't hear voices, nothing wack-job like that. I just had knowledge, *bam*, implanted in my mind, heart, and consciousness, like a light switch had been turned on. The answer to the first question had been clear: a successful writer. This struck me as odd at the time because I hadn't considered writing as a serious profession. I wanted, in fact, to be either a philosophy professor or a lawyer—please do not ask me how I thought those two things were anything alike, and also please recall that I was a kid. I liked to write and did it for my own enjoyment. But I hadn't thought a person could actually make any sort of a living at it.

The answer to the second question came as quickly as the first. It had been a man's first name, but also a certain shade of palest yellow. I remember thinking *ick* because I didn't much like guys with pale blond hair. Send me to Sweden and my gene pool would just die with me, basically. I'd thought *that* was what the yellow was for. Hair. Because it had not been just the color, but also a billowy, hairlike sense of length and breeziness to it. It was stringy yellow. Strandy yellow. Yellow streaks of stuff. There had also been a third bit of information given to me for this part of my query, and it was mysterious. Hollywood. That was all I got, a sense of Southern California. So in my mind, I assumed that this all meant that the love of my life would be a man with the first name I'd been given, that his hair would be palest blond, and that he'd be from Los Angeles. I'd gone through all of my life with this memory on the periphery, always wondering why the message had been so clear about who this man would be, and yet he'd never shown up.

Fast-forward to the second date with the cowboy. There I was, on a rural two-lane highway in the middle of New Mexico, driving from San Antonio toward Carrizozo, and all around me was mile after mile after mile of precisely that exact shade of pale yellow, a shade I had never seen before. It was so distinct that I remembered it instantly. The color came from the long, dry grass that filled the prairies. Strandy, as in strands of grass. (Which, I thought then, had a nicer ring to it than Leaves of Grass, grass not having leaves at all but certainly being strandy, and sometimes strandy enough to, like, braid or something.) Long and flowing. Windblown. It was *then* that I realized that the cowboy's first name was, in fact, the name in the premonition.

Two out of three, I thought with a shiver. *Weird*.

I knew it was silly, of course, to try to make this man and this place fit into some ancient idea I'd hatched when I was fourteen, and yet there was this sense, right in the center of my heart chakra, that it was true. But what, I asked myself, to make of the Hollywood element? From what little he'd told me so far, this cowboy had no connection to Southern California at all. He was from South Dakota and Kansas. He'd lived in Colorado. There was no mention in his online bio or in the conversations I'd had with him of Hollywood. I mean, I myself was doing business with Hollywood at the moment, having just sold my first feature film script. But the premonition had placed him, the guy, in Hollywood. So, you know, there you had it. My imagination was out of control. This was not the premonition. There was no such thing as a premonition, just like there was no such thing as Your One True Love. I knew better than all *that*.

I shook it off.

I drove on, still spooked by the wind-whipped faded lemon grasses on the plains, but determined to be more rational about things. More pragmatic. After all, cowboys weren't known for their New Age ideas or psychic tendencies. Or at least I didn't think they were. Truth be told, I didn't know *what* cowboys were known for. I thought they were pretty much extinct. The last interaction I'd had with anyone remotely resembling a cowboy had been back in high school, when I'd avoided the kids in the rodeo club at Del Norte High. Being a band geek and in the gifted program, I considered myself far above the incomprehensible boys and girls in that club, with their strange jeans and striped shirts and talk of majoring in agriculture at New Mexico State University. *Cowboy*, as a concept, had simply never been much a part of my life, other than the vague understanding that my mother's grandfather, a man named John Conant, had, in fact, been a real-life cowboy, with his own ranch near Mountainair, New Mexico. A long time ago. My mom had gone to the ranch as a kid, and she'd known how to ride a horse. But John Conant, my great-grandfather, had both sold the ranch and died long before I came along, so even though the whole cowboy *thing* was technically a part of my blood heritage, it was not anywhere a part of my socialization. I knew as much about cowboys as I knew about, say, sumo wrestlers, and probably held both groups in just about the same bemused elitist esteem.

Round about the town of Capitan, the geography began to change, getting more mountainous and greener. I was near the ski resort town of Ruidoso, which I didn't know much about but had heard was pretty nice, if you were a Republican. Which I wasn't. I was running out of gas, so I stopped in Capitan at the Shell station. Everyone else seemed to be in pickup trucks and jeans and cowboy hats and boots. Standing there with my pink debit card, Uggs, and jean shorts, with my hoop earrings and glamorous enormous superstar sunglasses, I drew some curious looks. So curious as to perhaps border on the hostile. So curious that I recall getting back into the car and texting the cowboy on his cell phone, about how it was probably a bad idea to wear shorts and Uggs to Capitan. His text back was succinct.

"City girls," he wrote, and I couldn't tell if he was joking or annoyed or both.

I was about half an hour from the meeting place now, so I

stopped off in the gas station bathroom to check my makeup and hair and to take some deep, soothing breaths. I was nervous. Incredibly nervous. I was in Billy the Kid country, literally. I knew this because signs all along the highway told me that this area was where he'd made his last escape, in the small town of Lincoln, just over there somewhere. It was also the part of the nation that had given us Smokey Bear. It was pure Americana, and as such it was absolutely foreign to me, who had been raised to think of myself as a "universal human being."

I was surrounded by people with rifle racks in their pickups, lost in a place that felt like a foreign country, dressed all wrong, on my way to meet the sexiest man I had ever seen in my life, but armed with the unsettling possibility that he was, in fact, the love of my life that my guardian angel had told me about all those decades ago. Well, I was either armed with that or with the equally unsettling knowledge that I was the crazy type of broad to believe something that ridiculous. Or he was a serial killer. Something like that.

Either way, I was unsettled, and it was all my own fault.

"You can do this," I told my reflection in the mirror. But I saw the doubt in my heavily made-up eyes.

The only thing I knew for sure was that I was about to find out, and I hoped I'd live to know the outcome.

THE PARKING PLACE

I managed to drive myself from that Shell station all the way to our designated meeting spot, at the T where the rural highway met the wide dirt county road. There was a road sign, just as the cowboy's extremely detailed written instructions had indicated there would be. I was somewhere between Ruidoso and Roswell, in a dry and grassy area that bubbled up in rounded cactus-pocked yellow hills all around. The sky was blazingly blue. A small river flanked the highway, and trees bounced up greenly along its banks. This place, I thought, was beautiful.

I did a quick final check of my hair and face in the rearview mirror as I approached the intersection in the less-than-sexy Elantra. My pulse sped up, and whatever squeeze bottle inside me held the adrenaline began to convulse and spurt in a way that made me feel breathless and insecure and sick. What was I doing there? He was pretty. I was fat. How could I measure up? I was nowhere *near* as pretty as he was. Even at my most fit—and I'd once been so fit as to have been the fitness director for a gym in Somerville, Massachusetts—I'd not measured up to a guy like *that*. How had he not noticed that I wasn't as pretty as he was? Maybe that was just the point. Maybe he didn't *care* what I looked like because his intentions with me involved not romance or a relationship but rather a sharp ax and pulleys and dental instruments and maybe a deep and wormy hole in the ground.

I slowed the Elantra and saw that there were two white pickup trucks parked on the dirt shoulder of the dirt road. *Two.* He had told me he'd be waiting for me in a flatbed Ford, white, and now there were two such things. One of them had dogs in the back. Were these to chase me with? Like the way good ol' boy prison guards did with chain gang escapees in the Deep South? To make sure I could not escape?

And then, there he was, standing in the sun, wearing his jeans and a white button-down shirt, his light-colored hat and expensive-looking sunglasses. He was leaning against one of the white trucks, the one holding the dogs, talking to the man who sat behind its steering wheel. *Oh no*, I thought. *There are two of them. He's ganged up on me. This isn't what we agreed upon.* I agreed to one cowboy, and one cowboy only. But my fear melted away when I saw the familiar cowboy had a genial smile for me and was nodding attentively to his friend the way people who listen well to others nod. He was chatting with a pal. That was all.

Relax, I told myself.

I pulled the Elantra up next to them. I parked, smiled as charmingly as I could, and looked over at him. The cowboy smiled back and waved slightly without missing a beat in whatever conversation he was engrossed in. This is when I noticed that the man in the white pickup was looking over at me, too. He wore sunglasses and a hat, just like the cowboy, but was about a decade older.

I took a deep breath, and that was when the cowboy excused himself from the friend, walked over to my door, and opened it for me, like a gentleman.

"Hello, Miz Valdes," he said in a flirty yet respectful way. I saw him grin just the tiniest bit as I unfurled myself—and my very buttery-soft moisturized legs—from my seat. He seemed to hold back a laugh. Pretty sure it was something to do with the shorts and Uggs and the JLo highlights and sunglasses. "C'mon over here a second, darlin'," he said.

Darlin'? Puh-lease. And yet . . . God, I loved it when he called me that.

I followed him to the white truck with the dogs in the back. The dogs were black and white, with ice blue eyes, and did not bark at me, though they watched me with great interest.

"This is my friend Alisa Valdes," the cowboy informed the man behind the wheel, then telling me the man's name. "He's one of our neighbors." The cowboy then told me I'd be leaving my car at this man's house, as he was the nearest neighbor to the ranch. I do not include either of the men's names here in this book because I have learned the hard way that cowboys are both not extinct and very, very private people who would not much like to have their names in a book, especially not in a book like this.

"Nice to meet you," I said.

"Pleasure to meet you, too," said the neighbor as he removed his hat in a most gentlemanly way that took me aback. I liked these old-school manners. You pretty much never saw them anymore in the city. I smiled and noticed that this gentlemanly man also spoke in a charming drawl so thick I almost could not tell what he was saying at all. He had a pleasant, handsome face, weathered and suntanned, much like my cowboy's. These were rugged people, men who spent their lives outside, in the fresh air and sunshine, doing . . . well, I didn't exactly know. Doing something cowboy. It gave them a certain healthy glow that you just didn't find in the city among the ranks of computer programmers, copy editors, and lawyers.

The two men talked a minute or two more, as though I weren't there, something about cow dogs, finishing up whatever conversation they'd begun before I got there, and then they said their good-byes and the neighbor drove away, leaving the unfathomably hot and sexy cowboy with his unfathomably excellent cheekbones and unfathomably strong jaw alone with me and my ovulation in the sunny silence.

It was now that the cowboy removed his sunglasses so that I could see his gorgeous blue eyes. He slid these up and down me subtly, with a self-confident look of approval and amusement. Shy, he was *not*. Lordy. Nor was there any part of him that seemed to doubt for a second that he could have me, or any woman on earth— and he was probably correct.

"*You* look nice," he said, and seemed astoundingly to actually *believe* it.

"Thanks. So do you."

And he did. Good God, did he *ever*. It wasn't *normal* for a man to look this good. I'd never experienced it, even when I'd lived in New York or Los Angeles, where there was no shortage of good-looking men, and I wasn't quite sure how to handle it. Surely he knew? He must have known what he looked like to other people. Did this make him vain? Did he pay attention to it at all?

I'm pretty sure he asked me about the drive, and we probably both made a little small talk, but all I can clearly remember from that moment is how completely attracted I was to this man, and how much this worried the monkeys out of me. I wanted to touch him in the helpless and passive way iron shavings might "want" to touch industrial magnets. I wanted to touch him the way the moon "wanted" to orbit the earth. I watched my own involuntary longing with a sense of horrified astonishment. I was drawn to him more powerfully than I had been drawn to any man I had ever met in my life. There was just something about him. A charisma, a confidence, a comfort with himself. He was a man, I realized. The first male I'd ever dated who actually felt like a man instead of a large boy. I'd been terrified to come here, and yet I felt safer in his presence than I had ever felt in my life until then.

"Follow me," he said. "Let's go get your car parked."

And so I trailed the white flatbed pickup in my Elantra down the dirt road, about a half a mile maybe. The pickup kicked up a smoky white plume of dust in its wake. I drove right through it, making sure the air conditioner was set to "inside" air because even though I lived in the middle of a smoggy city, I was concerned about the effect dirt might have on my breathing apparatus. Gravel pinged and popped like corn beneath my car, and the wheels shook and shivered as though in some strange vehicular ecstasy. Black cows chewed their cud and watched us pass by from their spots in the pastures at our sides. Their eyes were pretty and I pitied them because they would one day be eaten and this seemed horrible and cruel and yet I really liked beef. I hated myself for this, and so I pushed it out of my mind because I was encumbered enough as it was with the ethical dilemma at hand and did not need to compound my overthinking guilt with more thinking and guilt.

The road curved and snaked through those gently rolling, grassy hills, and it was bumpier than any road my city sedan had ever undertaken. I didn't know how to drive on a road like this, and it scared me. But I soldiered on. I was not about to let on that I was ignorant about this man's way of life. I mean, I had my ranch Uggs on!

I followed the cowboy as he turned off toward a house. It was a picturesque house, made of big stones and with a pitched metal roof. There was a windmill, and there were fruit trees in full bloom. There were dogs, and a fat orange cat running along a wall. There was nothing for miles around but this house, and another house, and a barn. That was it. That, and pastures and hills. If a woman *had* to be butchered, you know, by a complete and hot stranger, I thought, this was as pretty a place to have it done as any. At least I'd die in a Norman Rockwell painting, looking at a pretty man's face.

He exited his truck, leaving it running, and pointed me to where I needed to park, off to one side near a corral. He was direct with his gestures, commanding, and seemed to expect me to get it right. Stern, secure, sexy.

He was nothing if not a take-charge guy.

I'd never known a take-charge guy. I'd never dated one. This was exciting. *If he could be commanding in this context*, I thought as I tried to park well, *what might he be like, well . . . behind closed doors?* I gulped and pushed that thought out of my mind. *Don't get ahead of yourself, Alisa*, I coached silently. *Keep your cool.* And so I did, sort of. I parked, albeit in a somewhat inexpert way, driving and parking not being my strongest of suits. The cowboy watched with thinly veiled bemusement. I was starting to think he would always look at me rather like that. I was starting to think I wouldn't mind all that much if he did, even though it was supposed to be offensive to have a man look at a grown woman as though she were a child who didn't know what she was doing. It turned me on and I had no idea why and this bothered me immensely, but not immensely enough to make it stop.

I got out of the car, noticing immediately that there were dried cow pies everywhere around this house. I mean, everywhere. The cowboy walked right through them as though they weren't even there. I, of course, tiptoed gingerly around them. In my Uggs. He seemed to notice my delicate steps but didn't comment on them, just as he did not comment on my Uggs even though he seemed more than ready with an opinion on them. He seemed, in fact, to be consciously ignoring my tentative pleas for attention, as though he could not be bothered with sissies from the city. Cow crap, I realized, was a fact of life to this man. You didn't pay it any mind. And any woman who did mind it likely didn't much belong there. I wanted to belong there, at least long enough to maybe, like, touch him.

"Next time you're on a gravel road like that, you probably don't want to follow so close behind another vehicle," the cowboy told me. "That's a real good way to knock a hole in your windshield."

So much for seeming hip to his way of life.

"You got a suitcase or somethin'?"

"Yeah."

I popped open the trunk with my key fob, admiring my freshly manicured French tips, and the cowboy took my suitcase out as though it were as light as a box of cotton balls. He placed it in the back of the pickup and told me to leave the keys in my car in case the people who lived there might need to move it.

"But what if someone steals it?" I asked, astounded, a city girl to the bone.

The cowboy answered me by laughing, and opened the passenger door of the pickup for me, and that was pretty much that. I took this to mean that there wasn't much chance of my car being stolen out here, in the middle of nowhere, where everyone and their granny seemed to be armed, if not dangerous.

I approached him, my heart thundering like a hamster stampede. He held his hand out for mine, to help me onto the step that led up into the cab. I hesitated, then placed my hand in his. His hand was big, almost twice the size of mine, and strong, and rough, as though it were covered in tanned hide instead of skin. *A hand that could be counted on to keep you from falling down*, I thought. A man's hand.

"Thanks," I said, feeling very awkward as I got into the truck. I didn't make a habit of riding in trucks. In fact, I could not remember the last time I'd ever been in one. The closest I could think of was when I'd rented a U-Haul to move myself from California back to New Mexico, and I'd done that completely on my own, with no calloused hand to help me into my seat, much less to help me unload all my junk.

The cowboy closed the door behind me and walked around the front of the truck toward his own door. I watched him walk, and my breath sort of hung there in my throat. He did not look his age. Not even close. He was trim, fit, athletic, and his face bore few wrinkles. He'd aged the way Sean Connery or George Clooney had aged, with creases that only served to make him more angular, manlier, prettier. He looked wealthy, too. Something about the way he carried himself. He was spectacular.

"You ready, dear?" he asked, smiling over at me.

"As I'll ever be," I replied. I reached up to put my seat belt on, but he stopped me.

"Probably don't want to do that," he said.

"I'm sorry?"

"The road we were just on? That's smooth compared to what we're about to drive on. You'll be a lot more comfortable without it."

Being a writer, I wondered if this was some sort of foreshadowing. You know, city girl lives her life on pavement, meets a cowboy, ends up on the rocks. (It *was* a foreshadowing, by the way. I can tell you that now. But I'm getting ahead of myself, and there's nothing worse than that. Except, maybe, wondering whether you're going to survive the weekend in one piece, to return home to your son. That might be worse.)

With great worry, I released the seat belt. Throwing caution to the wind, I thought, in every way. Not taking care of myself. Putting my life in this man's big hands from the get-go.

"Something wrong?" he asked me as he eased the truck back

onto the county road and turned away from the direction we'd come from, toward the deeper and more remote canyons of this wild and untamed country that had nurtured then killed Billy the Kid and almost killed Smokey Bear.

"Not yet," I said.

The cowboy gave me a curious look and seemed to understand my trepidation instantly.

"I promise you, I'm a nice guy," he said. "You don't have to worry. Plus, I'm a good driver. Spent years driving semi trucks, in a lot worse conditions than this. Used to haul gas through snowy mountain passes. You'll be all right."

"I am *so* not worried," I lied. "Trust me, I can take care of myself."

He gave me a look then that is hard to describe. It was something like the look you might give a toddler who tells you the play sink in his room can actually be used for washing real dirty dishes. Something like the look you might give a Chihuahua that barks with extremely unfounded confidence at a huge police horse clomping through a park. Something like the look you might give an elderly woman with a broken leg and Parkinson's *and* slippery shoes who assures you she most certainly *can* make it down those icy stairs on her own.

He chuckled a little.

"I *like* you," he said as he turned his eyes back to the road, leaning back against his seat.

He draped one large, capable hand over the top of the steering wheel, at the wrist, the way the captain of a ship might casually settle in at his massive helm as the perfect storm approached.

He smiled to himself, almost imperceptibly licked his beautiful lips, and added, "But then, I knew I would."

THROUGH THE GATE

From the neighbor's house, it was a good half an hour over an increasingly rough and rocky road before we reached the first gate.

Yes, gate.

It was the metal kind you often find on ranches, and it was fastened with a heavy chain that was held in place with a substantial padlock.

Yes, *padlock.*

Until that point we'd talked casually about the area and the surrounding ranches through which we had to drive in order to reach the ten-thousand-acre monster managed by the cowboy. (Apparently such a road through someone else's property is called an "easement." I had no idea.)

I was struck by the cowboy's easy way of talking, and with his writerly attention to the telling detail. He held my interest, intellectually. Not a lot of men did that. This one did.

The conversation, so breezy and informal, suddenly stopped as the truck stopped, at this first gate.

"Wow," I said, looking at it.

"Be right back," said the cowboy.

He got out of the truck and fiddled with the lock a bit. It popped loose, and he pushed the gate open before returning to the truck to drive it through. Once past the gate, he got out to close it behind us and lock it again.

I watched him in the side mirror, nervous. I'd known I'd be in the middle of nowhere with a cowboy I hardly knew, but I had not known there would be nothing but miles and miles of hills and valleys, and this rough dirt road that felt more like driving along the bottom of a dry and rocky riverbed, and a locking gate.

Nonetheless, I was still more than a little bit aware of how great he looked walking back to the truck from the gate. The sun shone on him just so, and as he approached the truck he removed his sunglasses. He got behind the wheel again, and I just stared at him. I had literally never seen anything so attractive in my life. He caught me staring and sort of half smiled to himself before moving the truck a little ways. Then, just like that, maybe twenty yards from the gate, he stopped the truck again and set it in park. My heart pounded as he turned toward me and just took me in with his eyes.

"Hi," he said with a little twinkle.

"Hi," I said, weakly.

He touched my cheek, tenderly, his eyes filled with happiness. He leaned over to me, moving fluidly, confidently, and gently placed his lips on mine. Butterflies took flight in every part of me. His lips, so well formed and full and pretty to look at, were soft and warm—and oh so very competent. His breath was good. The kiss was perfect. A few short pecks, and then a longer, deeper kiss. My hand rose up to his smooth, tanned cheek and touched him. Such electricity I'd never felt with a man. Ever. It was like he'd been tailor-made for me. So absolutely perfect. He kissed me again, deeper still, and longer, and then, as I began to really get into it, he just stopped and pulled away.

He looked at me, cocky, happy, handsome.

"Wow," I said. "That was unexpected."

"Figured I'd let us get it out of the way now, so that if you think I'm a terrible kisser you still have time to get back to your car before dark."

I laughed. "Um, no. That is *not* the verdict."

He grinned back at me. "Good."

"And you? Is that your verdict about me?"

"No, ma'am," he said, sliding the car back into drive. He chuckled. "No. Not at all."

"That was very nice, actually," I said, shivering a little.

He walked his fingers across the seat to my hand and took it in his. He said nothing and began to drive again.

"So," I asked, uncomfortable in the new silence, with the changed dynamic of our relationship. "What are you, some kind of player or something? Do you do this kind of thing a lot?"

He laughed but looked at me as though I'd offended him.

"Darlin', I'm fifty-two years old and I've never been married," he said with a shrug. "So, no, I'm not what you'd call *inexperienced*. You'd be fooling yourself if you thought that. I like women. I have *always* liked women. Even in elementary school. I got in trouble for not staying on the boys' side of the playground. I was always going where the girls were. A lot of men don't really like women all that much. But me? I really do. I like women."

"Great," I said in a deflated sort of way. I released his hand. He withdrew his. I said, "Happy to be part of the harem."

He looked at me like I was getting on his nerves now. "Jesus, darlin'. Look around." He gestured to the empty land on every side of us. "You *see* this place. It's not like it's easy to get out here. It ain't like I've got women around all the time. If I wanted to be a player, this wouldn't be my first choice of a place to live, would it?"

"That's a pretty evasive answer," I said.

He shot me a warning look now, as though he'd had just about enough of this.

"Jesus," he said. His tone was firm, and his manner had grown just a little chilly compared to what it had been. "Just drop it. . . . Let's not do this."

So. We weren't going to talk about this. That's what he was saying. It was not a suggestion. It was a command. I cringed. I didn't much like being told what we could and could not talk about, and I truly did not like the idea of being part of some player's harem.

But I was on my best behavior, and that kiss had been so flippin' good that I didn't want to risk not getting another one by, you know, arguing or making unreasonable demands. Now that I thought about it, you know, it probably wasn't appropriate to be asking him about his dating life, and other women, just then. On our second date. After our first kiss—and a very romantic one at that, at least until I opened my big, insecure yap.

My suspicious interrogation had, in fact, probably been a massive buzzkill.

But I was Alisa, daughter of the 1970s, and it was pretty much anything goes, whenever I wanted. I was free, right? Free to talk about anything and everything. Free to control the men in my life, to suspect them, to make them do what I wanted and needed.

Except now.

"Sorry," I found myself saying.

"Just let it be what it is," he said, mysteriously.

My heart fell.

From there, it was another half an hour to the ranch, and there were two more gates. But there would not be another kiss on that road that day. No matter how badly I wanted one.

There would be polite small talk, and an ever so subtle—and masterful—retreat by the man who, I was learning, commanded complete control of his own destiny, all the time, and could read me better than I read myself.

THE RANCH

After an hour of bouncing and bumping along the hellishly rough road—and wishing the whole time that I had thought to wear a sports bra—we found ourselves passing through one final gate, which opened into a valley nestled among several large hills.

The valley held three modest rectangular houses that looked sort of like mobile homes, a barn, a couple of smaller buildings, water storage tanks, and a horse corral. There were large, tall elm and cottonwood trees. There was a windmill right past the gate, and an ATV and another pickup truck, the black Ford I'd first seen him in.

I don't know what I'd expected, but it . . . wasn't this. I guess when you see or hear about ranches on TV, there is usually something glamorous and sort of J. R. Ewing about them. I also guess that this man's wealthy appearance, or his movie-star looks, had made me assume he had money. I knew, from the small talk with the cowboy, that what seemed to be a large ranch to me (it had cost about the same as an average luxury home in Orange County, California) was actually small by big-ranch standards. I also knew that the owner was a man living in suburban Houston, a master electrician whose mother was a successful building contractor. The whole family had bought into the ranch as sort of an heirloom property and hired the cowboy to run things for them. I guess I'd expected the buildings to be more upscale. I wasn't disappointed, exactly, because I've never been the type of woman to judge a man by his wallet size, but I was surprised.

That said, there was nothing *trashy* about the place. Not at all. It was very clean, tidy, perfectly in order—and the land! Well, that was clearly the most majestic thing about it. There was so much of it, and it was so beautiful. The "camp" (not a campground, but cowboy vernacular for ranch headquarters) was very far removed from civilization, about an hour's drive from the nearest neighbors, and completely quiet. It was a sort of paradise, from a writer's point of view—or at least from this writer's point of view. I'd always dreamed of living somewhere this remote, somewhere that my imagination could run free and I'd have no distractions. I loved it instantly.

When the cowboy took my suitcase and led me into the central house, where he lived, I was as impressed by what I found inside as

I'd been unimpressed by the place from the outside. No, it wasn't large or particularly well built. No, it wasn't elegant. It was a small three-bedroom modular home—one step up on the housing food chain from a double-wide trailer—with two bathrooms, all of it built in the mid-1990s, you know, back when yellow-and-brown-flowered wallpaper was considered a fine and desirable idea. But the cowboy, much to his credit, had made it a *home*. A nice home. Much nicer than most men might have in the same situation. It felt loved, and comfortable, and clean.

There was a living room. The walls were of unfortunate faux wood paneling, and there was an older and fairly ugly brown carpet on the floor. Even so, the cowboy had made it as pleasant as possible. There was a very nice dark brown leather sofa and love seat, with metal stud trim the way you might expect in such a place. There was an armchair with a Mexican blanket thrown over it. The furnishings had all been arranged sensibly, appealingly, to maximize the limited space. He had a good eye for design, though I wasn't about to be the crazy person who dared tell a very manly and straight cowboy something like *that*.

There was a good, solid wooden coffee table, an end table, and another table. There were shelves, with books on them. Good books. Surprisingly good books, for me, who had assumed the cowboy would not read at all and would likely get all his information from Fox News. There were pretty coffee table books about cowboys. *Cigar Aficionado* magazine. There was a fake fireplace that balanced out the room and had a mantel, with a mirror over it. There were professional-looking handmade curtains, and paintings, and photographs, and a cigar chest. Horseshoes and spurs were used as decorations and paperweights in a charming sort of way. It was all very manly, and very clean, and very ranchy—but in the proper, non–Sundance Film Festival sense of the word. It was unmistakably cowboy, and this made it undeniably sexy.

I looked around, impressed by his attention to detail. The place gave off the same self-respecting energy as those kids whose families don't have a lot of money but they are nonetheless always very clean, polite, and getting good grades in school. There was nothing to feel sorry for him about here. There was also nothing to get excited about if you were, say, the type of woman who looked for a man to "keep" her. This wasn't your man. This man was a ranch manager. I didn't know exactly how much money such people earned, but it was pretty clear this guy was not going to make you a rich woman—at least not in the traditional sense. He had a decent place to live, and good vehicles, and he kept things going. But his value was not in his monetary wealth. It was in something else, something intangible. That was fine with me, because I'd never been the type of woman who required a man to support her financially. It had often been the other way around, which had sucked, too. I was basically just hoping to find a nice, smart, hot guy who could hold his own while I held my own and maybe, once in a while, we could hold each other's. (Parum pum.)

The first thing I noticed, after I noticed the neatness and artistry of the place, was the guns. The scary and many guns. He had a pistol of some kind on the mantel, and a couple of large, long guns in other places. Shotguns or rifles or something. I didn't know what the difference was between those two things, and at the time didn't much care, either. One of the longer weapons leaned against the fireplace. The other was on the bottom shelf of the side table beneath the television. After noting the guns, I saw the ropes. Stiff cowboy ropes. Hanging from the pegs on the coatrack behind the front door. Then I saw the knife. A pocketknife, on the mantel.

Crap.

My pulse raced. Guns, ropes, knives. And a man I didn't know. *Great*, I thought. *Just great.* My determined city-girl smarts wouldn't be much of a match for a man who towered over me and had hands twice the size of mine, especially not if he chose to use those guns, ropes, and knives. Plus, what kind of a man was quite this clean and neat? A serial-killer man, that's who. Right? Who else was so meticulous, especially in the middle of nowhere? A serial-killer man who was hiding evidence and bodies, that's who.

The cowboy explained to me that even though this was his house, it was the nicest one on the place and I would be staying there that night, in his room, without him. He'd stay at the hunting lodge, he told me, indicating out the window a house across the valley. He took my suitcase into the master bedroom and set it down on a leather ottoman in one corner. I followed, taking it all in.

Like the living room had been, the master bedroom was very neat and tidy. The bed was expertly made, with a manly but very nice bedspread that was reminiscent of the saddle blanket he'd hung behind the painting on the wall above the headboard. The pillowcases appeared to have been ironed, with a straight, starchy crease along the sides. There were photographs on the walls, collections of them, black-and-white photos of groups of cowboys. I didn't know what they were, exactly, but there was an interesting framed newspaper article near them, from *The Denver Post*, about how some local cowboys were making the big time because they'd been cast in a Super Bowl commercial. There were also paintings and drawings, of horses and cattle and that sort of thing. And another rope, on the shelf that was part of the headboard. And another long gun, this one behind the door. There was a framed photograph of an older woman in eyeglasses the cowboy told me was his recently deceased aunt. Her obituary had been cut out and placed in the frame with her photo. She looked smart and kind. He told me she had been uncharacteristically open-minded for that side of the family, adding that she'd lived in Spain for a while. This shocked me; I'm not sure why.

I got the tour of the rest of the place, and it was more of the same. Neat. Clean. Very cowboy. Very manly. Nicely decorated. Not a thing out of place.

"Would you like a glass of wine?" he asked, perhaps sensing my discomfort. I said that I would, and we went to the kitchen. It was an ugly kitchen, very 1980s, with ancient but spotless appliances. But it was spacious and terribly—almost unnaturally—clean. Things were where they needed to be on the shelves, arranged almost as though by straightedge, and everything was obviously very well taken care of.

As the cowboy took down a wineglass and opened a bottle of Shiraz, I noticed a stack of mail next to his computer. There was a pink greeting card on the top, with his name written on the front in girly handwriting. Naturally, this drew my attention because it was the only pink thing for miles around. I made a mental note of this anomaly, as well as recording to memory the name of the person who'd sent it, as it appeared in the return address area. A woman's name. Let's say it was Mary Pickle, even though it was most certainly *not* Mary Pickle. I am not going to put the real name here because I have had enough trouble with "Mary Pickle" at this point and do not seek to invite more.

But again, I get ahead of myself.

Let me back up, after I smirk for a moment at having chosen the pseudonym "Mary Pickle" for the woman who would turn out to be my nemesis. One's nemesis deserves a name like Mary Pickle.

Seeing Mary Pickle's pink card on the cowboy's desk, I had a sense of foreboding. My heart lurched in a familiar and lopsided way for a moment. I considered asking him point-blank about it, but I let it go, reminding myself of how badly it had gone when I acted suspicious and possessive in the truck earlier, after our first kiss. I'd only just *met* this guy, and yet here I was acting like a fool. So *what* if women like Mary Pickle were sending him cards in pink envelopes? What was wrong with that, exactly? I didn't own him, did I? Besides, for all I knew, that card could have been from his mother, or from a niece. I did not know who this Mary Pickle was, and it did me no good at that stage in the relationship or whatever the hell it was I was entering into to focus upon it. At all. Or at least not to let on that I was fixated on it, which I was.

Now, I suppose I should explain a little bit about why it was that I was so paranoid and alert to signs of other women lurking around. I won't go into too much gory detail, because frankly it would be depressing for both of us if I did that. Basically, I had been married once. To a man I was with for a total of twelve years. That man is the father of my son. That man was remarkable for many things, including his intelligence, handsomeness, and sense of humor. But he was most remarkable for his astonishing flexibility, and nowhere did he exercise this flexibility more than in his extraordinarily flexible relationship with the truth. He was a liar second to none. He once told me he was gay, just so that we would get a divorce that was, he later told me, without conflict. Forget that thinking the man I'd married was gay for five months had sent me into a deep depression and severe and almost suicidal self-doubt. If a lie made a thing easier for himself, my darling ex did it. It was that simple. And nothing was harder for him, it seemed, than being married to, and faithful to, me. There was a lot of lying, and a lot of sneaking, and a lot of general crap that I only found out about by being hypervigilant to signs of things being not quite right, things out of place, Mary Picklish signs of women having been sniffing around here and there, jasmine-scented scraps of possible betrayals sticking out at odd angles. I'd been practicing the fine and horrifying art of discovering deceptions for so long that it had sadly become habit, and I am ashamed now to say that I continued to practice my art upon any and all men who happened into my life, even long after the one who'd made such craft necessary for me had exited my world.

So there it is. In a nutshell. "Why Miz Valdes was a paranoid twerp."

I put the pink card out of my mind to the extent that I could but kept hope at arm's length until such time as I could assure myself that there wasn't heartbreak or heartache waiting for me at the end of whatever journey I would undertake with this breathtaking, intoxicatingly beautiful man.

"Here you go," he said, handing me the glass of deep red wine. "Shall we sit outside?"

And we did, on the little porch, on patio chairs. Then after a while the cowboy got up to go let his three dogs out of their kennels by the barn, to run freely around the large compound, including the yard by the house, where they paused to sniff me. I was about to pet one of them, but the cowboy stopped me, sternly. He held a hand up.

"Hey, now. My dogs aren't pets," he said. "Don't be hugging up on them and loving on them. They're working dogs. In fact, I'd rather you didn't touch them at all. Not yet. They need to know that if they're going to get attention, it'll come from me."

Naturally, I found all of this annoying and stupid and offensive, because in those days I had very little experience with dogs and no experience with working dogs whatsoever. My favorite book at the time was a memoir by Ted Kerasote called *Merle's Door: Lessons from a Freethinking Dog*, all about how dogs needed freedom and should not be told what to do because they are intelligent, sentient beings. I had no idea in those days that such a book might be an overly anthropomorphized bit of ponderousness that equated dogs to trust-fund college kids in SoHo, and so I naturally thought the cowboy was evil, animal hating, controlling, and mean. But I kept those thoughts to myself, along with the sickeningly pink sixth sense about Mary Pickle, because I was trying to suspend my judgment of him until at least I'd been able to kiss him again. I mean, I didn't travel all this way for nothing. In truth, I had mixed feelings about him. Like most people in the early delusion of impending love, I'd probably underestimated the cowboy in all sorts of ways and overestimated him in all sorts of others. I assumed he'd be all the things that my father thought people like him would be. That is to say, ignorant, brutal, sociopathic, lame. I assumed he'd also be all the things my ex-husband had been, which is to say dishonest, unfaithful, glib, and sneaky.

I sat there with my glass of wine, in the warmth of the late afternoon, and watched as the dogs came trotting and hounding out. There was a sleek black male that reminded me of a Dementor from the Harry Potter books, named Taz. There was a black, white, and brown one with ice blue eyes, a big giant of a male, named Beau. There was a brindle black and blond one, a female, named Effie, who was as muscular as a big old fist. Taz and Beau sniffed me. Effie circled me from a distance and watched me suspiciously. The cowboy came over with his beer and talked about the dogs at some length. I probably didn't listen as closely as I could have, because I was preoccupied with whether I was about to be bitten with fangs. The cowboy said something about how he was fascinated by their body mechanics. He'd studied them, and their personalities, and he told me that each of them had to be trained and handled slightly differently from the others.

"They're not all that different from people in that way," he told me, sipping his beer and sitting on the chair next to me. We watched the dogs romp in the green grass of his front yard. "Everything I've learned about people, I learned first from dogs and horses."

The cowboy then told me that when he'd first arrived at this place two years before, it had been an ungodly mess. He described a scene that was something like a garbage dump. The various owners over the past thirty years had neglected the place and just let it go to hell. He was a man who took pride in everything he did, no matter the pay, and had turned it around.

"I've always said that no matter what job you're doing, you should be so good that whoever's signing the checks feels like they're getting a bargain every time they do it."

It was the first of many wise statements I'd hear coming from this man's beautiful mouth. It stopped me in my tracks. I'd known he was smart, and flirty, but this was the first time I realized he was also deeply philosophical. This wasn't just your average human being who went through life without thinking too much about things. This was a man, something like me, who thought a lot about everything. Maybe even too much.

He asked about me, and I told him the basic outline of my life. Born in Albuquerque, raised mostly there but with a detour to Scotland as a young girl when my dad got his first teaching gig. Then another three years in New Orleans, when my dad got his first professorship at the University of New Orleans. Back to New Mexico, graduated from high school early, went to Boston to Berklee College of Music, studied jazz saxophone. The cowboy's eyebrow lifted up on that one, but he didn't say anything. Just let me keep talking. Graduate school in journalism at Columbia University. Staff writer for *The Boston Globe* and the *Los Angeles Times* after that. Then a novelist.

I was on to my second glass of wine then, and the cowboy was on to his second or third beer. He started some coals in the barbecue grill, with a copious amount of lighter fluid, and when they were hot enough he added a couple of steaks that had been marinating in the refrigerator since the day before. It smelled wonderful as they began to sizzle. The sun was starting to set behind the house, and the evening was cooling off. Birds settled into the trees for the night, and I saw groups of deer darting in and out of the brush, moving toward the low-lying pastures where they'd bed down.

Past the barn, a tall oak tree was filling up with buzzards, great black birds winging their way to roost, five, six, seven, then eight of them. A community of scavengers.

"Used to have some wild turkeys that roosted in the tree here by the house," he told me, as we both shared a sort of reverence for nature and the quiet of the world moving at its own pace. "Then I got the dogs and they found someplace else to go. It was pretty neat to hear them coming in at night, sounded like pterodactyls."

I looked at this man. He was no longer wearing the hat. He'd put on a pair of eyeglasses. He looked less foreign to me now. Yes, he was drop-dead gorgeous. Yes, he was exotic and sort of fascinating for his chosen lifestyle and profession. I knew all that. But now I saw something else, too. He wasn't just a hot, cocky cowboy. He was . . . a lot like me. He valued nature. Beauty. Solitude. Good books. Good music. He had a poetic streak. He was thoughtful. He was, in spite of his almost bombastic confidence, pretty much alone in the world, estranged from his family, taking this trip through life in that existential cocoon of solitude that so many of the world's most thoughtful and sensitive people find themselves within. *How strange*, I thought, sipping my wine, enjoying the peace I felt here. How very, very strange. How strange to find someone so much like me, who was to the outside world absolutely nothing like me at all.

"Interesting," I said, impressed with my own ostensibly deep thoughts in the way that only slightly drunk people can be.

"What is?" he asked as he poked the coals.

"This. You."

"How's that?"

I explained to him that he was more than I'd expected.

He smiled, in a way that communicated both patient annoyance and pleasant lack of surprise. "You'd be surprised how much thinking you can do spending your life looking at life through the ears of a cow pony."

He got up then, to go back to the kitchen, to prepare the rest of the meal. I sat outside a moment longer, listened to the screen door bang shut, and watched the vultures settling into their tree for the night. From this angle, they were almost beautiful.

Funny, I thought.

Vultures had their own kind of majesty. Yet I'd been taught only to think of them as vile, villainous, and cruel. I'd thought them ugly, but in truth they were not. They were doing what came naturally to them. They did work the rest of us needed but couldn't stomach.

In their own habitat, at the intersection of day and night, vultures were quite perfect, really, cooing gently to one another, flapping home from a hard day's work, oblivious to how the others saw them.

Vultures, it turned out, slept, too, at night.

And, I realized, they dreamed—just like all the other birds in the sky.

THE SECOND KISS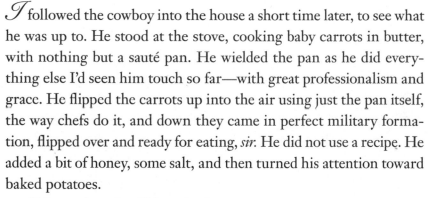

I followed the cowboy into the house a short time later, to see what he was up to. He stood at the stove, cooking baby carrots in butter, with nothing but a sauté pan. He wielded the pan as he did everything else I'd seen him touch so far—with great professionalism and grace. He flipped the carrots up into the air using just the pan itself, the way chefs do it, and down they came in perfect military formation, flipped over and ready for eating, *sir*. He did not use a recipe. He added a bit of honey, some salt, and then turned his attention toward baked potatoes.

"More wine, dear?" he asked me.

I declined, and composed myself. "Can I help you with something?" I asked.

The cowboy lifted an eyebrow in my direction and smirked a little, and said nothing for a moment. The lack of words did not impede his communication. He was saying, quite clearly, that he was sure there was something I could help him with and it had nothing whatsoever to do with dinner.

Butterflies.

"I got this under control," he said a moment later, enjoying the way I twisted inside at his unspoken intentions. It was nice to know he still wanted me, because since the kiss in the truck hours ago he'd not made a single move in that direction and I'd begun to doubt he would again.

"Okay," I said.

He smiled at me, as though I were funny. I probably was. I'm not sure what I must have looked like to him, standing there agape at the sight of a big old cowboy suddenly transformed into a chef without a cowboy hat. He looked like a guy, any guy—well, any guy who happened to be model-gorgeous and six foot four in boots. Everything about him was hot. That he could brand a calf and sauté baby carrots made me all sort of melty and goofy inside.

"Be right back," he said. He turned the burner off and went back to the steaks on the porch. I sort of piddled around the living room, flipped through a coffee table book on someone named Ian Tyson, waiting for him. He came back in, with the steaks on a plate, and went to set them down in the kitchen. I lingered in the living room, not quite sure what to do with myself, just sort of standing around looking at the artwork on the walls. Some of the professional-looking photographs of a cowboy and his horse appeared to actually be this man himself. In one of them, he is drinking out of a horse trough. *And I kissed that mouth*, I thought, quickly realizing that I would gladly do so again if given the opportunity. Even if it had just come fresh from a trough. That's how much I wanted him.

A moment later, he came into the living room and moved stealthily to stand behind me. I was going to turn to face him, but he stopped me, placing one arm around my neck and the other around my waist, pulling me in for a strange sort of my-back-against-his-front embrace. His grip was tender but nonnegotiable. Powerful. He held me in place, and then he moved me with him, ever so slightly, so that we were both facing the mirror above the mantel. I looked at our reflection and saw him behind me, felt him as he pressed himself against my back. He nuzzled my hair and kissed the back of my neck. I could not move. It was exciting but also frightening. All my life I'd longed to be held and controlled physically by a fantastically desirable man in just this way, handled by him, moved by him, wanted by him so much that he just made me feel all those things I was too ashamed to admit to feeling on my own. I'm sure there are deep psychological reasons for my secret longings, and I'm equally sure that analyzing them here and now will bore you as much as it would bore me. I am also sure that lots of women feel this way about men, for nothing more than simple biology. We are the vessel. They are the elixir and the funnel. We are the earth. They are the plough and seed. They give, we take. We open, they enter. Etcetera. It was intoxicating to feel so helpless, so desired, so at his command. And yet now, looking at the handgun on the mantel, the ropes, the knife, and realizing I simply could not escape this man's grip even if I'd wanted to . . . it scared me, too.

The cowboy looked up then, at our reflection, and he caught my gaze. He saw instantly the fear in my eyes, and released his grip— just like that. He saw my eyes on the pistol and on him. He came around to face me now, his own expression softening, sympathetic but not apologetic. He was all business suddenly.

"The keys are in the black pickup," he told me, holding eye contact. "It'll go right through those gates. You don't need to worry about that. You get to where you're scared, or you don't trust me, or you need to get out of here, you just get in and go. Understand? Just take the truck. You're not trapped here. I'm not a bad guy. You're okay."

I looked down at the floor, ashamed of how I'd made him feel. Ashamed of my paranoid former reporter's nature, my suspicious thoughts. And very, very sorry to have killed this second intimate moment with him just as surely as I'd murdered the first.

"I'm sorry," I said. "It's just, you know. If I were your friend, like a female friend, and I told you I was going out to some guy's ranch who I hardly knew, and you knew there'd be gates and guns and stuff, what would you say if she asked you if she should go?"

He smiled at me. "I'd say hell *no*, you shouldn't."

"Right. But I did."

He searched my eyes for a long moment before saying, "I'm glad you did."

"Thanks," I managed.

"And dinner's ready," he said, turning to walk back to the kitchen. "So you better wash up and get to the table before it gets cold."

And so I did. I washed up. When I returned to the kitchen I found the stereo on, Al Green playing. *I . . . am so in love with you . . . whatever you want to do . . .*

He showed me his CD collection and asked me if there was something else I'd rather listen to. I saw an old Pat Metheny album I used to love back when I was in college. That the cowboy would own such a CD surprised the heck out of me. What on earth was a rural cowboy doing with a vintage Pat Metheny album? Didn't guys like this limit their musical repertoire to, what, Merle Haggard and Roy Rogers or something?

I took it out and put it in.

"Wouldn't expect you to have this record," I said.

"Maybe you should stop anticipating," he suggested, knowing exactly what I meant, and exactly how offensive it was, but being too polite to tell me the plain truth, which was that I was as prejudiced as any prejudiced person had ever been, against rural white men, against cowboys, against those people Thom Hartmann would arrogantly call "low-information voters," against the people my father cynically referred to as "beef eaters." I was no better than Rush Limbaugh lambasting all Latinos as disease-riddled foreign terrorists.

I was an idiot after all, but not for the reason I had most feared

I'd be an idiot. He was a good guy. I was safe. And I was an idiot precisely because I was *prejudiced*.

The album had been my entire summer one year, the sound track to many solitary bike rides in the desert, many subway rides where I thought, and dreamed, and created art. It was uncanny that I'd find it again now, here, in this place, with this unlikely man. Uncanny and, I thought, a sign.

The cowboy stood at my chair, holding it for me to sit down in before he scooted me in. He served me my plate, then set his own down and took his seat. I'd never have thought that any man who described himself as a conservative cowboy would make dinner for a woman, much less serve it to her.

He made a toast.

"To new friends," he said.

"To new friends," I echoed.

It was the best steak I'd ever tasted, and the best carrots, too.

Maybe he was right, I thought. Maybe I *should* stop expecting, anticipating, prejudging. Maybe I *didn't* know what I thought I knew. Maybe the world wasn't as simple as they made it seem on *The Rachel Maddow Show*. Maybe conservatives were more nuanced and unpredictable than I'd been led to believe by Stephanie Miller and Hal Sparks and whatever other stunted adolescent had their own progressive talk show.

We ate. And we talked. I don't remember everything we talked about, but I do remember him telling me a little bit about his childhood, enough for me to realize that a weaker man might not have come out of it intact, or even alive.

"I'm sorry you had to deal with all that," I said.

"It is what it is, dear. And frankly, if I'd been in my mom's shoes, battling the demons she'd had to battle, I don't know if I'd done half as good as she did."

It was an uncharacteristically tolerant and generous statement, considering the source and the circumstances, and it surprised me.

He continued to surprise me now, by confessing to me, after he'd had a bit of alcohol himself, that he had done some modeling and acting. A literal model, in magazines and catalogs.

"That explains why your photos looked fake on Match.com," I said.

"They were all I had," he said.

Then he told me he'd done some commercials and, in his words, "minor film work," for Hollywood.

Hollywood.

(Note: As I wrote this book, the cowboy was uncomfortable about any of this being mentioned because in cowboy culture modesty is highly valued and he did not want to be seen as bragging or being impressed with himself. It should be understood that it is my desire, not his, that this information be known.)

My breath caught in my throat as I remembered the prophecy from when I was fourteen.

"Hollywood?" I asked.

He told me that he had been discovered by a talent scout in Colorado and cast in a commercial about herding cats. The commercial aired during the Super Bowl in 2000, and a star was born. The cowboy was signed to a talent agency in Denver. The owners gushed about how the camera loved him. I could not argue. The camera did indeed love this man. He knew it, but he didn't much care about it. Good looks were an accident of nature, he reasoned, nothing more than that.

"I wasn't born with the 'look at me' gene," he explained. "I don't like being stared at or looked at or noticed. I'm a guy who likes to be in the background."

"That's so unfair," I said. "So many people want to be looked at, and they'd kill to look like you."

The cowboy shrugged. He told me that some of the agent types were excited by how much the camera favored him, but he was only interested in it for the money, not his ego. His representative at his talent agency in Colorado was often frustrated by the fact that all he cared about was money. "Every time she had a job for me, I asked what it paid," he said. "Most of those people would have done it for free because they wanted to be seen, but I didn't give two shits about being on camera. I was only interested in what it paid and whether it could help me support what I really wanted to do, which was put together my own cow herd."

In other words, he only did the modeling and acting because it paid better than a lot of the other types of jobs he'd had. This list of jobs included but was not limited to the following: bar bouncer, bar owner, truck driver, horse-hauling business owner, cowpuncher, construction worker.

I asked him polite questions about his various jobs and tried to keep my classist knee-jerk tendencies in check. Yes, he'd mostly had blue-collar jobs. Yes, I'd been raised to theoretically defend "the common man" by a good socialist father; no, this had not made a dent in our family's elitist outlook on "respectable" jobs for a potential partner for me to have. My father had taught me well that although we were supposed to support and stand in solidarity with the working man, we (meaning me) weren't exactly supposed to, you know, share a bed with one. Or wedding vows. I'm not sure how those mixed messages took root in me, only that they did, and that I had to fight them.

"Tell me about when you drove trucks," I said.

This is when the cowboy launched into a story about having driven a "bull rack," a livestock-hauling trailer semi rig designed to haul cattle. Once, he transported pigs to a slaughterhouse in it.

"When I went to pick up these pigs, cull sows—a sow is a female, okay? These animals from an early age are warehoused, they're not outdoors, they can't see sunlight, anything like that. And what they're in there for is they breed them to raise more pigs. Once they reach an age where they can't produce any more piglets, they ship them off to be slaughtered. As these pigs were coming out of this building to load onto the truck, it was obvious to me that the sunlight startled them because they hadn't been out in the sun—it's a crappy life. And as they were pushing them on the trailer it's obvious this one sow has become crippled in one hind leg. She's having trouble walking up the ramp to get on the trailer and she's also a little shocked—they all are—about the sunlight hitting; they're squealing. I know that pigs are probably one of the smartest animals, and absolutely the smartest domesticated animal, and in my mind the smarter an animal is, the easier it is to drive it insane. So back to this sow, she's struggling to get on the truck. These guys that are loading her get impatient, and one of them hits her with a hot shot—an electrical charge—to get her to move. In my mind I know there's a vast difference between a pig's hide and a cow or a horse, so what's a mild buzz to a cow or a horse is painful to a pig. And while I had no problem making extra money on the side buying and selling killer horses [horses to be slaughtered], I am not about torturing an animal. So by the third time this guy hits her with a hot shot I get pissed and tell him if you hit her with that hot shot again I'm going to shove it up your ass and electrify your tonsils. They get them on the trailer and they tell me it's not like hauling cattle where you have to get there as fast as you can, that pigs will just lie down and go to sleep and you're going to have some of them die and just don't worry about it. As I've got to go all the way from southern Utah to western Tennessee, I can't tolerate the thought of having an animal die in my custody, so I run nine hundred miles an hour all the way, no stopping, no resting, to get them all there to the plant alive. It doesn't really matter to me that they're all going there to get butchered; they don't have to suffer en route. . . . By the time I back up to the unloading chute, it's like backing up to a house of horrors. You can hear pigs screaming, these guys are just brutal, they're kicking them if they're not moving fast enough, hitting them with hot shots, they become desensitized. It's pissing me off. Keep in mind the last one off the trailer is this crippled sow. She cannot come down the ramp because she's crippled and cramped. These guys come up with a cable attached to a winch and put it around her neck and they're going to drag her off the trailer this way. I stop them then and there and say put her fucking leg through there, you're not just going to drag her and choke her. So they engage the winch and it runs so slowly, dragging her off at a real slow rate of speed, they get her to the back of the trailer, baby, sits off the ground four feet high, no ramp, nothing, *whomp*, they pull her, she falls on a dead pig onto her side. She can't breathe because her lungs are compressed by the weight of her body, and they're just going to let her lie there until they're ready to take her in. I get pissed and say it isn't necessary to do this. They look at me like I'm from Mars because they're so desensitized. Until I'm tired of talking and I say either get her off that hog right now or I will whip your goddamned ass right here and right now, and of course I get this look like, jeez, what's the big deal, like I'm making a big deal out of nothing. Hence, to this day I will not eat pork products from this particularly well-known national processor of pork products."

I was ashamed, and astounded. Not five minutes before this, I had been smiling in a patronizing and awkward way because I didn't think that this blue-collar man could possibly have anything insightful or interesting to share with me, in recounting the details of his "career" with me. How wrong I had been. The color of the collar didn't matter, I realized in shame. The size of the heart did.

So there you had it. A story about a surprisingly empathetic and sensitive truck driver who handles the miseries of modern life by beating the crap out of someone for torturing a pig. Interesting, I thought. Few people in my white-collar world would have handled a conflict like this in such a direct and physical way, but this man wasn't so different from me, truth be told. I'd had plenty of battles in my years as a journalist, usually for reasons a lot like the one he outlined here, reasons of justice, or injustice really. I was the "crazy" person who stormed into morning editorial meetings, demanding a good reason for the paper treating victims of crimes differently de-

pending on what neighborhood they were from (meaning rich people got on the front page, poor people inside the Metro section
below the fold).

"That's an amazing story," I said, still covered in goose bumps
because the thing I'd been given knowledge of as a kid was unfolding
before me, live and in person. The name. The yellow grasses of his
prairies. Hollywood.

"Do you have any of your acting I could see?" I asked, changing
the subject because the thought of the tortured pig was almost too
much to bear.

He did. With some persuasion, he put in a video of himself starring in an Animal Planet reenactment, playing a criminal poacher.
He put little round glasses on to watch the video, and they made him
look very nerdy-hot in a way that this very nerdy girl absolutely
loved. We watched the video together on his sofa. He was quite good
in it, like a real actor. And so, so very handsome. Totally convincing.

"See, I was rushing my lines right there," he said, still disappointed with what seemed to me to be a very good performance.

"Looks fine to me."

"I could have done better."

"You could have totally been a *superstar*," I said.

"I didn't *want* to be a star," he reminded me, making a face as
though "being a star" were akin to eating garbage. "I like *this*." He
gestured to the room, and to the window to indicate the land outside.
"I don't *like* cities, or rude people. And most people, after a while, are
rude. I like being alone with my thoughts. I like a simple life."

"Sounds like you know what you want," I said. "That's good.
That's rare. Most people think they want fame and fortune, and
even when they get it they don't have what you have, which is peace
of mind, and happiness."

He looked at me for a long moment, as though what I'd said held
some special significance for him. Then he took my hand and spoke
directly to me, looking deeply into my eyes.

"You should know, Miz Valdes, that I'm not doing this Match thing because I'm interested in finding the *next* one." He paused before saying, "I'm interested in finding the *last* one."

He gave me a significant look, a look that made me think he might have been thinking that I could be the last one.

"Good to know," I said cynically, snarkily really, fully prepared to kill this third intimate moment for myself because, you know, nobody has ever been quite as good at messing up my life for me as, well, me. "For a guy who's never been married."

"No," he said, letting go of my hand. He got up, turned the video off, and went to put it away again in a cabinet. "But I wouldn't say it like that. I'd say I've never been *divorced*."

"Good point."

"I'm not afraid of commitment, Alisa," he said, returning to the living room but sitting a little farther away from me this time. "Plenty of women would tell you that I am, but they've missed the point."

"Which is?"

"Which is *this*: I'm not afraid of commitment. But I *am* afraid of marrying the wrong woman. I've thrown enough big loops in my life to know that I don't want to make a mistake that big again. I am one of those crazy people who think marriage is forever. I know what I'm looking for," he said, staring straight through to my soul. "And I knew for the longest time that I hadn't found it yet."

I couldn't think of anything to say, because his direct stare made me so nervous. It was almost like he was thinking that he had finally found it and that it was me. Or maybe that was how I wanted to interpret what he was saying. His eyes said he thought I was that elusive "last one" . . . didn't they? I didn't know. I wanted to ask, but it was too early for that. I was getting ahead of myself. I was imagining things, things I wanted to be true, romantic, silly, girly things.

And then he said, while looking deeply into my eyes, "But I can tell you this: I get just a little bit closer to what I'm looking for, every time I try. Real close."

He tipped his beer can in my direction then, and I felt my face flush hot and red. I knew better than to believe such a smooth line, so perfect a setup. Especially with Mary Pickle's card still in plain view. He was saying the kinds of words every woman longed to hear a man like him say. Words too shiny, too clean, too rehearsed. I should have known better than to drink them in like wine, and part of me probably did know better. A small part.

But the other part of me, the biggest part, the wounded part of me, the part that had survived a painful childhood, and then a terrible marriage, the part of me that had finally gotten up the nerve to date at all again, the part that had been broken enough to go from fit to fat in an effort to fill that horrible empty ache, the part of me who'd never had a wedding, who'd bought her own wedding ring, who'd tried and tried to make a normal life out of an abnormal marriage, the part that had staggered with monumental effort back to this thing called hope, in spite of being overweight and old and everything else—*that* part of me . . . *that* part of me felt like a little girl in a pretty pink princess dress, ready to stand up in front of everyone in the world and just spin and spin and spin, until she just fell down, giggling at the way the earth moved beneath her with the enormity of love.

I smiled across the table at the cowboy, and he smiled back at me as though I were the most beautiful and interesting woman in the world. The wine raced through my veins, and in spite of the nagging voice in my head telling me not to be stupid, I got stupid anyway. Really stupid.

Really, beautifully, happily . . . just . . . *stupid.*

For it was in that exact and recklessly premature moment, girded by wine and his (perhaps too slick) words, that I released my fears, broke all the rules in those outdated dating books, and began against all my better judgment to fall deeply in love with a handsome, wounded, hard-ass, difficult, brilliant, empathetic, poetic, pugilistic, literate, complicated, and solitary cowboy.

Bedtime came soon after that. I stayed in the cowboy's masculine house that night, in his bedroom, in his bed, as he'd planned for me to do.

Contrary to the original plan for him to stay elsewhere, however, he . . . um . . . joined me. And, to paraphrase a famous quote from *Seinfeld*, it was real, and it was spectacular.

Let me put it like this: Angels sang arias. The earth moved. I would love to describe in detail for you what actually happened, but one of the wonderful ways the cowboy has tamed the proverbial shrew that was once me, in the time that I have known him, is that he has pointed out to me that some things are better left unsaid in civilized company or, as he has suggested, left to the reader's imagination.

Somewhere along the way in our private happiness whose details you will never know, he looked me in the eye and whispered in a bit of happy astonishment, "It just feels right." And it did. And I felt something divine, something not quite of this world, a spirit, spirits, with us. This was meant to be. It was right.

And then we were still, and quiet, so very, very quiet, holding hands there in the darkness, side by side in the middle of nowhere, in a world away from people, cars, streets, and the disappointing, hopeless past. The crickets under the tree outside his window soon began their nighttime serenade. I listened, and my breathing slowed, my body relaxed, and sleep began to slink around the edges of everything. But I didn't *want* to sleep. I wanted to understand why I was so happy, so at peace. It was exactly as Dr. Seuss had once said, that you knew you were in love when you could not sleep, because life was finally better than your dreams. I resisted, looked around. The shades were open to the darkness outside, and for the first time I turned my eyes to the sky. I gasped at what I saw. Stars. But not the handful of stars I was accustomed to in the city. Billions of stars, smears of them, arcs of them, flowing in symphonic grace all across the universe. Twinkling. Blinking. Glowing. Being. A billion beautiful celestial princesses, turning and turning for all to see their skirts, whispering the name of God—Spinoza's God—to me, in this most unexpected and perfect place. *You see?* they seemed to ask. *We told you, didn't we? Someday, that someday you'd meet him, and his name would be his name, and yellow, and Hollywood, because all of time happens at once, and you experience it linearly because you are stuck to the earth, but out here, out here it has already happened, someday had already come and gone and would come again, and you'd meet him someday, just as you'd already met him before, when you heard that faintest echo of the beautiful thing that was to someday happen to you.*

Welcome back, and forward, my dear girl, to someday.

GIRLS' NIGHT OUT

Not long after my first weekend at the ranch with the cowboy, I had drinks with a couple of female friends, while my father babysat my son. In those days, my dad was pretty much my best friend, as he pretty much still is, and ordinarily I would have liked to share with him the information that I had begun to fall in love. One bonus to having parents from the countercultural 1970s is that you can talk to them about, well, just about anything. But I knew that the nature of the object of my affections was not one that my beloved father would or could understand—at least not *then*—and so, being filled to exploding with confused happiness, I enlisted the ears of my friends to spill my crazed-middle-aged-lady-in-love story. I was afraid to risk upsetting my dad with the disappointing news that his good leftist feminist daughter was falling for, well, the opposite of all that.

My friends were, respectively, an artist and a former television news anchor, both liberal like me, both single like me, both of Latina heritage like me, and both fond of trendy restaurants, like me. I will call the artist Brenda and I will call the former anchor Jessica. We met at a place called the Nob Hill Grill, in the selfsame and achingly emo-yuppie never-met-a-piercing-it-didn't-like Nob Hill neighborhood in Albuquerque, near the university and near the house where I was living. This would be a good time to confess to you, metaphorical tail between my metaphysical legs, that I was in fact living with my father at the time. That particular arrangement arose for a complexity of reasons, but suffice to summarize it thusly: In the world of a writer or other creative artist, salary can usually be described in terms of either feast or famine, and neither one tends to last forever, the pendulum swinging with cold glee from one hot pole to the other. I'd feasted for a few years, quite nicely, in fact, but was now in the throes of a prolonged and painful famine. My Lexus had been repossessed. I'd had to short-sell my half-million-dollar house. My student loans were nearly in default. I had terrible credit and mountains of medical debt due to a mystery illness from a couple of years before that turned out to be lupus-like and thyroidy.

And it was all only getting worse on the financial front, though I mercifully did not know it then. I was at the start of a year in which I would eventually earn *less* than I'd made as a part-time receptionist back when I was in college twenty years before. It wasn't pretty. It wasn't a thing to be proud of. But my father had a large house, the newer and bigger portion of which he had given over to me and my son. He was collecting a retirement pension that was substantial, and sharing it with us, hugging me as he handed me money and telling me that life was about taking care of other people, sharing what we had, and that he did not believe this American idea about always having to prove oneself by being utterly independent in times of need. He enjoyed helping us, and this, my friends, is one of the beauties of true progressive-minded people; they are, at root, no different from truly Christian people, in their desire to redistribute the excesses to those in need, or, as conservatives might call it, "charity."

And my son and I were in need of charity.

I felt guilty about it, and I felt like a failure. I promised to pay my father back someday, but he shrugged this off and reminded me that more adults than ever were having to move back in with their parents at this point in American history, "through no fault of their own." He explained to me the banking crisis, something about Goldman Sachs being the bastard child of Satan and Mussolini, I think, something about the way that huge corporations had knowingly misled and bankrupted people and the entire nation so a handful of yachting types could do even more yachting. He understood economics as an academic, and what he said was true in some ways. People were hurting. Lots of people. And books were a luxury item, something that consumers gave up buying when times got tough—well, most books. The consumer always seemed to make an exception for anything written by Stephenie Meyer or James Patterson, but that was another story for another day. Point is, I was homeless and broke, technically, but knew that I'd never be truly homeless or truly broke as long as my father was alive, because my father, a die-hard socialist to his marrow, lived his values and gave everything he had to anyone who needed it and asked, including me and my son.

In retrospect, I can admit that while my decline in income was due to lagging book sales, I have to be honest and say that a big part of that was not actually due to the economy sucking. A big part of it was due to *me* sucking, as a person. I had badly mismanaged my very promising literary career a few years before, by being a woman without proper boundaries, an angry woman, and self-destructive on a grand scale. Readers came to love me from my books, and then they got to know me through social media, blogs, and the like, and soon came to hate me because, basically, I was bat-crap nuts. That's really the best and most honest way to put it. I censored nothing. I spoke openly about all of my views, which, considering how narrow-minded and combative many of them were and how out of step with the mainstream, did nothing to help build my fan base. If anything, I seemed to be working very hard to diminish my fan base, and succeeding with warp speed.

But I didn't know any of this. The day I had drinks with Brenda and Jessica, I just thought I was in a temporary dry spell and that book sales would be picking up again any minute now. I blamed the banking system, and George W. Bush, and God knows what else for my failures. Alberto Gonzales. Jennifer Weiner. Jodi Picoult. It was all their fault, right? Somehow. Jennifer Lopez. I don't know. Someone. Anyone but me. It was easier to hold my head up that way.

Back to girls' night out.

The Nob Hill Grill is trendy, for Albuquerque. This statement is sort of like saying "The seafood is fresh, for Afghanistan." The joint might actually seem like an upscale restaurant and bar in any city in the land, as long as you went back in time five or ten years before going there. The décor is dark and modern, all leather and squares, with deep-chocolate wood floors. The clientele are young, hip, fashionable, attractive, snarky. The cocktails are creative, and the bartenders tend toward the female and the flat bellied, but with an edge best described as "rude." The one we got had a tattoo around her navel, which was exposed thanks to the low pants and short shirt. The tattoo was dark blue and starlike and gave her the overall look of someone who might have just been shot in the gut with a rifle, or so I thought at the time, the time being a time in which I still had no clue about the differences between, say, rifles and shotguns, or pellets and buckshot.

Brenda is a beautiful woman, with deep brown soulful eyes and pretty, thick hair that is always flying off on a new adventure of color and style. She has one of those pretty heart-shaped faces that can handle just about any hairstyle, short or long. She is a visual artist of uncommon skill and intensity, and her work makes me feel intense and frightening emotions that are normally drawn out of me only through orchestral works by Hector Berlioz. She has had a tough life. It started out tough, and stayed tough, getting even tougher in recent years as she got sidelined by a disease that is usually reserved for people who are much older. She is not old and she has always taken very good care of her beautiful self. She did not deserve this disease. No one deserves this disease, except for maybe Stalin, or Stewie from *Family Guy*. Brenda most certainly did not, and watching her struggle through it was very painful.

As we sat there with our cocktails that evening, Brenda was in remission and I was happy about that and yet still not terribly comfortable talking about it with her because I did not know how to bring a thing like that up. What do you say? "Gee, hope you don't get sick again?" Anyway, she wore a scarf. She does that, and they always look marvelous. You don't think a funky, beautiful artist who can make you feel emotions as big as the sky and whose jokes make you fall out of your chair laughing can ever be so gravely ill as to scare you that she will die, and yet that was Brenda's story. And yet Brenda still came to listen to me talk about a cowboy, as though she had all the time in the world to be burdened with such useless information as Alisa's Ridiculously Dramatic and Oft-Pathetic Love Life.

Jessica, meanwhile, is tall and thin, with short dark hair. She is prone to animal prints and manages to be elegant anyway. She resents men and rightfully so because they have been notoriously rotten to her, and at that point this mistrust of humans with Y chromosomes was one of the strongest cements that bound us together in friendship. She is a single mom, just like me, and we shared tips about raising boys without men around. She is a dynamic woman, the kind who always has something outrageous and interesting to say, and sometimes says it loud enough to invoke stares from other tables in the bar.

There we sat, at a table in the bar, with a big pile of nachos spilling off the plate before us. I ordered a screwdriver. I don't remember what the other women ordered. Pretty sure Brenda had a gin and tonic. Pretty sure Jessica had something fruity and strong. But I wouldn't bet my life on the accuracy of my memory, though I am 100 percent sure of the nachos because the chips were blue, red, and yellow and the cheese was ooey-gooey goodness.

We talked a bit about work, projects we were each working on, asked about one another's families and children. Asked about health, exercise, talked about the weather. And then, after a couple of drinks, I told the girls that I had something important to tell them and I wanted their honest opinions. Brenda and Jessica perked up the way pampered cats perk up when they hear the can opener. They waited to hear what might come next.

So I told them. I told them basically everything that I've told you so far, only in far fewer words, and punctuated by increasingly nervous and sloppy slurps from my unadventurous cocktail. I ordered a third drink and asked them if they thought I was crazy.

"I can't believe you'd date a conservative," said Jessica. "I mean, I've dated some out-there guys, no doubt about that, but there are a few things that are deal breakers for me, and politics is one of them."

"I know," I moaned, taking another nacho and stuffing it into my gaping maw. "But he's not what you'd expect. I mean, he is, in some ways he totally is. He's got guns, and ammo, and knives." I think I paused here to grunt the way Tim Allen used to on his first sitcom, the gorilla-man grunt.

It was then that I detailed some of my new concerns about the cowboy. Although he had certainly surprised me by being more literate and compassionate than I had expected of a member of his exotic and unknowable tribe, he had said some things, voiced some opinions, that unsettled me.

"Like what?" asked Jessica.

Like the way he called undocumented immigrants "illegals."

"He got pretty angry," I said. "He was all, 'what part of illegal don't you understand,' that whole nightmare."

"Ugh," said Brenda.

"Yeah, I know. But he *did* say that it doesn't matter if you're Mexican or Irish or Russian or Canadian, if you're here undocumented, you're here illegally. It's not a skin-tone thing for him, like it probably is for some of them. He said he knows we probably need immigration reform, but as it stands now, 'the law is the law.' He says if you start out your time here illegally, you get desensitized to getting caught and you're more prone to commit more illegal acts."

"What else?" asked Jessica.

I told her about the way he told me that he understood why some "white men" whom he called "less sophisticated and less questioning minds" might be prone to scapegoating "Mexicans," if that was what was happening, because they felt, perhaps wrongly, that the days of their sole supremacy were numbered. This did not mean he agreed with them, but it did mean he understood where they were coming from. He said he believed people, all people, were inherently tribal at a base and biological level and would tend to align with those they perceived to be their own even when it wasn't in anyone's best interest to do so. It wasn't that he thought darker people were inferior, he'd told me, but rather that some people feared that *any* people who gain a majority are inclined to oppress and subjugate those who look different from themselves, and he understood why some less critical thinkers would think that white people were running out of time.

"And he said something about how he was among those who were going to prepare for the potential economic collapse of American society by having guns handy and ready for when the swarms of desperate and less principled people came to take what was his."

"Wow," said Jessica. "How very Ted Kaczynski."

"So I'm conflicted," I said. "We disagree on so many things, but I swear to you, I want him, physically want him, more than I've ever wanted a man in my life. It's not just the way he looks, even though there's clearly nothing *wrong* with that. It's something else—I can't put my finger on what it is. Something totally just, like, biological. I can't really explain it. I swear it's like I can smell the testosterone coming off him. It's like he's an actual grown-up man. He's a man who you could trust to get things done. To take care of you. To take care of business. To protect you. I sound so old-fashioned, don't I?"

At this point, we stopped to talk about how even though we were all independent women, none of us liked wimpy guys. By wimpy, we meant everything from how they walked to whether or not they could support themselves or even, you know, pay for our dinner. We mused aloud about what the roots might be of our desire to be with men who could take care of themselves, economically. I recounted for them the fact that in my marriage I had been the only breadwinner, and that while I certainly appreciated the effort my ex-husband had made at home (he was a good housekeeper and did his best to raise our son), it was still a biological turnoff for me to feel the pressure to be the one financially providing for the family while also being the one who had to carry the child in her womb and nurse it once it was born. I had tried. For nearly a decade I had tried to accept this role reversal in my marriage. I had even bragged about how great it was to have such an enlightened husband. I credited him with making my novel-writing career possible because he did everything on the home front. I'd gone seven years without once doing my own laundry, for instance. And yet, I gradually over time lost all sexual attraction for the man I was married to, and I knew deep down inside it was because I couldn't see him as a real man if he was doing traditionally female things. I wanted to be the one home with the baby, not the one out jetting around doing book signings. I wanted to be the one doing the shopping and the cleaning. I didn't really like the way my husband cleaned, and I found myself always repairing it. He just didn't have an eye for design like I did, and of course I wanted to be with my son as much as I could. My friends and I sat there in the bar and tried and failed to come up with the names of any friends of ours who were women who might feel okay with being in the traditional man's role, economically. I ventured to say I thought this was evolution speaking, somehow, and we agreed that while it wasn't ideal to feel the way we did, we felt that way nonetheless. It wasn't fair to men, probably. But it was truth, or at least it was our truth.

I said, "I know this sounds really stupid, but I've been thinking about it, and I think there's a biological reason I'm attracted to a guy like the cowboy, like an evolutionary reason. Guys like that, the alpha males, you think you shouldn't like them, but you do anyway. Right? We evolved for it, and I think it's time that I just admitted that and got on with, like, being a girl. I'm tired of the men in my relationships getting to be the girls all the time."

Brenda smiled at me, which surprised me, and then she got that look people get when they discover something, the lightbulb-over-the-head look.

"Exactly!" she said.

"Sorry?"

"I can't remember the last time I met an actual man," she said despondently. "I swear to you, what we have in this country right now is a crisis in manhood. Every man I meet is a goddamned giant boy. Or, like you said, a girl."

Jessica gave a high five now, and an amen.

I mentioned then to my friends that I had been thinking long and hard about the way women in our generation—which is to say women born in the late 1960s or early 1970s—had been raised with ideas that no other generation of women had been raised with. I talked about my belief that most of these ideas were good—you know, that women should be able to do just about any job they liked, that we should be able to choose whether or not to have kids, that we should be paid the same salary for the same job as a man, etcetera.

"But it maybe went too far in a lot of ways," I suggested.

My friends, who were both about the same age as me, listened.

"Think about it," I said. "The paradigm never changed. That's the problem. The paradigm, or the system of value ascribed to people, didn't change. It's like feminism just decided that women would be determined to be equal to the extent that we were able to do what men did, and men were able to do what we did."

"So?" asked Brenda.

"That's not real liberation," I posited. "Because it presumes that we were all exactly the same to begin with, right? Able to do the same things with the same skills. But we're not. Science shows that we're not. There are some serious and major differences, but second-wave feminism, the way we were raised, or at least the way I was raised, with a sociologist professor for a dad, was to assume that all of our major differences were learned, not inborn. Nurture, not nature. We acted, as a society, like the very idea of innate sex differences in men and women was offensive. We're still acting like that in this country."

"How so?" asked Brenda.

"The whole honorary man thing. Look at Hillary Clinton. All these women politicians. To be taken seriously, they have to hide their attractiveness and dress like men. But in Argentina, you have a woman like Cristina Kirchner, who is feminine and beautiful but still allowed to be powerful. That doesn't happen here. We act like it's an either-or thing here. I think the whole reason Sarah Palin was so popular with so many women is that she was the first woman in American political history to actually look feminine, and act feminine, without shame. Before that all we had was Geraldine Ferraro. Condoleezza Rice. Women who didn't quite act like women. Janet Reno. Women who were forced to act like men, really, and only women in theory."

My friends nodded as though they understood what I was saying.

"And it's not just women!" I exclaimed, my brain racing. "Think about the pop-culture sex symbols we had growing up, as girls. They were girly, every single one of them! It was like our whole society and culture in the 1980s was doing everything in its power to make men women and to make women men. Prince? Seriously?

That was supposed to be sexy? A tiny little man with no body hair, running around in fucking thigh-high stiletto heels, singing in the highest falsetto in the world about how you were a 'Little Red Corvette'? Are you fucking kidding me?"

They laughed.

I was on a roll.

"David Bowie? Are you shitting me? Who the hell in her right mind would actually want to have sex with that . . . thing? I won't call him a man. He wasn't. Oh! And all the hair bands. You're telling me that the height of masculinity was a bunch of men who were prettier than us, with long flowing hair, and makeup, tons of makeup these guys wore! In spandex pants? That was supposed to be manly and sexy? Glam-rock guys? Oh my fucking God!"

"You're right," said Jessica.

"We didn't know any better!" I cried. "They were experimenting on all of us. Boys and girls. Duran Duran? How many guys in my high school tried to Dippity-do like those guys? And Flock of Seagulls? It's insane. We all felt this pressure to act like the other sex, just to atone for the goddamned sins of our grandfathers. Adam Ant? Seriously! The manliest one of the bunch was Billy freakin' Idol, and I loved him. But I only loved him because he snarled at you. He looked like a stinkin' girl, but he still acted like a guy. That's why I liked Billy Idol.

"You know what songs we went around singing? In high school and college? Cyndi Lauper's 'Girls Just Want to Have Fun' and Janet Jackson's 'Control.' It was all about being independent, not needing a man, being in control. You add that to the way I was conditioned by my family, the way I had to fight patriarchy because it had made my mother so miserable and because it was the only way to get my dad's attention, by fighting 'the man' that he spent his life rebelling against, and then you add to that this whole MTV generation thing with Prince as the ultimate sex symbol of a guy? My God, no wonder I've failed at love all my damn life! No wonder I'm excited that I finally found a real man, who happens to be eleven years older than I am, meaning he missed out on the whole MTV thing."

Brenda looked around. "We're still suffering the repercussions of what you're talking about, aren't we?" she asked.

"There are no men in our generation. They're all afraid to be men. Except when they're alone, which is why everyone's addicted to porn. This is why men are so confused, too! They want us, but they hate themselves for wanting us, and they want to be men, but hate themselves for wanting to be men, so they push it all down and act like freakin' Prince, but then they end up treating women like garbage because they have this aggression that has to come out somehow, and they're not being allowed to express it in the healthy ways men used to be able to express it."

"Deep," said Brenda.

It was then that I realized something profound. It wasn't men's fault that they were turning into women. It was our culture's fault. In the wake of the radical second-wave feminism of the 1970s, it was almost like everything in our culture was pointing them in the direction of being less like men, in order to be seen as desirable. So, acting on their male impulse to find and get women, they had remade themselves as music, TV, and movies had told them we wanted them . . . as wimps. As nonthreatening. Where was a man going to even find his sense of masculinity anymore? He wasn't being valued as the breadwinner, because here we were, telling men that we didn't need them for that anymore and, furthermore, we expected to compete with them for the best jobs around. They couldn't be demonstrably masculine anymore, because fashion and pop culture had elevated effeminate men. While both men and women had certainly made some important gains from feminism, it was obvious to me then, as clear and crisp and painful as a lightning bolt, that both sides had lost something important and fundamental, and that we were all feeling unhappy about it. Women bemoaned the lack of real men in the world, and men simmered with resentments for women that they were not free to express in any arena of their lives, except, perhaps, in the secret enjoyment of pornography, which had interestingly become both rampant and increasingly degrading to women during this same era.

We sat there with all this for a while, and looked at the giant boys all around us, men who looked like they'd be in frats forever, even though they'd been balding for years, men who were so painfully insecure that it hurt to look at them. Sniveling little boys, with crow's-feet and online-porn addictions.

"So this is what it has come to?" I asked them. "That there are no men left in the city, and so we have to start trolling the countryside for men in camo?"

"Girl, if he does the job, what the hell does it matter who he votes for?" asked Brenda. "If he makes you happy, it doesn't really matter if you agree on everything, does it? You found a man. That's not so easy to do anymore. You're right."

Jessica stiffened. "I don't know. I don't care how manly a guy is. If he votes Republican, I've pretty much lost my erection, know what I mean? That party hates—hates—women."

"Sometimes a little hostility goes a long way in the bedroom," I suggested.

We laughed. We'd probably drunk too much. The joke reminded me of the weekend, and I told them, without too much detail, just how amazing it was. You know, all the stuff I'm not supposed to tell you, my dear readers, but which I am still free to tell them, my dear friends.

"Best of my life," I said. "I swear to every God under every sun."

"Really?" they asked in unison.

"Like, a whole nuther level of good," I said, knowing now that I had absolutely drunk too much because of my use of the nonword *nuther*. "I didn't even know it could be like that."

More high fives.

"Is it weird?" I asked them, desperate to understand what was happening to me. "Why am I attracted to this man? This caveman? This big, tall, strapping, manly caveman. I think it's because we're supposed to be attracted to men like that, and no matter what happened in the wake of second-wave feminism, we still are."

"What does he look like?" asked Brenda.

I pulled up his online dating profile and showed them the photos. They were impressed. Brenda was as impressed as I was. Jessica was not as impressed as I was, but still impressed.

"That could explain a big part of it," suggested Brenda. "Hard to turn that down, even if he votes Republican."

"He's more of a libertarian," I said.

"Whatever," said Brenda.

"I could turn it down," said Jessica. "No problem."

Right about then, the cowboy sent me a text message. His texts were heating up a bit, getting bolder, sexier. One that he'd sent earlier in the week had stopped me in my tracks in the middle of Target, where I'd gone for socks, and I'd just kind of stood there in the laundry-detergent aisle fanning myself and blushing at the vivid, exciting details he provided for my fertile imagination to run with.

This newest text was very simple. It read: "Hmm. Wanna wrestle?"

"Oh my God," I said, showing the text to my girlfriends. I felt my belly get fluttery. Even via text he had a way of exciting me. "See what I mean?"

"Do you?" asked Brenda, with a grin.

"Do I what?" I asked.

"Wanna wrestle," she said.

I gulped. "You have no *idea* how much I wanna wrestle that cowboy. You have no idea how good this man is at . . . 'wrestling,'" I told them. "I didn't realize men could be that good at it, actually."

"So you play with him for a while, get you some," said Jessica. "His side lost the election last time, anyway, and they're going to lose again. As long as you don't let him convert you over to the dark side, it's all good, girl."

"He's *not* a neocon," I said. "He's a libertarian."

"Same thing," said Jessica.

"I don't think so," I said. "But I don't really pay attention to things on that side."

"Are you going to see him again?" asked Brenda.

"Should I?" I asked her. "I want to, but would it be stupid? That's what I'm trying to figure out."

Brenda looked around the bar, and pointed out, under her breath, how sorry and slim the pickings of urban men seemed to be in the liberal enclaves of Nob Hill, Albuquerque. She then pointed out that I had stumbled across a six-foot-two former model and actor with a great book collection and a natural talent for "wrestling" and opened her eyes wide at me as though I'd missed the point.

"And?" I asked.

"You should follow your heart," she said.

"Just don't marry the guy," said Jessica.

"She's not talking marriage. She's only just started dating."

"You guys won't lose all respect for me if I start seeing him?" I asked for clarification.

"We're your *friends*. We'll support you no matter what," said Brenda.

"Unless you marry him and start pumping out new Republicans," said Jessica.

I sat there with that thought for a long moment. I had not even thought about marrying this man. I'd barely begun to consider dating him. But when my friend mentioned it, I considered it for a brief and drunken moment. What would marriage to a man like the cowboy look like? Would he ever live in the city? Could I ever live in the country? Did he *have* kids? He said he didn't, but somehow that seemed hard to believe. He was nothing if not virile. What would he be like around my son? Why was I even going there with any of this?

This was insane.

"I don't know," I said.

"What have you got to lose?" asked Brenda.

"I like the guy," I said. "But I really dislike a lot of what comes out of his mouth sometimes. God help me."

"Then it's settled," said Brenda, with a warm hand to my arm. "Stop worrying so much. I'm sure it'll be fine."

And so I texted him back. One word.

It was: "Affirmative."

A WORD ABOUT FEMINISM

Okay. The time has come in this book, right now, for the public-service-announcement part of this whole thing. You and I both know that in the title of this memoir I clearly say, "feminism stole my womanhood." I have just recounted for you the conversation I shared with two of my friends over cocktails that was the start of me exploring how feminism had defeminized me and made my personal and romantic life hell. I feel, therefore, that I owe you a sort of flow chart on feminism, so that we're all on the same page.

First let me say this: Words are symbols, and like all symbols they are imperfect and incomplete. Words merely represent ideas, and because ideas can never mean exactly the same thing to any two human beings, we can all be using the exact same word to mean vastly different things. For this reason I want to state as clearly as I can what feminism means to me, what I mean when I use that word for the purposes of this story, and where I stand about it.

Second, let me say that this is not intended to be an academic treatise, mostly because I actually have hopes that lots of people will *read* it. I am admirably capable of waxing pedantic and of obfuscating the simplest of ideas in the most grandiose of terms, but I'm not going to do that to you. I have no doubt, however, that my critics will do exactly that. I have no doubt of this because they have already begun to do so on my blog, which I put online around the topics in this book about a year before the book was published. My in-box has since been regularly filled to the vomiting point with all manner of academic garbled miseries, made "legit" with reams of official-sounding footnotes, intended to prove how wrong I am about, um, my own life story. Which they know nothing about, just as I know nothing about their lives.

Which leads me to the third thing.

I don't intend for this book to be anything but my own life story and my own personal observations and change. I'm not writing a handbook. It's more of a diary.

Now then. Let's get to the meat of this feminism thing real quick, and then promptly return to the romance and cowboy and ranch and, hopefully, take his clothes off.

Feminism.

I have heard feminism described as all sorts of things, depending on who has been talking. For the purposes of this book I am sticking to the following basic outline and definitions.

Feminism is a big old umbrella term that is used to describe and lump together a bunch of different movements from all over the world. The basic gist of it, in theory, is to promote the equality of women in education and employment.

It should be noted that, in theory, I have absolutely no problem with this basic premise or purpose. It should also be noted that I think lots of places on earth—the Democratic Republic of Congo, and countries run by the Taliban, for instance—are still in desperate need of this protozoan manner of feminism.

I am going to limit our discussion of feminism to my country, the United States. I will give a shout-out and high five to the first wave of American feminism here, because it kicked ass and I wouldn't be writing this book if it hadn't happened. Nor would I be voting. For the record, "first-wave" feminism took place mostly in the nineteenth century and focused on really basic things like the rights of women to own property, vote, hold jobs, and control their own money. Things like that. I have absolutely zero problem with any of this stuff, and if anyone anywhere thinks it's a good idea for us to revert to the "good old days" that took place *before* first-wave feminism, you can pretty much bet that I'll be first in line to beat them senseless with a rubber chicken. We clear? Good.

Moving right along.

The mid-twentieth century brought us second- and third-wave feminism. Second-wave feminism started, like me, in the 1960s. It's still going on. We can basically thank Simone de Beauvoir and Marxism for it. The idea behind second-wave feminism is essentially that we need to get rid of all discrimination and level the playing field for men and women. The best way to do this, many such feminists argue, is to, you know, destroy all existing power structures and get really pissed off about our personal lives and insist that men and women are exactly alike except for the whole pesky private parts thing.

Second-wave feminism is where you see the phrase *the personal is political*, coined by an activist named Carol Hanisch, popping up. It is also the birthplace of radical feminism, which ended up spawning such disturbing ideas as antisex, as in "sex is bad." Under the furious banner of second-wave feminism, everything about life as a woman comes into question and gets analyzed to death, and more often than not the solution these feminists come up with is to overthrow everything about patriarchy or anything that even remotely smells like patriarchy. There are lots of theories born of this type of feminism, and lots of arguments. Some of it makes sense. Lots of it doesn't—for instance, the assertion by radical feminists of the time that all forms of sexual intercourse with a man were tantamount to rape.

Third-wave feminism is a lot like second-wave feminism, except that it supposedly expanded the conversation to include so-called women of color, because apparently only see-through women had been having their needs addressed by the movement until then.

Second- and third-wave feminism are where most of the women whose ideas my mother whispered to me in secret and whose books she bought for me came from. Audre Lorde, Gloria Steinem, Cherríe Moraga, bell hooks. This is where you get women insisting that true liberation would come only if they stopped spelling *women* with the word *men* in it, opting for the much more enlightened *womyn*, because, you know, everything about men was evil.

Because I was raised in a radical Marxist academic household with the weird mixed messages my particular parents threw at me about gender relations, anger, etcetera, I wholeheartedly embraced extreme radical second- and third-wave feminism in my youth. I mean, big time. I was radical. Very. I was combative, angry, and on a mission. I was mean to the men in my life. I wrote angry poetry and read it at places like the Women's Center in Cambridge, Massachusetts. I thought nail polish was evil, a plot designed to keep us down. I related almost everything in my life to my victimization because of my sex. I was straight, but I tried (and failed) not to be because I was *so* insanely radical that I couldn't honestly imagine being sexual with men anymore because it just seemed like such a betrayal of the cause to, like, open up and let them *in*. I fought, a lot. For example, at Berklee I wasn't all that crazy about practicing my instrument. Other people practiced a lot more. But I blamed the fact that other people got more gigs than I did on my sex. I railed against sexism at my school and even wrote a piece about it for *The Boston Globe*, which kick-started my journalism career. I was really good at blaming men for all my shortcomings as a person. It was much easier to do that than it was to, say, work really hard instead. I was so radical, in fact, that I got angry when a man opened a door for me, and wouldn't hesitate to stop and read him the riot act then and there.

I will never forget the afternoon in Havana, where I'd gone on assignment for my job as a reporter for the *Los Angeles Times*, when I stopped a group of men on the seawall. They'd just catcalled me in the time-honored *piropo* tradition of that island, saying, "If you can cook like you walk, I think you're the woman for me." I was furious! I stood there, tears in my eyes, and asked them if they thought I was less human than they were. I demanded to know why they felt the right to talk to me like that, like I was a dog. They stared, dumbfounded, because in their culture it was a compliment to toss *piropos* at women. The stupidest and saddest part of all is that in private, in moments that I could and would never have admitted to anyone, I replayed those *piropo* moments in my mind, and liked them. They made me feel pretty, and wanted. But I was unable in those days to understand that this was okay. Instead, I pretended I didn't feel what I actually felt, because to feel what I felt made me a traitor to the cause.

I dealt with sexuality in the same way. I was so radical that I had closed myself off from my sexual biological self. This is because that person, the sexual me, thought about things that were absolutely unacceptable in a just and egalitarian world. I had domination fantasies. I mean, how disturbing! Or so I thought then, in the days before I had learned that the Kinsey Institute for Research in Sex, Gender, and Reproduction had documented quite well that domination fantasies were exceedingly common among straight women. This was probably due to evolution, as anyone who has ever watched any number of mammals mating might attest to. Koala bears, those cute and cuddly little creatures, are known to engage in rough mating, with the male biting the female's neck and holding her down. And I bet she likes it.

But I digress.

Radical second- and third-wave feminism, by and large—but not always—espouse the view that the only real differences (other than a penis and a vagina, which they often dismiss by citing the fact that these organs start out as the same tissue in utero) between men and women are due entirely to socialization. We are socialized, they believe, by an evil patriarchal system to look and behave differently from one another when, in fact, men and women are essentially just the same. Women can do anything men can do, and vice versa. (I've even had a radical feminist write to me to "inform" me that men have nipples and can nurse babies if they only take the right hormones, as "proof" that we are the same.) This craziness was the view I held for most of my adult life until now. I firmly believed that everything that seemed different about the sexes was totally about socialization, and that if we could only change the way we socialized boys and girls we'd be able to liberate all those downtrodden women like my mom from those raging oppressors like my dad.

What meeting the cowboy began to teach me, however, is that a lot of the assumptions made by radical second- and third-wave feminism, while nice in theory, are simply not viable when you look at them scientifically, which is to say from an evolutionary biology standpoint. The reason I was open to changing my mind is that the more I learned about life, and about myself, the more I knew, deep down inside, as I think many of us do, that men and women *are* different, and that this isn't a bad thing. There are people who will rise up now and try to tell me that feminism has never been about saying that men and women are the same, but that's nonsense.

I'm going to digress into pseudo-academic territory now, but only for a minute or two, to show you what I'm talking about in microcosm. Let's take the idea that women are more emotional than men. This perception is widespread in our society and has been used to argue against allowing women to vote, fly airplanes, engage in combat on the battlefield, and many other things. But is it true? Are women more emotional than men? And if we are, does that make us less able to carry out certain tasks?

Most studies that look at this issue come away concluding that, yes, women are "more emotional," but the reasons for that conclusion vary quite widely. As with so many issues in the politically charged arena of gender distinctions, the answer to "why" depends on whom you ask.

In general, second- and third-wave feminists in the social sciences will tell you that no, women are not inherently more emotional than men, arguing that any observable differences in how men and women react emotionally is due entirely to socialization. In other words, they say, women act more emotionally because we're taught to. That is the basic conclusion with studies such as "Are Women the 'More Emotional' Sex? Evidence from Emotional Experiences in Social Context," by four female research psychologists— Lisa Feldman Barrett of Boston College; Lucy Robin of Indiana University; Paula R. Pietromonaco of the University of Massachusetts at Amherst; and Kristen M. Eyssell of Pennsylvania State University.

Now, this kind of thinking was all fine and dandy in the 1970s and maybe even in the 1980s, because we didn't have machines that could actually measure what was going on inside people's heads. Now we have those machines. And science is starting to prove, much to the dismay and denial of radical feminists, that you can't explain everything away through mere socialization.

For this reason, neurobiologists are more apt to attribute differences in our emotionality to brain structure and emotional hard wiring and evolution. This is the conclusion reached by scholars such as Larry Cahill, a professor of neurobiology and behavior at the University of California, Irvine. Cahill's research has found that the emotional wiring of men's brains and women's brains is fundamentally different. Modern technology is allowing for the observation of actual brain structures and response to stimuli and suggests very strongly that it is not merely socialization that makes men and women behave differently, but rather, evolutionary biology.

It is important to note that no study has surfaced that shows men and women responding the same way emotionally. The only differences have been the reasons scientists and social scientists give for the discrepancies.

So does this mean that women are less capable than men in handling certain types of stress or in performing some jobs? Again, the answer depends on whom you ask.

Unsurprisingly, feminist social scientists tend to say women are not inherently hindered by their emotionality because it is socialized and can be overcome. The study conducted by the four psychologists mentioned earlier concludes that "women's 'greater emotionality' is a culturally constructed idea, based on observed differences in emotional expression—differences which are socialized from a very early age," and says that observations in their own studies ought to be discounted because of this, because they "may provide a skewed picture of the emotional life of a person—a picture skewed in the direction of supporting gender-based stereotypes about emotion."

Studies of brains themselves, meanwhile, suggest that differences in emotional response are biologically based but that they likely pose no significant risk of women being incapable of responses that are as intelligent and reasonable as those of men. Neurobiological research out of the University of New Mexico and the University of California, Irvine, concludes that men have nearly six and a half times more gray matter related to general intelligence than women, but that women have nearly ten times more white matter related to intelligence than men, according to the journal *Live Science*.

The lead author of that study, Richard Haier of the University of California, Irvine, said, "These findings suggest that human evolution has created two different types of brains designed for equally intelligent behavior."

So what I take away from stuff like this (and I obsess on it, trust me) is that it is probably safe to conclude the following: Studies show that women react more emotionally than men, but radical feminist social scientists and neurobiologists disagree about the reasons. Regardless of the reasons, most social scientists and neurobiologists tend to agree that in spite of the differences in how men and women process and react to information—and regardless of the reasons for this—neither gender is better, more capable, or more intelligent because of it.

Which leads us to what I anticipate will be the pithy, neat end to this little digression in the middle of my memoir, which is to say, an explanation of where I stand now.

Now, I am proud to say that I consider myself to be among those people who are increasingly identified in "the literature" as "difference feminists." I didn't even know there was such a thing as "difference feminism" until I started writing this book, which is to say that I went through my personal transformation entirely on my own, only to later discover (much to my joy) that there were lots of other people who have come to the same set of conclusions.

Difference feminism, which is rooted in the Catholic Church, basically says the following, and it makes a lot of sense to me: Men and women are different, either created that way (if you think God did it) or evolved that way (if you think nature—and to me nature is God—did it). Being different makes us complementary and equal versions of the same species. Catholic theologian Michele M. Schumacher, one of difference feminism's leading voices, describes it beautifully when she says that there is only one human nature, with two modes of expression, and that together men and women "form a communion of persons to exist mutually one for the other."

It is no coincidence that I've experienced a bit of a spiritual awakening at the same time that I have come out from beneath second- and third-wave feminism's dreary shroud of lies. I have come to embrace a philosophy that is called complementarianism, taught in several religious traditions, including my own Christian one. Christian complementarianism interprets Scripture as teaching us that God holds men and women to be of equal worth but did not create us to be the same. This view is in stark contrast to the Old World interpretation of my faith, which was biblical patriarchy. One of the strongest and most beautiful voices in Christian complementarianism is Joyce Meyer, a woman I admire greatly and whom I consider to be a true leader of women in the world today.

If asked for my view on gender roles in relationships today, I'd say it is a difference feminist view that sticks closely to the Christian complementarian ideal that says God (or nature, if you prefer) designed men to be loving leaders of their families, to love their wives as they love themselves, and for women to submit to their men lovingly and voluntarily. In this paradigm, both the man and the woman live fully as nature made them, and both live in a selfless and loving way that complements the other. It's really pretty simple.

That is what the cowboy showed me. *That* is what he helped me to understand. By being the perfect yang to my yin, by making me whole when we were together, he helped me understand that men and women were not designed differently so that we could battle one another for dominance in a patriarchal paradigm; we were created differently so that we could complement, care for, respect, love, support, and honor one another in a human paradigm.

Having lived among radical second- and third-wave feminists for so long, having in fact been one of the movement's little darlings, I know that my new views will be met with extreme anger and resistance, because they will be mistaken for backpedaling to a time before first-wave feminism when religious ideas were used to subjugate and oppress women. That is not what I'm about, at all. But there will be little room for any other interpretation of my words in many circles, and that's okay. I knew as much going into this, and I have no doubt that I will be demonized by those who simply don't understand what the frack I'm saying. I also know that when I was among those resistant and angry women, I was miserable in life and love, and now that I have accepted and embraced difference feminism, and with science proving more and more that men and women truly are very different at almost every level of our existence, I feel free. Now that I embrace the notion that I am not the same as a man, though I have equal *worth* to a man, I have finally found a spiritual peace and balance in my life that had eluded me for—well, for always. Until now. No matter what becomes of my relationship with the cowboy, I myself have been forever changed for the better because of it.

So there you have it. When I say feminism stole my womanhood, I am referring to the radical feminism of the second and third waves, the feminism that actually agreed with ridiculous statements like this one, made by feminist icon Audre Lorde: "The true feminist deals out of a lesbian consciousness whether or not she ever sleeps with women." Puh-lease, girlfriend! That's so stupid I would almost believe SpongeBob SquarePants said it. And yet for so many years I tried to live by this and other absurd, soul-sucking radical feminist credos.

No more.

When I say the cowboy helped me find my womanhood again, I am describing the often difficult journey that this most manly of men took with me, leading me to a place where I could finally, joyously, admit what my biology had known all along: I was a woman who loved men, real men, men who were different from me and complemented me. Men who walked like men, smelled like men, talked like men, thought like men.

Freedom would never come from trying to force men to be women and women to be men, as so many radical feminists seemed to believe it would. Freedom came when I connected to the ancestral feminine womanhood that I carried in my DNA, and stopped feeling guilty for all that it spoke to me.

Freedom came when I finally embraced my own sex and stopped pretending it was just like theirs.

And now, back to our regularly scheduled program, wherein the cowboy and the city girl fall in love . . .

TELLING MY FATHER

So a couple of weeks passed, and the cowboy and I kept texting and emailing each other. (Even though there is no cell service on the ranch, the cowboy does have a cell phone that he can use to text me when he's running errands in town; also, he has a function on his email account whereby he can send text messages or emails, both of which came to me on my smartphone.) We didn't talk by phone much, because he was reticent to make long-distance calls from the ranch (the ranch owner paid the phone bill and the cowboy wanted to be respectful and not take advantage, he said), and I didn't believe in calling men so early in the relationship, having decided that the rules book was somewhat right, or at least having decided that all of the non–rules book things I was doing *didn't* work. I wanted the cowboy to chase me, not the other way around. I didn't want to be the one in charge. I also didn't want to seem too desperate, even though, truth be told, I might have registered somewhere on the desperate-o-meter. I wanted to play it cool.

So life went on. I did not date anyone else. There were a couple of men I'd either agreed to meet a while back, or that I'd dated once or twice and might have dated again if nothing more interesting came along. I let them all fall away, like skin flakes that would turn to dust under the piano. I did not *want* to date anyone else. I wanted the cowboy. All the time. I thought about him constantly. And though we didn't physically see each other much because of the distance, and though most of our communication was via the written word, we got to know each other pretty well. Two writers, writing, will always come to know each other better than they would if they sat in a room together talking.

I felt like I couldn't get enough. It was a strange and sudden addiction, an obsession, I suppose. I wanted more. But I knew enough by then to understand that you did not get more from most men by demanding or forcing more. You waited. If they wanted to give you more, they would.

So I waited.

I continued to work on some projects that took a lot of time—the racy memoir I would never release, a script that I technically sold but still hadn't earned a dime for. I began nosing about for a day job, because this writing thing wasn't going as I'd hoped. I mean, I was writing. A lot. Some of it quite good, from what I could tell. But I wasn't making very much money at it. Okay, I was making nothing at it.

I also continued to be a mom, doing mom things. Taking my kid to karate. Helping with the science fair. Planning my son's upcoming birthday parties, and, yes, there would be two of them. One at the rock-climbing gym during the day, and a slumber party with my son's closest friends—"close friend" meaning, at age nine, those boys with whom you shared fart noises made with various hand and mouth contortions. There was always something to do, as a mom, and it seemed that as time went on my son began to have more and more difficulties at school. He was undisciplined and had begun to hang out with a group of boys who were somewhat merciless to other boys. I didn't know how to handle any of it, and more than once I wished that my kid had a stronger male role model in his life than he had in the part-time dad he mostly played video games with. I was mom and dad to my kid, and I was coming up short.

I tried not to think too much about this new man, who sent me a good-morning greeting every single morning, without fail, via email, sometime between six and seven in the morning. "Good morning, Miz Valdes. Wanna wrestle?" Something to that effect. Or "Good morning, dear. Thinking of you." I'd message back. He'd text back. Always he gave me something clever and sexy, something that made me pause and feel appreciated, special, wanted. I got used to his attentions and the consistency of them. He was reliable, like clockwork. I also got used to the good-night texts, which were similarly predictable and on time. He was steady, he seemed very interested in me, and I could count on him.

I was in a good mood, naturally. I began to jog again. I began to eat better. When I'm happy I tend to take good care of myself. I had hope. It had been a long time since I'd had hope. I was enjoying hope. I whistled around the house. I walked with a spring in my step. I smiled a lot, in public places where I had not been accustomed to smiling, such as the food co-op. To my great surprise, people began to smile back at me. It was almost as though I were . . . *friendly*. This all manifested in an almost immediate loss of weight. I dropped ten pounds in a month, without trying. Or at least without thinking about it. I was happier, so I was living better.

My father noticed my weight loss and elevated mood one evening as we sat watching the series *Lost* on Netflix. We had become addicted to that show and enjoyed our evenings together on my overstuffed French Country sofa in his living room (my father really had no decent furniture to speak of until my son and I moved in). I was knitting a scarf, even though summer was coming, because I'd only recently gotten the urge to learn how to knit—right around the same time I started being open to, you know, dating a conservative. Pure coincidence. It was yellow and full of holes, my second scarf ever. But the knitting calmed and soothed me, and to me the sense of peace and happiness I had that evening, just sitting there on my comfy sofa, watching a good show with my beloved dad, knitting and knowing that my son was safely sound asleep and knowing too that I had a sexy cowboy sending me text messages every so often (that being the reason my BlackBerry was close at hand on the sofa next to me), felt good. I felt better than I had in a long time.

"It's nice to see you happy," said my father. I knew that he was fishing, maybe wondering what had happened to boost me so. I also knew that I'd have to tell him, sooner or later, about this new man. It wouldn't be that night, though. I was too scared. I wasn't sure what I was scared of, exactly. Just that I was. I guess it was the fear that I'd disappoint my dad, that I'd be doing something that was against the family rules. The only thing I can compare it to is the way you might feel if you were raised in a racist household and fell in love with someone outside your own race. Having to tell the family wouldn't be easy, and you'd risk banishment and shunning. We were supposed to be the loving, tolerant side, but I realized with a sick feeling that we had our own prejudices. I'd never seen them before, having been so wrapped up in them myself.

I knew it was stupid to be afraid of what your father might think of you when you were in your forties, but I'd always valued his opinion—so much so that I had taken it as my own for most of my life.

I told him the next morning.

My dad was sitting in the sunroom off the kitchen, the room that he used for his home office, doing something online for his Listserv related to Cuba. I sat at the round wooden kitchen table nearby and asked him if he had a minute to talk. Now, I know that I have indicated that my father, in my youth, was something of a brute in some ways, and controlling, and all of that is true, but it does not negate the fact that over the years and with maturity coming for both of us, we were able to move past our issues in many areas and go on to become very close friends. I am one of those lucky people who actually like their fathers. He's a smart guy, a decent guy, a nice man in many ways. He has always been extremely supportive of my writing career and has in fact been a pillar of encouragement in my life.

"What's up?" he said, turning in his swivel chair to face me. He is about my same height, with white hair, and bears a striking resemblance to Anthony Hopkins. Anthony Hopkins in sweats and hiking shoes, that day.

"I have to tell you something, but I want you to keep an open mind," I said, wincing a little.

My father's face hardened almost imperceptibly.

"You're not going to like it." My pulse raced. "But I don't want you to think I've lost my mind or anything like that. So, just, you know, try to be open-minded."

"What is it?" he asked, starting to lose patience with my preparatory monologue and perhaps annoyed by the fact that I'd already decided how he'd react to something he had yet to hear.

"Well, you know how I've been on this Match.com dating site?" I asked. "Well, and you know that I've mostly had some disappointing experiences through it, right?"

My father nodded and waited.

"Well, a few weeks ago I met someone new, and I really think I like him."

My father looked at me as though confused about why this would be upsetting to him. We'd often talked about the men I dated, and my father had been supportive, generally. He was a good counselor at times. He was also, I could tell, irritated with the drama of my disappointing dating life.

"See, the thing is, this new guy's not anything I thought I might like. And I don't think you're going to like him at all."

My father scowled, perhaps scrolling through his memory of the various men I'd dated over the years whom he was not fond of. There was not a shortage of them.

"I didn't want to meet him at first," I said, almost as a way to save face, I suppose. "I mean, okay. Here's the thing. He's very conservative. And he's a cowboy. And he's got some pretty traditional views about gender roles, things like that."

My father considered this. "Anglo?" he asked.

"Yes," I said, annoyed that this would matter to my father, who himself had married an "Anglo," that person being my mother. I said, "He lives down near Ruidoso, on a ten-thousand-acre ranch, by himself. He's a literal cowboy. Not just some guy who wears a hat or something. You know, he's pretty clear about how wrongly the media and everyone use the term *cowboy* when all they're talking about is a guy in a hat. He's actually a guy who tends cattle, on the open range, on horseback. He's ten years older than I am, and he's never been married."

My father's scowl deepened, and he removed his eyeglasses in order to rub the bridge of his nose as he sighed heavily. "But he's not a neocon! I swear!" I tried to sound upbeat. "He doesn't identify with the neocons. He doesn't like extremism on either side."

My father replaced his eyeglasses with a weary look at the floor, and then up at me. "You're a grown woman," he said with an exasperation he tried hard to conceal. "Your personal life is your own."

"I know. I *know* that. But I wanted to let you know, because it's been bothering me to keep it a secret. And because he makes me happy."

"How long have you known him?"

"About a month."

"That's not long enough to know if someone makes you happy. Take your time. Don't jump into anything with haste."

"I stayed at the ranch last weekend, Dad. We had almost three days together, all the time. I got to know him pretty well."

"I don't need to know everything about your life," he said, growing uncomfortable. I wasn't sure if his discomfort was because I'd stayed with a man at his house or because that man was an "Anglo" conservative cowboy. Probably a bit of both. We are all bundles of contradictions that intersect in surprising ways, but no one is perhaps more contradictory pertaining to women (and daughters) than a progressive American professor who was raised in socially conservative Cuba.

"I know. But I wanted to tell you that this man is the reason I'm so happy all of a sudden. He's really smart, Dad. He's a really good writer. That's what I like best about him. He engages my mind. He's a poet."

My father looked doubtful, and I found myself thinking of Robert Frost, who was both a conservative and a poet, and also of Dean Koontz, who is a libertarian and also my favorite living fiction writer.

"He does!" I cried. "I know what you're thinking. I thought that, too. But he's not as ignorant as you might think. See, I think we're maybe guilty of being as prejudiced about his kind of people as we accuse them of being toward us. Don't you think?"

"Alisa," he said simply. "As I said, you are an adult. You make your own decisions. But I am speaking to you now as a friend, and as your father, as someone who knows you and has watched you over the years as you tried to find a relationship."

I gulped and braced for whatever was going to come next.

"You are very intelligent," he said. "And like most intelligent people, you like a challenge." He paused to weigh his words. "Challenges are good things, in many arenas of life. But in the personal sphere, in our relationships, romantic relationships, challenges are not the way to go."

"He's a libertarian," I said. "Not a Republican."

My father sighed again and seemed to be patiently enduring my interrupting him. "Be that as the case may be," he said, "it is irrelevant. Sociology tells us that the relationships that last, the ones that work the best, are those that are forged between two people of similar socioeconomic backgrounds and belief systems."

"I know," I said miserably, because I'd read the same data.

"I'm not saying that you and this cowboy won't be able to work it out, I don't know the man; I have never met the man," he said carefully. "But I am posing the following question to you, for you to consider. Just to think about it. Okay?"

"Okay."

"Ask yourself, why is it that you choose the most difficult path in your relationships? You are a risk taker. This is something I and many other people admire about you. In your career, you have taken huge risks, tried new things, followed a new path that no one else had ever followed before, and that was something a lot of people didn't understand until after you'd done it and found success. I've watched that with great admiration. But you do it in the men you pick, too. You pick men that are the least likely to be right for you. The long shots. You seem to do this in part because you like a challenge, but also in part because you almost seem to want to sabotage yourself."

"It's not like that with him," I said. "He's different."

My father hesitated, deep in thought. Then he said, "You say he is a libertarian?"

"That's what he told me."

"Alisa, what do you know about libertarians?"

"Not much. Honestly, nothing really. I know my favorite novelist is a libertarian. And he seems pretty centered and compassionate."

"Do you know this Ayn Rand, the writer the libertarians are always quoting?" he asked.

"Not really. I've heard Thom Hartmann talk about her on his show. He doesn't have anything nice to say."

"That's because Ayn Rand was a sociopath," he said, matter-of-factly. "And I hate to say this, Alisa, but most of the people who are drawn to her writings are somewhat sociopathic themselves. I'm not saying all of them, but how anyone can subscribe to a philosophy of selfishness and be proud of it—that is beyond me."

"He did mention that book," I said. "*The Virtue of Selfishness*. But he said it was less about being greedy and self-centered than it was about, like, the way, and this is how he said it to me, okay? When you're in an airplane, right? And they're going through all that safety stuff at the beginning? They always tell parents to make sure to put their own oxygen masks on before they try to put them on their kids. It's like that. That's what he said. That you can't be of much use to anyone else if you aren't at your best yourself. That it's okay to be selfish, to the extent that you strengthen yourself so that you can help others better."

My father looked dubious. "That is not my understanding of Ayn Rand."

"Have you read her?"

"Yes."

"Okay, well, I don't know." I began to doubt my own opinion of the cowboy. I began to question myself, as I'd so often done throughout my childhood and life, in the face of my father's very strong and well-reasoned opinions.

"Just be careful," he told me. "You are a strong woman, Alisa. You are an independent woman. You are a successful woman. There aren't many men who can handle that, and this kind of man, the kind you're describing, is among the least likely to be able to deal with someone as modern and independent as you."

Was I really that modern and independent? I wondered. I knew that my father had always told me I was. I knew that I had never been taken care of by anyone, except for now, when my father was taking care of me for a time. But I didn't know if the woman he was describing, the strong and independent one, was quite how I felt inside. I wasn't sure, either, whether the cowboy would be resistant to such a woman in his life. After all, he'd told me over and over that he liked me. When I'd told him a story about me taking on my employer and succeeding in my battle, the cowboy had grinned from ear to ear and told me that he knew he'd like me, that he liked my spunk. But my dad knew me well, better than just about anyone. He couldn't be wrong about me, could he? And I'd been such a failure at relationships; maybe I was doing it again, making a stupid choice.

My father looked sad for me. Like he pitied me. "I watch you trying to find love, and it makes me think of Sisyphus, pushing the rock up the mountain, only to finally get there and have it come rolling back down again."

"So you think I'm making a mistake?" I asked.

"I don't know the man," he repeated. "But I can tell you that you are setting yourself up for a lot more conflict and struggle than you need. You would be better off trying to find someone with whom you shared core values and culture."

I thought about this and realized, with a bit of a shock, that at forty-two years of age I wasn't entirely sure what my core values were. For most of my life, they had simply been my father's own core values, which had been given to me the way religion is given to any child, and I spewed them back at the world from my mouth as my own. I'd assumed, because of his rigidity and confidence, that there was no other choice, rather like a child raised in a cult or with a strict minister for a father. I'd longed for his approval and had been his perfect clone in many ways in hopes of getting it, too afraid of banishment to question the family faith.

I realized, too, that in admitting to him that I had begun to enjoy the company of a man who was his opposite on so many levels, not only was I risking my own relationship with my father, a man who had long required that those in his orbit agree with him and never challenge him, but also I was risking a step into an abyss where I'd have to figure out on my own what I actually believed.

"He opens doors for me," I told my father. "And when I sit at a table, he holds my chair for me and scoots it in for me."

My dad seemed unimpressed by this. I had never seen him do either for any woman, and especially not for my mother.

"And I *like* it," I told him, as my heart raced, preparing for a fight.

I had never said anything so defiant to my father in my life. A man held doors open for me! *Me!* The girl who'd been taught by her parents to resent such patronizing behavior from men who clearly just wanted to take my power away. And yet, what was actually more patronizing, I asked myself? Having the cowboy hold a door open for me, or having my father tell me my thoughts and feelings were all wrong . . . ?

Which of these two men in fact respected me more?

"I'm going to keep seeing him," I told my father. "And I hope you can handle it."

I was challenging the very fabric of my upbringing. Yes, it was risky to date a conservative cowboy. But it was far riskier, I realized, to tell my father I liked it.

"You are an adult," he said again. "And you are going to do what you think is best. I cannot tell you what to do."

And with that, he turned back to his computer and I was dismissed. He'd said he couldn't tell me what to do, and yet that was exactly what he was doing. He was telling me not to date the cowboy, not to be so stupid, not to set myself up for the rock to come rolling down the other side.

I got up and said I hoped he enjoyed the rest of his day.

Then I went to my room and called up my email. I sent a note to the cowboy, asking him if he would like to attend my son's birthday party at the rock-climbing gym in Albuquerque that coming weekend, making some excuse about needing big, strong adults to belay. The cowboy wrote back to say that he had cattle coming in sometime in the next week. If the cattle came before the party, he would not be able to come, but if they came after, he'd be there. I felt incredibly defiant doing this, truly independent for perhaps the first time in my life, inviting this man to a place that I knew my father would be. I needed to see them in the same room together, to see what I truly felt, to see where the truth of things was.

With a strange pang of misplaced guilt, I realized that I was being independent for the first time in my life—independent of my father. I realized, in a stunning epiphany, that my "feminist" upbringing had taken place in the most unyieldingly patriarchal of homes and that my "independence" was nothing but a display designed to please my father. It wasn't freedom at all, and it never had been. It was just another flavor of obedience, incongruously *called* freedom.

For the first time in my life, I heard the orders from my father and refused to obey them.

CLIMBING ROCKS AND DRIVING TRUCKS

The cattle came to the ranch the day before my son's party at the Stone Age Climbing Gym. I didn't know what this meant, until the cowboy explained it to me on the phone. (He had called me.)

The ranch he operated was leased out to a man who owned a bunch of cows. The man brought the cows over to the ranch from his own ranch, in a cattle drive that he charged non-cowboys who wanted to learn how to be cowboys to come and participate in. You know, cowboy camp for grown-ups. They brought the cows in, stayed in tents on the land, cooked over fires, just like in the old days—except that none of them knew what they were doing because they were tourists. The cowboy, naturally, had to stick around to make sure nothing stupid happened. He was sorry. He'd been looking forward to the party, to meeting my father and son.

In retrospect, I realize that one month is not much time. That we zipped ahead so quickly in that span, going from a first date over quinoa salad to having the cowboy attend my son's tenth birthday party, is pretty amazing. I would not have advised such speed to any of my friends, and yet when I think back on it, it felt somewhat natural at the time. I guess it was the torrent of beautiful, thoughtful emails. The texts. The increasingly frequent evening phone calls. He *felt* like my boyfriend, even though we didn't call it anything like that yet. I think I was starting to think of him as exactly that, though. I hadn't dared to use the word *boyfriend* with the cowboy so far, though. But I do remember telling my former mother-in-law about the cowboy, at the rock-climbing party, and showing her his photo. I wasn't doing this in hopes that it would get back to my ex, who from what I understood was quite happily in love with a woman he intended to marry. Rather, I liked my former mother-in-law and knew that she'd be the kind of woman to appreciate an alpha male like the cowboy. She commented about how handsome he was, and I felt very good, invincible. And, yeah, okay. Maybe there was a part of me that did want it to get back to my ex that I had a boyfriend who was taller, hotter, stronger, bigger, and manlier than he ever was, because, you know, you lie to a girl long enough and hard enough, she's bound to want to exact some sort of revenge at some point, unless she's Mother Teresa or something. Which I wasn't. For years, I'd seen my ex at these types of functions for our son, and I'd longed for the old days. I'd missed him. I'd found him handsome and funny, and I'd wished things had not ended up this way. But this year, the year of having fallen in love with the cowboy, I felt nothing whatsoever like that at all. I felt nothing for my ex. At all. It was amazing. It was great. It was good.

I remember walking to the car after that party, with a text from the cowboy buzzing through on my phone. He'd been with me, in email or text, through the whole party, celebrating with us even though he couldn't be there physically. He had very quickly become the rock in my little world, the thing that gave me hope. The sun was setting, and the breeze was warm and scented with the distinctive, sweet smell of New Mexican spring—cottonwood fluff, melting snow in the river. It was lovely, and all was good and right in the world. I was content, for the first time in a long while. I didn't have money anymore, or really much stuff at all. But I had friends, and I had a happy son, and I had finally found a real love, unlike any I'd ever had before.

The following weekend, I headed off to the ranch again. This time I packed food in a cooler, so that I could cook for him and return the favor he had so deftly provided for me with the flawlessly flipped carrots. I planned an arugula salad with sliced flank steak and Argentine chimichurri sauce, made with garlic, olive oil, and fresh basil. I had thought long and hard about what I could possibly make for this cowboy that would be a statement of the potential for our two very distinctive worlds to meet and meld into something delicious. I was known as the nation's leading Latina author of commercial women's fiction. He was a cowboy. Argentina was a Latin American country known for its cattle ranching and beef. I was a health-conscious city dweller who liked unusual and spicy greens, so the arugula was me. The beef was him. I got red wine and crusty sourdough bread, all at the Whole Foods in Albuquerque, and then I set off for the ranch.

I wore a flowing long white linen skirt from Banana Republic, with a pale yellow short-sleeved top that was flattering to my figure—to the extent that I had a figure. I wore strappy high-heeled sandals. Somewhere during the time we'd been communicating in email, the cowboy had mentioned something about liking when women looked like women, with skirts and heels. He'd also said that he liked women curvy, and if that meant a few extra pounds, then great. I was curvy. I had a few extra pounds. He found me attractive anyway. This made me feel attractive. I'd had my nails freshly done, and my hair highlighted and styled. I was pretty sure I looked good, and this was confirmed for me when I realized I'd forgotten a food processor and so I stopped at a Walmart in the town of Socorro, en route to the ranch, and a group of very young men catcalled me. It had been a long time since anyone had done that. It was a good feeling. I was still desirable, both to my new man and to random men in random Walmarts. I know, it doesn't sound like much to gorgeous young things in big cities, but to a middle-aged mom in New Mexico, a mom who had been single for quite some time and convinced that it would likely always be that way, this was all very, very good news and went quite some way toward boosting my ego.

I blasted the iPod as I drove. Again I played salsa. I also played reggaeton and merengue. I played some jazz and rock and pop too, but there was something about the Latin stuff that I really felt that day. As I sped across the desert listening to Daddy Yankee, I sort of danced in my seat, singing along. I felt giddy with the juxtaposition of the cowboy's world with my own. A hybrid myself, I'd always loved hybrid anything. Music that combined two different traditions, like the merengue hip-hop of Fulanito, excited me. I liked people who took the best of different genres, cultures, cuisines, whatever, and made something new and amazing with it. My father had been right in saying that I liked a challenge, but it wasn't because I liked a fight. It was because I liked creating something new out of nothing. I was an artist. I liked the creativity of hybridization.

I got to the T in the road near the ranch, feeling much more confident than I had the first time, but nonetheless still quite nervous. It had been two weeks since I'd seen this man. I had photographs, but as soon as I saw him standing there next to his white truck waiting for me, I fell in love all over again. He was absolutely stunning. I know I say this a lot, and it probably sounds not just redundant but also sophomoric and hyperbolic. But it was true. For me, this was the absolute most attractive man on the planet. The jaw, the chin, the lips, the cheekbones, the smile, the way the sun had kissed him just a bit, the laughing blue eyes.

Again we drove to the neighbor's house, this time with me in the lead and him trailing protectively behind. I kept sneaking looks at him in the rearview mirror. Something about a hot cowboy following you down a dirt road in his pickup truck. Lordy. I'd never thought myself the kind of woman who'd be impressed by something like that, but this was only because I'd never actually experienced it. He was manly, capable, strong, sexy, and coming for me. It made me melt.

I parked the car and got out. The neighbors were there, in the yard, and they'd come to say hello. I met the wife now, for the first time. She was nice, friendly. We made a little bit of small talk. I wanted to jump into the cowboy's arms, it having been a while since I'd seen him and we having been engaged in this constant verbal flirtation for weeks now. But he was pretty clear about boundaries. He was not going to touch me, not here, not in front of his neighbors. I wasn't sure why this was. Maybe it had something to do with that pink card I'd seen the last time I was there. Maybe there were lots of women who showed up here like this. Maybe it was just plain old manners. I didn't know.

We said good-bye to the neighbors then, and the cowboy opened the passenger door of the pickup for me. I climbed in, and as I did so he subtly, very subtly, looked me up and down. He took just a corner of his lower lip into his mouth, and grinned a little, letting a low, almost silent chuckle out. He silently whistled through his teeth, impressed with me.

"You look nice," he said, with an arched brow.

The passenger side of his truck faced away from the neighbor's house, and this is probably why the cowboy felt safe touching my thigh, ever so lightly just running his fingertips along the fabric of my skirt as his eyes looked at my lower body briefly and with great longing. Then, with a confident smile to himself, he snapped my door shut and came around to take the wheel.

We talked during the drive, which, you might recall, was about an hour from the neighbor's over a bumpy road through hills and valleys. Again we stopped once inside the gate, and he kissed me. It was good. *So good.* A little more intense than the first time, now that we were both pretty sure we liked each other and were starting to get a little more comfortable with the idea of us together. I felt electrified, in a good way. I could not recall feeling like this ever in my life before. This was the first time it occurred to me that there was something powerful and chemical going on when I was in his presence. He exuded something, some scent—what did you call it? Pheromones? He had, like, these undulating waves of testosterone coming off him, lapping at me, drawing me in. It was palpable, and real, and I could literally sense a masculine magnetism rising off his skin. It was magical, intoxicating.

On he drove, wincing a bit as the bumps jostled his shoulders. He told me then that his shoulders were completely shot. He had only a tiny percentage of rotator cuff left in each one, and they were always at risk of popping right out of the socket. Bumps and especially holding the steering wheel made them hurt. He didn't complain about it. He just seemed to bear down and wince. It had to hurt a heck of a lot, I realized, for this most stoic of men to show any discomfort at all.

"Want me to drive?" I asked. "Would that help?"

He laughed out loud, and I was taken aback. "No," he said, as though I'd asked an absurd question.

"What? I'm a good driver."

"I'm sure you are, but no," he repeated, laughing again.

"What?" I cried, growing indignant and offended.

"Darlin', you might be a fine driver, but there are a few things you should know about me, if you want to date me."

I sat there, trying not to stew but feeling my blood pressure rising as the anger bubbled in my chest. I didn't much like being underestimated, and if anything had motivated me to fight in my life, it had to be that. Underestimation of me. I'd been underestimated all my life, for the usual reasons of being a girl, or a member of a supposed minority group, or whatever. I hated it.

"Do tell," I said, crossing my arms over my chest and turning my body so that I was no longer facing him but rather was facing forward.

"If I'm in a relationship with a woman, I'm going to be the one driving," he said.

"What?"

He looked over at me, in a stern and serious sort of way.

"That's ridiculous!" I said.

"I'm kind of a traditionalist," he said. "Some things I'm just going to stick to, regardless of the new mores of society."

"Oh my God," I complained, starting to regret having come here. Sad to my bones that I had given this man so much benefit of the doubt. "How can you say that if you don't even know whether I can drive well or not?"

"I don't care how you drive," he said with a shrug. "That has nothing to do with it. I don't like for anyone else to drive. That's just how I am."

"That's stupid!"

His face grew dark and he gunned the engine a little bit, started driving a little faster than I was comfortable with. My mind raced to all of the material I'd read in my years as a journalist, covering domestic violence stories, for example, about controlling men. Driving recklessly in order to scare their partners was one of the telltale signs. What, I wondered, had I gotten myself into now?

"Stop it," I said.

"Stop what?" he asked, driving faster.

"I get it, you drive well, you don't have to scare the crap out of me to prove your point."

He slowed down a little. "We all have things we're comfortable with," he said. "And whenever you get involved with someone, you have to find out what those things are and decide whether they're things you can live with or not."

"So you're saying you will never let me drive, as if it's up to you to 'let' me, is that right?"

"Pretty much."

"Oh my God," I repeated.

He sighed with frustration. "I'm sure you're a good driver," he said, measuring his words. "I'm not saying you're not. And I'm not saying you'll never drive anywhere. If there's some reason I can't, then you'll drive."

"Gee, thanks," I said sarcastically.

He frowned. "I'm trying to be a gentleman, to protect you, to take care of you. It's how I was raised and it would make me very happy to know that you could respect that."

"I'll think about it," I said.

At the time, I was very annoyed.

Very.

At the time, I thought he was a caveman.

Total caveman.

I was offended.

But I still liked him enough to try to think hard about whether it made sense to have that reaction. So we sat there in silence and I thought. And here's what I came up with, in a nutshell. I had been married to a man I was with for more than a decade, and we had shared the driving responsibilities, and most other responsibilities, too—except earning money; that had been my domain, sadly. In fact, my ex-husband had often preferred that I drive. Come to think of it, the last time he and I had moved from one house to another, he had insisted that I drive the moving truck even though I was afraid to, because he had been even more afraid than I was. I remembered then just how much this had bothered me at the time. I had resented him for it but hadn't understood why. It had made it very difficult for me to see my husband at the time as being much of a man. He'd been much more like a child. I had hated it.

I looked over at the cowboy as he very capably drove his pickup, with me in it, and realized he'd never make me feel the way my ex had made me feel—like I had to hold the sky up over everyone's head, including my man's head, all by myself, or the world would cave in on us. *This* man would hold it up himself. He'd hold it up so high, and so powerfully, that I might not have to hold it up at all; I might even be able to . . . relax, now and then.

And stop worrying so much.

Hmm.

"Well?" he asked.

"Still thinking," I fumed—or pretended to fume. In truth, I liked the idea. But I did not like that I liked the idea, if that makes sense. It was unbecoming of an independent modern woman to like the idea of a man driving her everywhere they went together. Wasn't it?

Plus, I was still angry at him for basically telling me how we would do things. I didn't like anyone making rules for me like I was some kind of a child. I didn't like someone setting limitations on me, at all.

So then *why*, I wondered, was it exciting, sexually exciting, to see him driving and know that he was in charge? That no matter what I said or did, he would always be in charge?

You're nuts, I told myself.

No, I told myself, *I'm . . . complicated.*

Why *did* I *really*, when it came right down to it, kind of like it that he would always insist upon being in command when we were in a truck together?

It made no sense.

But then, so much was starting to unravel in my life that I just kind of let the thread go, to see what happened.

"So you're saying that even when we go somewhere in *my* car that you're going to have to be the one driving?" I asked.

He laughed again. "Um, no, dear. Because we'll *never* be going anywhere in your car. *Ever.*"

"What? Why not?" I felt my heartbeat accelerate. I was furious about the indignity of this man insisting that he drive, and yet his very demand for control made me want to sit on his lap and bounce up and down.

You, Alisa, are an idiot, I told myself.

No, I answered back, *you are*.

Jesus, I thought, *am I one confused broad or what?*

"What's wrong with my car?" I asked him.

"It's not American, for one," he said.

I laughed out loud, thinking he was joking. No one I knew bought American cars anymore, or at least no one who had a choice. Everyone in my social circle knew that American cars were lame. If you wanted a good car, or a car that you could actually pull up to a valet with some sense of self-respect, you bought a Lexus or an Infiniti. At least a Honda or a Toyota. Even my Hyundai looked good and ran well enough.

The cowboy shot me a hostile look. "I always buy American," he said.

"Seriously?" I asked. "Half the cars you think are American these days aren't even made in this country anymore! And half the ones you think are foreign were probably made here."

"Listen, I'm a guy who's going to buy American, no matter what. That's just my culture; that's who I am, and you damn well better get used to it or keep on walking. You think it doesn't matter, but it does. That money needs to stay in America."

"This is insane!" I cried. "You think that in a world of multinational conglomerates and offshore tax shelters, with the gap between the rich and the poor growing bigger than ever, with the middle class disappearing, and with so-called free trade shipping all manufacturing out of the country, that it's going to make a difference where the company is supposedly based? You think your money is actually staying in this country anymore? Wake up. There are only two nations on earth anymore, the haves and the have-nots."

"We're not debating this right now," he said.

"Good."

"Plus, your car is too small," he said. "It's too small for a guy my size. And not just my size, multiple knee surgeries." (Note: At six-two, and six-four in his boots, the cowboy actually does not fit into my car or most sedans comfortably.)

"Please. What are you, from Pandora? They make cars and trucks all the same inside, so anyone can drive them. The seat is adjustable, sir."

He shot me a look, an annoyed, severe look. "No," he said. "They don't. Trust me. I wouldn't be comfortable in your car. I like my own vehicle. I will always drive my own vehicle if given that choice."

"I can't believe this," I muttered.

"It's not too late for me to take you back," he said, and I could tell from his tone of voice that he was angry, too.

We were angering each other. A lot.

He continued, "If this isn't workable for you, I respect that and we can turn around."

He stopped the pickup in the middle of the dirt road and looked at me. I looked at him back. I thought about what he'd said, for a long moment. I tried to understand what was going on in my heart and mind.

My knee-jerk mental reaction was to be offended, but my instinctive physical reaction was to be turned on. And my emotional reaction, which was very hard for me to admit to, was that I felt . . . relieved. I might not have agreed with anything he was saying, but I respected him for having and defending such strong opinions. I considered his desire to help his country, and to drive "his" woman, and realized they were both probably rooted in the same impulse this man had to protect others. He was an alpha male. It was that simple. No, wait. It wasn't that simple. He was an alpha male, a patriotic American alpha male, a cowboy with an American pickup truck and guns, and he wanted to drive me around and protect me, and I actually really liked it.

All of it.

You, Alisa, are an idiot, I reminded myself.

And you, Alisa, will not touch this man again if you keep acting like a moron, I reminded myself back.

Nor will he touch you, I reminded myself.

And as we recall, you really liked the way he did that, last time, I reminded myself.

So maybe you should stop acting like such an elitist liberal bitch, I suggested to myself.

Look who's talking, I answered.

I thought about it all.

There had to be something bigger, something biological, going on. Something emotional. He wasn't saying I was forbidden to drive. He wasn't even saying I was incapable of driving, or that women in general couldn't drive. He was saying that he, as a human being, liked to drive, and to drive his own vehicle, for his own reasons. One of those reasons appeared to be that he wanted to feel like he was doing everything in his power to protect me when we were together, and this included driving a large truck, and driving it well. Truth be told, he was a great driver. A professional driver.

I thought back to my conversation with my father and to the realization I'd had then about core values. What *were* my core values? Had I ever considered even for a moment that I could dare to have different values from my domineering father, who had demanded that his daughter be a freedom fighter? Did I really need to be the one driving all the time? Did I really need for me and whatever guy I was with to split everything fifty-fifty?

I kept thinking, lightning fast, while the cowboy kept looking at me, waiting for an answer.

What I thought about? This: One of the remarkable things about my former marriage had been the nearly complete lack of sex. We'd once gone for seven months without doing anything at all, not even kissing. I had not been attracted to my husband at all once it had become clear to me that I would be the breadwinner and main grown-up in the relationship. I'd found him unappealing. In retrospect, he'd always seemed less appealing the more we shared everything equally, and least appealing when I was the one who had to be in charge, whether it had been driving or carrying groceries into the house or whatever.

I realized that there was a louder voice than my socialization speaking now. There was an ancient voice, in the heart of my DNA, that was talking to me. I realized with a shock of recognition and horror and relief that I was programmed, sexually and emotionally, to get excited by a man who took charge. It was part of what made me a straight female. I realized this with a thud of disappointment in myself, even as I felt a strange thrill at being actually reconnected with an ancient part of myself that I had for too long subsumed. I was supposed to be more enlightened than I was being, more independent. But I wasn't, and it had nothing to do with how I'd been socialized. It was visceral. Instinctive.

Animal.

The dirty little secret of feminism, I suddenly understood, was that it could never go as far as it aimed to, because we were, all of us, fundamentally shackled to our own biology whether we liked it or not. Hundreds of thousands of years of evolution could not be erased in one bra-burning decade, just because Gloria Steinem or Alice Walker said so.

"So?" he asked me, growing impatient. "What'll it be?"

I gulped, hard, and pushed through what I knew I was supposed to say, until I arrived at what I wanted to say. I scooted across the seat, closer to him, and touched his warm, pheromoney cheek with my hand, tenderly.

"It's fine if you want to drive," I said. "I accept that."

He looked at me doubtfully, surprised by my sudden turn of attitude, and so I moved in closer still and planted a kiss on his lips.

I told him, in a whisper, "I don't know why, but I have to admit that I kind of like it when you drive. It's . . . sexy."

He paused and then laughed.

"Jesus," he said, and kissed me back before saying, "You're sort of a piece of work, you know that?"

"Yes," I said, kissing him again and feeling myself ignite all over. "So I've been told. It's a good thing cowboys are hard workers."

MEET JOHN DOE

We got to the ranch in the late afternoon, and the cowboy suggested I go in the house and relax while he let the dogs out of their pens and unloaded my belongings from the pickup.

"I'll help you," I said, feeling the need to participate. My ex-husband had rarely, if ever, fetched my belongings for me without having to be asked to first (and in those instances would likely have rolled his eyes at the inconvenience of it). I'd worked for wages since I was fifteen years old. I'd always taken care of myself and had never been taken care of by anyone in this way. It felt strange. I felt guilty. I wasn't sure how to handle it.

"No, darlin'," said the cowboy sweetly. "Let me handle it. Go get settled in."

And so I did what he said. I went into the house, and I sat down and relaxed while he took care of business outside. I stood at the screen door and watched him walk across the clearing toward the barn. He was graceful, strong. And maybe, just maybe, starting to be . . . mine. I felt undeserving of his attention, his assistance, yet loved it at the same time.

There was something very pleasurable about him taking care of things for me that I had always had to take care of for myself, for the same reason letting him drive was pleasurable. Neither of these things, I realized, was something I would be able to brag to my girl-friends or family members about the way you bragged about, say, finding a guy with a great intellect.

I wondered if my friends, too, deep down in their biology, had a longing to be taken care of by a strong man, an alpha. I wondered if they, too, were ashamed of this. I wondered why I was ashamed, what that meant. So many questions arose in my mind and heart then, so many contradictions between my socialization and the person I was slowly starting to recognize was my true, female, woman self.

I'd be lying, however, if I didn't say that even in the midst of this pleasure at my new ability to act more like a traditional woman, there was still a nagging sense of worry. This worry was augmented by the fact that he seemed to me at the time to have yelled at his dogs. A lot. In a very angry tone of voice. Loudly. It threw me at first, this yelling, and I am pretty sure that was the first time I heard it. One of the dogs had taken off after something and was getting too far from the house, and so the cowboy yelled, and cursed. This bothered me. It reminded me of what a friend of mine from college, a guy who'd once trained wolves and who was very protective of women, had once told me: *All I need to know about the way a man is going to treat women and children I can figure out from the way he treats dogs and busboys.*

What if it didn't stop at driving and hauling suitcases, and yelling at dogs? What if this man became so emboldened by his new-found domination over me that he started to make other, more unreasonable demands? What if I one day wandered too far from the house and he yelled at me like a dog? What if he, say, thought I should do all the cooking and dishes? Or thought I should stay home and not "embarrass" him by having a successful career—not that I was having one anymore, but, you know, a girl could always dream. Anyway. Wasn't that the risk? If I peered into it, might not I fall headlong down the rabbit hole and disappear altogether? I promised myself I'd be vigilant and that if he began to do anything—anything at all—that I found reprehensible or sexist, I would end this thing and carry on with my life.

The cowboy came in after that, as his dogs, now safely hovering nearby, bounded about happily in the front yard of the house, and he hugged me. The dogs did not seem to have had their spirits crushed by the yelling. I put it out of my mind. I didn't want to start finding fault with this man, not yet. I liked him. I liked his touch. I'd never been touched like he touched me. It felt so good to be held by this man, this very tall, very strong man. I burrowed into his chest and breathed him in. Copenhagen, dust, laundry detergent, denim. He smelled like a cowboy, and cowboys smelled good. At least this one did. I'm sure somewhere there was a cowboy or two who smelled like death on a putrid platter. But this was not one of those.

He kissed me again, with his lips closed because of the dip he'd put in his mouth since our first kiss. To my surprise, I didn't mind the tobacco smell. I actually kind of liked it.

And then he got started unpacking the food I'd brought in the cooler.

As with the week before, we got a couple of drinks and went to sit on the porch in front of his house as the late afternoon turned into evening. This time, the drinks were Cuban mojitos, the cocktails favored by Ernest Hemingway, made of rum, bubbly water, sugar, and fresh crushed mint, over ice. It was the perfect drink for a warm evening. The cowboy sipped his mojito politely after giving it a suspicious look, but I don't think he liked it all that much because once he'd finished it he returned to the kitchen to prepare himself some Pendleton whiskey on the rocks, with just a dash of water in it.

"I'm not good with rum," he explained when I raised a brow and smirked. "Rum and tequila, any kind of oily liquor."

"Oily?"

"I don't know, darlin'. Something about it is oily to me. Tequila tends to make me 'ten feet tall and bulletproof.' I usually avoid it. The drink was good, though. Thank you."

It was warm out, and beautiful, and peaceful, and we just talked. We had thus far never found ourselves at a loss for words. He had stories, lots of stories. I liked this a lot about him. My ex-husband had pretty much never talked. He'd been one of those shy, quiet, socially awkward guys you had to kind of push to start talking, and when he finally started, all that would come out were single syllables, except for when he ventured to say something bisyllabic, such as "Uh-huh" or "Dunno."

This new man was full of stories, and I found them all fascinating for different reasons. First of all, there were the fights in this man's past. *Lots* of fights. To him, it was just "his share" of fights, because it was "a way of life" in a rural environment. He liked talking about them and got a bit of a gleam in his eye when he did. I'd never known a man to either get into fistfights with other men or brag about it. This was a man who'd gotten into so many fistfights in his youth as to have lost count. He'd even slammed his boss's nose into a desk while working as a broker in Colorado because he felt the man needed to "learn some manners about how to treat female employees."

This fascinated me. This excited me. This also scared me.

A lot.

Especially when combined with the angry yelling at the dogs.

I told him so.

"Oh, baby, it's been more than twenty years since I hit anybody," he said.

"Have you ever hit a woman?" I asked.

"No," he said with offended conviction. "I hate bullies. And any man who hits a woman is a bully. The fights I've tended to get into have usually involved me and a bully who really needs someone to show him what it feels like to be on the other side of what he's doing to people."

Naturally, I didn't want this to excite me. But I'd be lying if I said it didn't. I did not respect myself at all for finding the idea of this man fighting other men—and usually winning—intriguing. I scared myself. I knew better. After all, I knew the statistics, and I'd read material about abusive men back when I was a newspaper reporter covering domestic violence. There were physically abusive men who enjoyed telling women about the fights they'd been in, and how they'd won, as a way to let the women know that they were capable of physical violence. It was, to those men, a warning of sorts, a form of mental terrorism. A way to keep women in check. I wondered if that was what was going on here. I didn't know this man well enough to have a well-formulated opinion on the matter.

"Why did you think violence was the way to solve your problems?" I asked instead. "I don't mean any disrespect, but it's not generally how people in my world solve their issues. We talk it out, or avoid the fight."

This is when the cowboy told me about growing up in South Dakota and Kansas, in communities he promised me valued fighting among their boys, at least at the time.

"It's just what everyone did," he said. "And if you were big, and if you could hit hard, you got rewarded for it. Trust me, darlin', people in Kansas have good manners, because in Kansas you know that if you aren't polite, you could get your ass whipped."

I did not detect pride, exactly, in what he was telling me, though I did not detect shame, either. He was simply telling me facts from his life.

"You got attention for fighting," he said. "And I was a kid who needed attention. I was big, over six foot and over two hundred pounds, when I was playing football. I liked to crush people. I was rewarded for it. People back in Kansas thought you were pretty cool if you were a big guy who could win fights. I'm not saying I'm proud of it, baby. It's not something I do anymore. That was then. I know it's not the best way to handle things. I understand that now."

It was time, then, to put the dogs back up in their pens. The cowboy didn't let dogs in the house. Instead, he'd built runs for each of them, on the side of the barn. I went with him and watched as the dogs obeyed him perfectly, taking their treats once they'd "kenneled up," as he called it.

Then I spotted the cute, fat-faced orange tomcat rubbing himself along the side of the barn.

"General Sterling Price," said the cowboy by way of greeting the cat.

"Meow," said the General.

"Oh my gosh! He's so cute!" I cried, rushing over to pet the friendly, pudgy kitty cat.

"Don't you dare touch him," said the cowboy.

"What?" I stopped, hurt, and looked back at him. "Why not?"

"The General's a filthy fleabag."

"But he's so cute. He wants to be petted. Look at him. He likes attention."

"He's a dirty, no-good, rotten barn cat," said the cowboy with affection.

"Please? Can I please pet him? He's begging!"

The General, sensing a friend in me, began to twirl in circles at my feet, rubbing himself on the wall of the barn some more, purring loudly enough for me to hear him.

"Damn rotten cat," said the cowboy.

I bent down to scratch the General behind the ears. The cowboy shot me a serious look.

"I told you, he's probably flea covered and everything else."

I stopped petting him and felt sorry for him. "Poor General," I said.

"Come on," said the cowboy. "The General's fine. He's fat and happy, with more mice than he knows what to do with. And birds. He's got a life any cat would love to have. My animals aren't pets, dear. They serve a purpose. The General's a mouser."

He walked back toward the house and I joined him, trying to respect his world and the role animals played in it. The General padded after us, sorry to see me go now that he knew I was the type of person to pet him. The cowboy noticed this and picked up a rock. He threw it toward the cat. (As I wrote this, the cowboy insisted, "I did not throw a rock at the cat. I tossed a rock in his general direction. I like the cat. I'm not going to try to hit him with a rock. Jesus, baby, you make me sound like an ass. I'll be amazed if any of your readers like me at all after reading how you write about me.")

"What is wrong with you?" I cried as the General ran away, back to the barn to hide.

"You're gonna get that cat killed," he told me.

"What? No I'm not."

"Baby, there are predators out here. Coyotes, bobcats, mountain lions. If the cat gets used to coming over to the house, out in the open, he'll be eaten. See, you think I'm cruel, but that's just because you don't understand how things work out here. The kind thing to do is to train the cat to stay near the barn, where he's safe."

"You can't train a cat," I said incredulously.

"You can train anything," he said. "It's all about negative and positive reinforcement."

We settled in on the porch again, as the sun went down. I tried not to be annoyed at the way the cowboy treated animals. I tried to keep an open mind. It wasn't easy. Dogs and cats had always been house pets in my life, companions. I wasn't used to them being so separate from the people who owned them.

I told him about my life. He told me about his. We did what we could to understand each other. It wasn't going to be easy, and it wasn't going to be quick. Nonetheless, he was a good listener, an active listener, unlike a lot of men I had known. He seemed to take an actual interest in what I was saying, and beyond that he seemed to understand things about me and my stories that I hadn't even considered yet.

Like?

Well, like when I started complaining about my ex-husband not being what I would have considered to have been a good father in some ways to our son. The cowboy refused to commiserate with me the way my other friends did. Instead, he narrowed his eyes at me.

"*You* married him," he said.

"What is that supposed to mean?"

"It means that we all make our choices in life, and we deal with the consequences. It's not his fault that you married. It was your choice."

It was a painful blow, at the time, and I probably got a little defensive, something about it having also been my ex-husband's choice, which only made the cowboy laugh at me. There was difficult, enormous truth in what he was saying. I'd married my ex when he was too young for such things. That was stupid. I should have known better. In retrospect I think I picked such a young and passive man to marry because he was so nonthreatening. I'd been raised to fear and avoid real men, so who better to marry than an unformed man-child? He was male, but he wasn't a man. It was obvious to me then, for the first time, and humiliating.

"I'm not saying it's not frustrating for you, sharing a child with him now," he amended. "I'm sure it is. But the way I approach life is that people need to stop complaining so much and start taking responsibility for the role they've played in their own misery. The way I see it, the world doesn't owe us anything. It's up to us to protect ourselves. And it's probably not been a joyride for your ex, either."

I liked what he was saying. It wasn't easy to hear, but it was smart, and, I realized, if I could endure it, I might actually learn something from this man.

Mostly I recall that conversation as being pleasant, and fun, and flirty. I also recall that he was breathtakingly beautiful in the sideways slanting shafts of afternoon sunlight. There were times that I looked at him and simply didn't understand what someone that unbelievably, irrefutably hot saw in plain and pudgy little old me. I'd always had attractive mates, or at least I thought they were attractive initially, physically, but I'd never been in a situation where I felt like my mate was this far out of my league, physically. Being me, and being a little tipsy, I told him as much.

The cowboy observed me carefully for a long moment and shook his head. "You don't get it, dear," he said.

"I don't get what?"

"You don't see what I see, do you? When you look in the mirror?"

"I don't know."

"You're beautiful," he told me. Then he smiled. "You also happen to be smart and talented and funny. And a little nuts, and a whole lot neurotic. Shall we get dinner started?"

We went back in and began to prepare dinner. He got the coals going for the flank steak, and I made the chimichurri sauce in the little food processor, realizing as I did so that something so heavy on raw garlic, while certainly well intentioned as a poetic statement of our distinct backgrounds, probably wasn't the best choice of fare if I hoped to, like, get *lucky*.

As the flank steak cooked, the cowboy put the Al Green CD in again and cued it up to "Let's Stay Together," the song he'd played for me the last time I was there.

I-yi-yi-yi . . . I'm so in love with you. Whatever you want to do is all right with me . . .

The cowboy sang along, and his voice was strong, in tune, and good. He could have been a professional singer, I realized, on top of everything else. Was there anything he wasn't good at? If there was, I hadn't yet figured out what it might be.

He started to sway to the music, in the middle of his kitchen, and came over to me, taking my left hand in his right and putting his other hand on my waist. We began to dance, with him still singing this very sweet love song, while looking me in the eye.

Loving you forever is what I need . . . let me be the one you come running to . . . I'll never be untrue . . .

I got sappy and melty. He was singing to me, looking me in the eye, as though he meant the lyrics, as though they were ours and ours alone. With great effort, I snapped myself out of my delusional state.

Don't give in to this, I told myself.

It was too perfect. Picture perfect.

I felt myself blushing at how he was so effortlessly open, emotionally, at his very romantic, playful, confident nature. I'd never experienced a man acting this way, the way leading men did in movies, and I didn't know how to handle it. My ex-husband had been so cynical and belligerent and sarcastic that he'd actually rolled his eyes during our wedding vows. That's what I was accustomed to. That's all I felt I deserved.

It was insanely beautiful, dancing there in the kitchen with the cowboy, as the scent of the steak grilling wafted in, as the mojito went to my head. I wanted that moment to never end, and I fought back the tears. I didn't care if it wasn't genuine, if he had a million girls he was doing this same thing to, I told myself. It was lovely, and I wanted it, and I was going to hang on to it for as long as I could.

He kissed me, and we danced, and it was completely unlike anything I'd ever done in my life. I had given up on thinking in terms of finding a forever mate again, but here he was, I thought.

The man of my dreams.

When the song ended, the cowboy went back outside to check on the meat on the grill, and I began to ferret around in his cabinets for a bowl big enough to make a salad in. As I did this, I stumbled across something that I hadn't seen the last time I was there, and it stopped me in my tracks. It was a gift bag for a wine bottle, from Whole Foods.

There was no Whole Foods anywhere near this ranch.

The closest one was up in Albuquerque, where, to my knowledge, the cowboy had not been since the last time I was here.

I felt a pit in my gut, because the bag also had a little red chiffon ribbon on it, as though it absolutely had been a gift, or an offering at the altar of cowboy, and almost definitely picked out by a woman, or a gay man. Definitely not by the cowboy. The pink card with Mary Pickle's name on it came back to me, and I warned myself to stop.

Stop.

Stop getting so serious about this smooth operator.

Stop thinking this is going to end up being something real.

Stop thinking he is actually falling in love with you just because you are falling in love with him.

Stop thinking that just because this man looked you in the eye and sang "I'm so in love with you" that he actually is in love with you.

Another woman had been here. And recently.

I was convinced of it now.

That said, I knew that it was stupid to be upset about such a thing. Even though we'd texted, emailed, and spoken every day for the past month, and even though he was acting like he was my boyfriend, and even though he *felt* like he was my boyfriend, that did not mean we had come to any sort of agreement about anything like that. We hadn't discussed it.

But we would.

Tonight.

I made up my mind to confront him.

The cowboy brought the steak in, whistling happily and still dancing just a little. He had a goofy side, I saw now. A giddy, happy, boyish side that belied the cold, hard, manly side. It endeared him to me even more.

Stop it, I told myself.

Stop falling without a safety net.

He cut the meat, and I put it over the greens with the garlicky chimichurri dressing. We warmed the bread. And sat down to eat while more music played. I worked up my courage.

"I need to ask you something," I said.

"Sure." His face was open and trusting.

"Are you seeing anyone else?" I asked him.

The cowboy seemed caught off guard as he forked some salad into his mouth. He chewed and seemed to be relieved to have that extra little bit of time with his mouth full in order to think of how to best answer me.

"Not since we met," he said.

I looked at him doubtfully and said nothing. I felt my cheeks flame red with the discomfort of the situation. All of the old hurts and betrayals washed back through me. I had barely survived them. I could not survive a new batch of that sort of thing again. I wanted to think that men could be honest with women, but it was difficult to go there for me, the same way it might be difficult for a war veteran to endure the backfiring pop of a car when it sounded like gunfire.

"But," he said, smiling playfully, "in the interest of not lying to you, I'll be honest and tell you that there were a few gals I was seeing when I met you, and I've been trying to figure out the best way to break it off with them."

"Oh." I paused inside at his use of the word "gals," because no one in my universe of living human beings had ever used that word in a nonironic way around me. He was folksily charming. Foreign. Exotic. A throwback.

A throwback who was seeing other gals.

Crud.

"I really like you," he said with a most charming smile.

"I like you, too," I said, thinking, *I love you, actually.*

"I already told one of them, this nice gal from Las Cruces, that I couldn't see her anymore, and she pitched a fit because I did it over the phone, and she chewed my ass out. She thought I should have done it in person."

"Oh. And the others?"

"I'll take care of it," he said.

"You don't have to," I said, testing him. "I mean, we only just met, really."

He chuckled a little. "I *like* you, Miz Valdes. And I want to do this right. I don't have the time or energy for more than one woman at a time."

I assumed he meant he didn't have energy for a relationship with more than one woman at a time, though casually dating more than one didn't seem to be much of a problem.

"Okay," I said, satisfied with the answer but nonetheless feeling less than happy to know that there was more than one other woman out there who considered herself to be dating this man. So I asked him, "Do any of these women think you're their boyfriend? I mean, am I the other woman? Because I hate that. I don't do that. I *won't* do that."

"No!" he said. "I told you, you're the one I want, and I'll take care of it. Now, if you don't mind, let's just drop it."

I didn't want to drop it. I wanted to know who they were. What they looked like, how I stacked up in comparison. It was stupid. I knew it was stupid. So I dropped it, and finished dinner, and then the cowboy suggested we watch a movie. He had one already picked out.

"It made me think of you," he said. "And what you were saying about Fox News and all that."

For the record, I had, somewhere in our texting and emailing and phone talking, told the cowboy about how Fox News was little more than a Republican propaganda machine. He'd countered by saying that Fox News was no less biased than MSNBC. I'd disagreed and said that NBC, being owned by General Electric, was actually extremely conservative, too. He'd laughed and told me that even though he didn't agree with my points of view, he respected me for having strong opinions that I was able to defend. We'd agreed to disagree and I'd given up.

The movie was Frank Capra's 1941 *Meet John Doe*, starring Gary Cooper and Barbara Stanwyck. The film is about a fictional news media company that concocts the perfect American everyman hero in order to manipulate the masses to do its bidding. As I had been before, I was stunned that this conservative man was showing me a film that was so clearly progressive in nature. It seemed to predict the Fox News phenomenon, decades before it actually happened.

I said as much when the film was over.

The cowboy thought about it and said, "Well, that's probably why I don't like the term 'conservative' very much. People have all sorts of misconceptions about me when I say that. I think of myself as more of a traditionalist. I like traditional things, including freedom of the press. I think there was a lot to value in many traditional ways of life and thinking. That doesn't mean I'm opposed to women's rights or equal rights for minorities or anything like that. It just means that I value the old ways of doing a lot of things. In fact, I'd like it a lot better if you didn't call me conservative at all, and just call me a traditionalist."

"Slavery was a tradition," I pointed out in my typical obnoxious form.

The cowboy made a face. "Just because I'm a traditionalist doesn't mean I think all traditions are worth keeping. I just think that sometimes to be a liberal you think you have to destroy all the traditions and come up with something new, and sometimes the old way is better. That's all I'm saying."

I'm pretty sure this is when the conversation turned toward whether or not there was value in the traditional setup of the nuclear family, wherein the woman stayed home and the man went to work. While I agreed that it was probably best for kids to be raised in two-parent households where one of the parents stayed home to raise the kids, I did not agree that the stay-at-home parent should preferably be the mother. Well, no. That's not quite right. Deep down inside I knew that I would have preferred to be the stay-at-home parent when I had been married, and that I'd resented the hell out of my husband for being such a wuss when he did it. But I couldn't admit to anything like that openly, at least not then, because it was so completely unfair to feel the way I did. So at that moment, with the cowboy, I toed the feminist party line about men and women being equal in their rights to choose to be at work in or out of the home.

The cowboy said that even though it was fine for men to stay home if the couple decided that made sense to them, he doubted that biology and evolution had designed human beings for that particular setup and said that he suspected that in such situations both partners probably felt resentful. I argued and argued, even though I really didn't believe, at a gut level, any of what I was saying. He argued back.

"My ex-husband was a stay-at-home dad," I bragged. "I was the breadwinner."

The cowboy grinned, his expression noting that I was on a date . . . with him. And he wasn't my ex-husband. "Yeah. And how'd that work out for ya?"

It hit me. It hadn't. It hadn't worked out for me. At all. It was one of the many things that destroyed the marriage, in the end. I hated the cowboy for being right. He knew the role reversal hadn't worked for me. It hadn't worked out for me, not at all, or I wouldn't have been here right now, with the cowboy.

Duh.

"There were other reasons," I offered, weakly.

"Sure," he said. "But I don't think any woman, deep down, can truly respect a man who stays home with the kids while she's off working some nine-to-five all day. It's not natural. I'm not saying there aren't great dads out there who can pull it off, and I'm not saying there aren't women who were born to run companies."

"As long as they share things fifty-fifty, it will work," I suggested.

Somewhere along the way, the cowboy said that no relationship worked where the man and woman shared every responsibility fifty-fifty.

"Someone has to be in charge," he said.

"That's ridiculous," I said.

"It's life. You can't have two leaders in a couple at the same time," he said.

"What about gay couples?" I countered.

"One of them is going to emerge as the natural leader," he said. "You can't have more than one alpha in any given group. It's not the way nature works."

"So you think the woman should be submissive to the man?" I asked, incredulously.

"Not all the time, but sometimes, yes. Most of the time that's the natural way it plays out. I'm not saying there aren't couples where the woman is the alpha—there are, but you couldn't beat me hard enough with a stick to want to be in one of them."

"That's not fair at all."

"Life's not fair, darlin'," he said. "There's the way things should be, and then there's the way things are. Human beings evolved for men to be bigger and stronger."

"But not smarter," I said.

"At some things we are smarter, actually."

I huffed angrily. "Name one."

He grinned, liking how feisty I was getting, savoring the duel.

"Seeing motion," he said. "Men evolved for hunting. Studies show that men are better at detecting motion in the wild than women are."

"Puh-lease!" I griped. "Prove it!"

"Look it up," he said.

"I will. And I'll prove you wrong!"

"By the way, you guys are smarter about some things."

"Yeah, like arguing about who's smarter."

"No," he chuckled. "You're better at hearing babies crying in the night. You wake up faster than we do. That's evolution. That's why you're the better primary caregivers for children. I'm not saying men are superior to women, just that we're different, suited to different things."

I'd had enough. This was too much for me to take. I demanded that he take me to my car. He said it was far too late to disturb his neighbors.

"I can't stay here," I said. "This was a mistake."

"Fine," he said, retreating to the kitchen to get himself a cold beer. "You can stay in the lodge."

"No, I'm going *home*," I said, grabbing my suitcase and heading out into the very dark night. "If you're not going to take me, I'll walk." (Note: It was six miles to the county road and another six miles to where my car was parked, all through pitch-black unlit wilderness.)

I marched out across the dark front yard, past the cowboy's trucks, toward the first ranch gate by the windmill.

"This ain't the city, darlin'," he called out to me. "There's coyotes, bobcats, mountain lions, bulls, all sorts of things out there, rattlesnakes. You don't want to do this."

"Quit telling me what to do, you Neanderthal!" I screamed, heaving my suitcase over the first gate.

"Okay, bye."

I heard the screen door shut.

I looked back, thinking he'd be walking toward me to drag me back. After all, that's what my boyfriends and my ex-husband would have done.

But he wasn't.

The cowboy had turned and walked back into the house like nothing.

I was so irritated by him! He wasn't just supposed to ignore my tantrum! *That wasn't how it was supposed to go*, I thought, incensed. He was supposed to fight with me and force me back, right?

Not just let me go.

But that's what he did.

I began to pick my way along the rocky dirt road, under the incredible stars, listening with worry to the creepy, scary sounds in the night. This was stupid, I realized. I was going to die out here, and he knew it. Why wasn't he coming to save me? Didn't he care about me?

I made it maybe twenty feet before I got too scared to go on.

Was that something moving in the brush? I couldn't tell. Could I not tell because I was genetically inferior to him in seeing threatening predators hiding in the trees?

Ugh.

I turned around, dragging my heavy suitcase with me. As I trudged back to the house, the metaphor of the entire situation wasn't lost on me. This man was close to nature. He lived in it, saw it for what it was. And nature, I understood then, was entirely unfair. Everything about life in our universe was unfair.

That's where his attitudes about most things sprung from, from a deep and intimate understanding of nature, and the life cycle. He hadn't learned it in any book. He'd learned it watching the world.

Men and women should have equal rights, but we weren't equal. They were bigger than we were. They were hairier. We had the babies and the milk ducts. We menstruated. They were fertile all the time. They liked to fight or flee. We liked to tend or befriend.

He was freakin' right.

And I hated it.

I looked at the stars, and another metaphor struck me, like a meteor.

Gravity itself was a glorious expression of the inequality inherent in all of the natural world. The bigger body forced the smaller one to crash into it, or stay near it. There was nothing you, as the smaller body, could do about it. If you were the smaller body, you orbited the bigger one, or you crashed into it. You stuck to it, no matter how high you jumped, no matter how hard you flapped your wings against it. The bigger body determined your fate, just by being there.

I had always liked to think that the *nature* of things was *fairness*, when in reality the nature of nature was ruthlessly brutal, every bit as much as it was gorgeous, and fairness never came into the equation.

This "buy American," tobacco-dipping, gun-toting, horse-riding, dog-training cowboy was . . . right.

I dragged myself up the steps to his porch, humiliated. It was then that I noticed the General creeping toward me, still hoping to be petted. I sat down on one of the porch chairs, feeling sorry for myself, and patted my lap for the cat to come sit on it. The General leapt up and obliged me, purring madly.

I hugged the cat, and scratched him, and nuzzled him.

"He's mean to us," I told the General. "He's a hard man to get along with, isn't he? He doesn't understand love."

The General purred and purred, and I muttered sweet nothings to him while looking through the screen door at the cowboy inside the house. I saw him sitting calmly in front of the computer at his desk, reading the news off Yahoo!. After a bit, he heard me talking to the cat. He looked up casually and laughed. He got up and walked confidently to the door.

"Back so soon?" he asked sarcastically through the screen door, opening it for me. When he saw the General on my lap, though, his kindly condescending attitude changed to irritation. "Baby, are you stupid?" he asked.

"What?"

The cowboy stomped on the floor of the porch. "Yah!" he yelled at the cat. The General trotted back to the barn.

"You don't listen, do you?" the cowboy asked me.

"When what's being said makes sense, I do," I said.

"Lord," said the cowboy in frustration. He took my suitcase from me with an easy strength that I had to admit I simply could not match and would never be able to match even if I took copious quantities of steroids and did nothing but lift barbells for the rest of my existence.

"You gonna stay out there all night?" he asked.

"Maybe," I said, sniffling a little still.

"Suit yourself."

He went back inside, and pretty soon I joined him. I sat on the sofa. He stayed at the computer, still reading the news, but spoke to me without looking up. "Glad you came to your senses. Wouldn't have much liked having to find your carcass half-eaten on the road in the morning."

I sat on the couch and looked at him. He turned his head now, looking at me.

"Oh, come on," he said. "I wouldn't have really done that."

"You'd have ignored my carcass?" I asked.

"No. I'd have given it an hour or two, and then I probably would have gone out looking for you."

"Why would you have to wait that long?" I asked.

"To give you time to learn something."

"Yeah, well I think I learned something anyway."

"That's what I like about you. You're quick."

"Shut up," I said.

It was then that I felt the bite. A flea bite. In a certain place, where hair grows. Hair few people ever see. Then another. And another.

"Ow!" I cried, scratching said nether region. I was wearing black Lycra yoga pants.

The cowboy observed me in amused disgust. "Got an itch?" he asked.

More bites. Painful, awful insect bites.

"Oh my God," I cried, jumping up. I felt as though I was on fire.

The cowboy shook his head. "I told you. You don't listen. I do not want fleas in this house. Take off your pants."

"What?"

"Take them off. And your panties. Give them to me."

He was very no-nonsense, matter-of-fact about it.

"Usually when a guy tells me to do that he's a little more romantic," I joked.

The cowboy was not amused. "We've gotta throw them in the washer immediately. And you need to get in the shower."

The fleas bit me again, and I screamed. "I'm infested!"

"I know," said the cowboy.

I took my pants and underpants off and handed them to him.

"Shirt too, probably."

I took everything off and handed it to him.

"Shower," he commanded, holding the clothes at arm's length and going to the laundry room. "Now."

I did as he said, as the bites burned. I was allergic to fleas. I remembered that now. I stood there in the shower, trying to see if I could find the critters in what little hair I hadn't shaved off. In desperation, I took my razor and removed it all. Then I scrubbed, and scrubbed, and scrubbed.

I got out of the shower and was relieved to discover that the biting had stopped. I was humiliated, though, looking in the full-length mirror on the back of the bathroom door. I looked like I'd developed a pox, in a place where decent girls shouldn't have a pox.

I wrapped myself in a towel and carefully exited the master bathroom. The cowboy was reclining on his bed, with his hands behind his head, when I came out. He looked at me in amused triumph and shook his head. His anger was replaced by complete and utter pity and a wry grin.

"City girls," he said.

"Shut up."

"Did you get 'em all?"

"Yes."

"Let me see."

"No!"

He playfully tugged at the towel.

"Don't!" I cried.

The cowboy began to laugh, very hard. "Amazing," he said.

I shimmied into my nightgown and tried to avoid being seen in my current state.

"Think you might listen to me now?" he asked.

"Maybe."

"Think maybe I might know what I'm talking about out here now?"

"Maybe."

"Good girl," he said in a patronizing tone designed to annoy me.

I got into bed next to him. He was still chuckling at my expense.

"Like I said, you can train anything. Positive and negative reinforcement."

"Even fleas?" I asked.

"Maybe not fleas."

"There are flea circuses," I suggested.

"You'd be good in a circus. *The amazing Alisa, who listens to no man!*"

"Shut up," I repeated. "Seriously. It's not funny."

He chuckled again. "It so *is* funny. Dork. You're such a dork."

"Shut up." I pouted at him in a way I hoped was more cute than stupid.

"I think you've had your negative reinforcement for the night," he said.

"Great."

"Might be time, now that you're being so good, for some positive."

He grinned at me, turned out the light, then rolled over to me, and just . . . took charge of me, in a very strong, very good, expert sort of way.

Easily the best such experience of my entire life.

It was good because he did everything right, everything I needed him to do, without being asked, without being told.

He knew what to do, for both of us, because he paid attention. And was confident. And enjoyed giving as much as receiving.

He was *very* giving, in an assertive, alert, and attentive sort of way. If I grew too self-conscious or shy and tried to squirm away or cover myself up, he stopped me, held me in place, without a word passing between us, because somehow he knew what I *really* wanted, and he was strong enough to overcome my own insecurities for me. He pinned me, forced me past my own unwanted barriers, and gave to me.

Afterwards, I lay spent on the bed next to him. He propped himself up on an elbow and looked at me in the eerie blue light from the moon outside the window.

"That's better," he said. "Right?"

"What is?"

"You do understand, right? This right here, this is why we get along," he said.

"Because we have good sex?" I asked.

"No. The reason we have good sex is that here, in bed, you're completely submissive and cooperative. You don't feel the need to fight me all the time like you do everywhere else. Here, we work as a team. It's like this is the only place where you're free to be your true and genuine self."

I thought hard about this and wondered if the bedroom wasn't where most of us expressed our truest spirits. Stripped down to our skins and our souls, with nowhere left to hide. If so, then this meant that my true spirit was . . . submissive? I recoiled at the idea, mentally, but emotionally it made perfect, beautiful . . . *terrifying* sense.

I liked being submissive, at least to this man, because he . . . took care of my needs. Thought about them. Took them seriously. And I don't just mean in bed. I mean everywhere, in every part of our lives.

"You're actually a really sensitive guy," I told him. "If you think about it."

"Good night, Miz Valdes," he said, placing a kiss on my cheek. "Promise me you won't go out walking down the road if I go to sleep now?"

"I promise," I said.

"Promise you won't be out petting that rotten cat again?"

"Promise."

That's when he turned me gently onto my right side, then positioned himself on his right side, and tucked my back up against his front. His top arm wrapped protectively, gently, around me, and he kissed the top of my head with the greatest and sweetest of care.

"I knew I'd like you, you crazy girl," he whispered, with just a hint of a laugh in his voice.

He was curled all around me, like a shield.

I closed my eyes, happy and safe, and fell into a deep and restful sleep.

THE BIG FIGHT

$\mathcal{I}$ was conflicted all the next day, thinking about what had happened the night before. I was ashamed of myself. On a few different levels. But happy. Disappointed in myself, but hopeful, all for the same reasons.

It made no sense.

The day went fine, though. It was very much like the day before, all the way up to the point when we were lying on the bed again in the night, talking. I was very happy with that. It felt natural, and comfortable, and I was amazed at how fast the day had flown by and how we'd

162 | ALISA VALDES

never seemed to lack for something to talk about. I was content. Or at least I was until the conversation turned to a time in high school when a star football player tried to force himself on me in the back of a car and I kicked him, pushed him, got out of the car, and ran home.

"Stop," he said, holding his hand up.

"What?"

"I told you, I don't like bullies. There are some topics that I don't like to talk about, and I have my own reasons for that, and rape is one of them."

I was furious. Here I was, trying to share a story of how I triumphed over a bully, and the cowboy was trying to shut me up, and shut me down.

"I'm not *talking* about a rape. I'm talking about me beating a bully," I said. "I'm trying to tell you about how I took this guy on, and won. Triumph of the underdog."

"I don't care," he said, growing angrier.

Now, this would be a very convenient time for me to take a little break and tell you that no man in my life has ever scared me with a facial expression the way the cowboy has. He is beautiful, yes, but he also has a scary ability to shut down all his emotions and just grow cold. He is strong, direct, and very decided when he takes action to do something. He also has an ability to get extremely angry, and I was just starting to see corners of that rage for the first time.

"That's not fair!" I said.

"This ain't about fair," he said, getting angrier and coming closer to me, pointing his finger at me in a way I hated. "This is about you respecting my boundaries. I'm telling you, I don't want to talk about this. You don't want to go there."

"Why not? What happened to you?" I asked this because I assumed that a person would only act this way if they'd been harmed as a child—which did not turn out to be the case.

"I don't want to talk about this, Alisa. I have told you, but you just keep pushing. Don't do this." He was growing exasperated with me.

"I can't believe you're doing this!" I cried. "This is crazy! You're not even listening to what I'm telling you, and you're trying to control me!"

This was the red flag I had warned myself earlier to be alert to. If this man started to make demands that I felt were unacceptably controlling, I needed to see them for what they were. If he started to poke his finger at me in the air between us, I needed to pay attention to that, and how it made me feel.

"I've had enough," he said.

He got up then, and went off to the guest bedroom, closing the door behind him. I sat there on his bed, stunned. I felt so violated! I hadn't done anything wrong, and yet he'd treated me like I had. Things had been going so well with us! And now it had all suddenly just come crashing down. I was trying to get him to understand me a little better, what motivated me, how I'd gone from being a musician to being a journalist. I was telling him my life story, and he was censoring me.

It was upsetting, to say the least.

I didn't know what to do with myself. My negative emotions got very intense then. Perhaps it was the wine I'd had with dinner. I didn't know. But I started to feel very, very angry. Insanely angry. And anger of that magnitude tends to make me do one of two things: cry or . . . hit.

I wasn't proud of the latter.

Sadly, I'd hit my ex-husband once when things got really bad. I was not proud of it. I hit him just as I myself had been hit by my father when I was a teenager. You don't think those things are going to recycle in your life that way, but then they do and you can either admit it and deal with it, or pretend it never happened and keep some semblance of self-respect. For most of my life I have denied it. No more.

I cried for a long time in his bedroom, big dramatic sobs that I was sure would bring the cowboy to his senses and bring him running back to apologize for having hurt my feelings. I kept one eye on the door.

This did not happen, however. He ignored me. Completely ignored me.

This made my anger escalate. I was so angry, I felt dizzy with rage. My heart was about to burst from hurt.

I went to the kitchen, unable to handle the intense emotions I was feeling, and I grabbed the bottle of rum. I started to take sips from it. I'd never done anything like that before. Except for now. Since meeting the cowboy, probably because the whole situation was so scary and unfamiliar to me, I'd had more drinks than I normally did, almost to try to calm myself down. And now I was drinking to deal with this conflict. I knew this was stupid, but I did it anyway. Faced with these new, intense, terrible feelings, I just wanted to numb myself. I just wanted to make it through the night and leave in the morning. Actually, I wanted to leave then and there, but I was in no condition to drive and we were an hour away from my car anyway. And the cowboy was ignoring me, locked away in the guest room.

I brought the bottle of rum back to the bedroom with me and sat on the floor in the corner, with my iPod on, listening to music and swilling the bitter clear liquid, thinking about what a complete failure I was. Here I'd thought I finally found a good man. I thought I'd finally gotten it right. Days before, I'd been dancing with him in the kitchen as he sang Al Green to me. And yet, look what was happening now.

It always came to this.

I'd screwed it up somehow.

That's what I told myself then. That was how I felt.

I went back in that moment to a bleak place that I return to from time to time, when faced with very strong, very negative emotions. It is a place I first visited when I was sixteen years old and my father threw me out of the house after a major conflict, the details of which

I don't really want to get into right now. Suffice to say that my father had a long history of throwing people out of the house whenever there was a major disagreement. He'd done it to my brother. He'd done it to my mother. After he did it to me, he went on to do it to girlfriends. It was part of the personality of a narcissist, I later learned, to deal with any kind of challenge or criticism by simply shutting the offending person out of their lives, as punishment for not always boosting the narcissist's ego. It is, in fact, part of the diagnostic criteria for narcissistic personality disorder to "react to criticism with rage," and that is absolutely how it usually went down with my dad. I can say all this now because, happily, most of these issues are long gone from my father's life and he is truly a great guy who is one of my best friends. But back when I was sixteen, it had been devastating to be thrown out, locked out, faced with finding a way to survive without my parents. And if you remember, my mother had abandoned me three years before, for her own reasons. At sixteen, all alone in the world, I had been forced to go live with my best friend and her family, and I had felt terribly alone and suicidal. It had wired my brain and emotional system to overreact in moments where I felt rejected, as I did at the cowboy's house then.

That grief returned like a tsunami.

That big, fat, enormous, unending grief.

I hated myself.

I hated my life.

I hated the cowboy.

I was drunk.

Everything sucked.

There was no hope.

And I was very, very sad and very, very angry.

I drank more rum and cried louder and louder, trying to get some kind of a reaction from him through the imposing walls. He gave none. He ignored me. He stayed in the guest room, done with me, and for what? He had bragged about the fights he'd won, but when I tried to do the same, he stopped me as though I'd done something wrong.

It was so damn unfair.

Emboldened rather than numbed by the rum, I staggered to my feet and then down the hall, and banged on the door of the guest room with my fist. I called his name, loudly. A part of me sat back watching myself, thinking this was stupid, hating what I was doing, how I was behaving. It was exactly the way my father had treated my mother, and me, and it was how I, at various unfortunate times in my life, had treated other boyfriends or my ex-husband. I was becoming my father, when he acted like his own stepfather, who had been a brutal loan shark.

I was losing control.

I knew this, but knowing it did not stop it from happening. I'd been so happy this past month, so sure I had finally found something worth holding on to, and look what was happening! It was ending. Of course it was. Everything I ever loved ended up ending. Everyone I ever loved and started to trust hurt me. That was just how it was for me. I was cursed, doomed to always hurt. I hated it. I hated life. I hated myself.

And most of all, in that crazy, drunken, pathetic moment, I hated the cowboy. I hated him for having given me false hope, for having tried to control me, for ignoring me, for failing to hear what I was trying to tell him.

I knocked and knocked, and called his name. I told him to open the goddamned door and talk to me. When that approach failed, I begged him not to ignore me. He gave no response and did not open the door, so I opened it myself. It was locked, but it was flimsy and the lock gave when I put enough pressure on it.

I found him asleep.

Asleep!

How could this man be sleeping with me sobbing in the next room or bellowing like an elephant seal in the hallway? Did he have no heart at all? Was he deaf? First he'd told me I couldn't drive, then he told me he had a history of physical fights in his youth, and then he yelled at his dogs, and then he told me what I could and could not talk about in my own life?

I let him have it. I began to scream, to yell. I turned the light on and demanded that he look at me. I felt enraged by how he was trying to make me invisible, and I was unfortunately completely, totally out of control. I thought at the time that I was clever, powerful. That I was going to teach him a lesson. That I was going to make this man respect me, the way I had thought I'd made my ex-husband respect me by abusing him in the past.

I told him he couldn't control me. I told him he would never be able to control me, that I was my own person, that I could decide for myself what I would or would not talk about, and when I'd do it.

The cowboy responded calmly. "That's fine," he said. "We'll take you back to your car in the morning, and you can talk about whatever you want, whenever you want, without me around."

This infuriated me even more. He wasn't even trying to engage with me, to talk to me about this.

"I didn't do anything wrong!" I screamed. "How can you do this? Things were going so well with us, and then boom! You decide that you don't like what I'm talking about so you just tell me to shut up? No one tells me to shut up!"

He ignored me some more and acted like he was going to go back to sleep.

I came closer to him and shoved him.

"You understand? No one. No one tells me what I can and can't say, least of all *you*."

That finally did the trick. The cowboy was pissed. But he still wasn't going to dignify my idiocy with a response, so he got up, pushed past me in spite of my efforts to block the doorway, and went to his own bedroom again.

"Get away from me," he said. "You're nuts."

"I will *not* get away from you," I said, smiling like a madwoman. "You can't tell me what to do, see? You think you can. You think just because you're a man and I'm a woman that you're going to order me around like a slave?" I laughed insanely. "No, that's not how we're going to do this. You understand?"

It all came back to me, the upbringing, the indoctrination, the anger. My mother's anger. My own anger at the way she left me. The hollow sense of not having anyone in the world to care about me or love me except myself. The anger at feeling invisible most of my childhood, the anger about the way, no matter how good I was, no matter how much I excelled at everything I did, it was never enough to get the attention and approval of the people who were supposed to love me.

It. All. Came. Back.

I began to curse at him, spitting mad, and I shoved him again because more than anything I hated the cold way he just ignored me. It felt too familiar, too horrible.

"You don't want to do that," he said, turning to narrow his eyes at me.

"You don't tell me what I want," I hissed, and I shoved him again, hard, into the wall. He fell into it and nearly knocked a framed photograph off the wall.

In that instant, I realized what a grave mistake I had made. The cowboy's face changed. Where he'd been annoyed and guardedly controlled before, he was now extremely angry, his own demons swimming up from the depths of his soul where he'd locked them away. I had finally gotten through his walls, as I'd wanted to, but the result was not going to be what I'd thought. There would be no sensitive apology or remorse. There would be no epiphany where he realized I'd done nothing wrong. There would be none of that.

There would be strength, and a magnificent fury.

The cowboy grabbed me by the wrists as I was about to shove

him again. He clamped his enormous, powerful fingers around my wrists, not in a way that hurt me, but in a way that made it clear I was no longer in charge of my own extremities. It occurred to me then that this man had spent decades wrestling with bulls and steers, stallions and broncos, animals much larger than me, and that he understood very well just what it took to control another living being, physically. He understood body mechanics, and how to incapacitate someone. I was helpless in his grip, unable to squirm loose. I tried. But he met my every move with equal force as we locked ourselves into this macabre ballet. He did not meet my moves with greater force, ever. He simply kept me still, in check, unable to move as I wished, at his command.

I would never be able to push this one around, as I'd pushed my ex-husband around.

Ever.

He moved me across the room, to the bed, looking me hard in the eye in a blazingly intense, intelligent, and displeased way that was like a punch to the center of my soul. His eyes made it clear: *You will not control me, little girl. You are not in charge.* No one would control this man. I saw that now. He was completely in command. It was stunning to me because I had always been able to control the men in my life. The Dippity-do, Adam Ant, "Little Red Corvette" men. Always. They had always done what I said, what I wanted. They had always given in to me. Me, the bully.

They had been afraid of me.

The cowboy wasn't.

At all.

"You do *not* want to do this, Miz Valdes," he said in a simmering rage. I'd never seen that kind of angry yet controlled focus in another person's eyes. He had fury in him, deep fury of the kind that only came from having suffered great abuse earlier in life, but he was able to keep it carefully in check. This was not a man who lost it.

Ever.

I cursed at him, resisted in a weak and futile sort of way, thrashed in an attempt to get away. I threatened him verbally, the anger inside me literally spewing out like a volcano. He'd tried to control what I said to him, and now he was controlling what I did to him physically. I did not react well to this, not in that anguished and desperate state. The reptile part of my brain had completely overwhelmed the higher-functioning parts, and I was spinning out of control like a top wobbling to a halt.

"Stop. Now," he said, with a strange and eerie calm.

He pushed me down onto the bed, effortlessly, released my wrists, and stood over me, watching, waiting to see if I could rein myself in. The gentle yet determined power with which he'd pushed me down and away from him was impressive. He hadn't been rough. Just firm. He wasn't going to put up with my crap. I looked at him and saw that he had within him a rigidly controlled capacity for extreme violence that I had never come across in my life.

It scared me quiet.

"You have no idea what I'm capable of," he said softly yet clearly, his gaze not deviating from mine. "I've worked very hard, for many years, to keep this thing at bay, and I'm not about to let you ruin it for me. You do not want to open that box. Believe me."

"What are you going to do, hit me?" I cried. "I'll call the police."

"I have never hit a woman in my life," he said. "But I will not let anyone, man or woman, disrespect me in my own home."

He turned away from me then, and began to leave the room.

"Take me to my car!" I cried. "I want to go home."

He looked back at me and said, "I understand you don't want to be here. But I'm not going to wake my neighbors in the middle of the night, especially not for something this embarrassing. It's inconsiderate."

"What is wrong with you?" I cried, beginning to sob in frustration and ancient sorrow. "I don't want to be here!"

"Jesus Christ! I don't want your ass here, either," he said. "*Believe* me. But if I take you now, their dogs will start barking and everybody will come out to see what the commotion is. This ain't the city. Out here, you have consideration for other people. It's called manners. You might want to learn some."

He looked at me coldly, as though he could not remember what he'd ever seen in me in the first place. I saw then that he detested me. He felt nothing for me. He wanted me out of his life.

I felt terrible and sat up, reaching my hands out to him. I had lost him. I saw this now. In the past, this sort of display on my part had always brought the men in my life closer to me, as they tried to rescue me. With the cowboy, it had backfired. There was no affection in his eyes for me anymore. He was done with me.

"I'm sorry," I said, realizing that I had never wanted to do this, to make him this cold toward me. I had simply been going through the out-of-control motions that had always seemed to work before, the angry-damsel-in-distress routine. This was the first man I'd met who wasn't about to engage in this destructive dance with me.

"Please," I said. "Let's not do this. I'm sorry. Can I just hold you?"

"Too late for sorry," he said. "We're done."

"No, please." I reached for his hand. He recoiled and gave me a stern look.

"Stay away from me," he instructed, before going back into the guest bedroom. "You're not right in the head. If you try any of this shit again, I won't hesitate to hog-tie you with duct tape and haul your ass down to the sheriff's office. Are we clear?"

I felt the tears spill like lava out of my eyes, and nodded, for the first time in my life defeated.

He let out a deep breath, and said, "Good. Tomorrow I'll take you back to your car, and you'll never have to see me again. Get some sleep, Alisa. Good night."

"How can I sleep like this?" I wailed, miserable. More miserable than I'd ever been. "You don't understand."

"I understand perfectly."

"No," I said. "You don't understand that I—I think I love you. I'm just . . . I never drink this much. I'm sorry. I've been stupid. I love you. I do."

He laughed in disbelief and shook his head.

"I do," I cried. "I love you. I wish you hadn't seen me like this. I wish you loved me."

The cowboy sighed deeply, and blinked once, slowly, before saying, "You want to impress me, Alisa?"

"Yes," I said miserably.

"Okay. If you want to impress me, go to sleep. That will impress me a lot, if you can rein yourself in enough to do that. If you can show me you have any self-control at all."

"Okay," I said sadly, sure I couldn't do what he'd said, but happy to have the opportunity to at least try to redeem myself.

"Good night," he said.

"Good night," I replied, curling into a ball and wishing I weren't so completely, totally, and transparently screwed up, and so completely, hopelessly alone.

THE NEXT MORNING

I woke up on the sofa. Somewhere in the night, or in the four hours of darkness that had to fill in for a complete night after my incredibly insane tantrum, I had gotten up and moved myself from the cowboy's bed to the living room. Sleeping in his bed without him had felt unbearable.

I woke up because the light in the adjacent kitchen was on, and the cowboy was rummaging around in there, drinking a cup of coffee or water or something. I was too fuzzy brained to comprehend just what he was doing. I looked up, bleary-eyed, and realized I was still just a tiny bit drunk, and hungover at the same time. I felt the room spin. I wanted to puke. It wasn't good.

The cowboy was fully dressed, in his usual jeans and boots, long-sleeved shirt tucked in, belt and hat.

"Good morning," I said.

He didn't answer me, though I knew he'd heard me. I sat up and looked at him, hoping he might look at me. But he didn't.

"Get your things," he said. "Truck's warming up. Time to go."

"Go where?" I asked.

He still did not look at me, just grabbed his wallet and cell phone off the counter next to the computer. "You're going home."

"But I slept!" I cried. "I did what you asked."

He ignored this and went to the bedroom, returning with my suitcase and my purse. Without looking at me, he took these out the front door. He returned moments later for the cooler in which I'd brought groceries.

"Please don't do this," I moaned.

"*You* did this," he corrected me.

I got up and came toward him, holding my arms out. "Please. Look at me. At least look at me. Please. Let's talk about this."

He moved away from me and seemed almost afraid of me, dodging me without looking directly at me.

"Are you scared of me now?" I asked. "Big strong alpha man is afraid of me?"

"Nope," he said, putting his sunglasses on. "Just don't want you near me. Get away."

"But I love you."

"Let's go," he repeated.

At this, I fell to the floor, unable to contain my emotions again.

I began to weep. It didn't work. He did not come to scoop me up. Instead, he sat on the sofa and waited, with his elbows on his knees and his fingers laced together.

"I can't do this," I said. "I need you. I can't lose you."

Silence.

"I know it's only been a little more than a month, but I've fallen for you."

"That may be," he said. "But we're not suited to each other. I think you proved that last night."

"I'm sorry! I didn't mean it. I'm never like that."

"I've seen all I need to see, darlin'," he said. "Like Maya Angelou says, when someone shows you who they are, believe it."

"So that's it? You're resigned to this?"

"Yep."

I began to cry harder.

"Jesus Christ," he muttered, annoyed.

"I thought I found someone amazing, and now he's gone! I blew it. I'm so stupid. I thought what we had was good."

"It *was*. Until it *wasn't*. Time to go."

I realized that it was useless to try to change his mind. He was firm. I gathered what little strength I could and went to the bathroom to clean up a little. I returned to the living room, but he wasn't there. I looked out the window and saw him waiting behind the wheel of the flatbed truck. Ready to go. Ready to be rid of me.

I kept crying and couldn't stop.

I staggered droopily toward the truck and climbed in with great dramatic fanfare of sobbing. The cowboy said nothing as he pulled out and started down the road and through the gates. I talked and talked to him, tried some more to convince him to change his mind, or at least to look at me. He didn't budge.

Finally, he spoke, after I'd flung myself onto the floor of the truck and begun to sob into the cushion of my seat.

"You know what your problem is?" he asked. I didn't answer the rhetorical question, though I did think to myself that there were far too many problems in my possession to narrow it down to just *one*. "You don't know when to shut. Up."

This woke me up. "Shut up." That was a phrase I had taught my son never to use, because it was so insulting and rude. It just wasn't said in polite company. Then again, polite company didn't drink too much rum and shove you into a wall, either. I wasn't polite company. At all.

"Sometimes, the best thing a person can do is just stop talking," he said.

"I have a lot to say," I countered.

"Yeah? Well, how about this? I don't want to hear any of it. None of it. I would appreciate it if you could please be quiet. I'm sick of listening to you."

Taken aback, I decided, for the second time that morning, that it was useless to try to get through to this man. He still hadn't looked at me. Not one glance.

"I don't want this to be over," I whined. "I can't do it. I don't want you to be done with me."

"I *am* done," he said, more to himself than to me. "I'm done, with you, with all of you. I'm too old for this. I'm sick of trying. Don't need the stress."

I kept crying because I didn't know what else to do, but I did manage to get myself up into the seat again. I watched the land roll by outside, and I felt sick and sad thinking that I'd never be back here. I loved this place. And this man. And how I'd felt with him in my life. I loved the ways he made me surprise myself and reassess what I believed to be true about conservatives, men in general, and myself.

"I hate this," I said.

"Shut. Up," he said through his teeth. "Please. You're repeating yourself. Just stop."

And so finally, I did. I stopped. I . . . shut. Up.

He took me to my car. He left the truck's engine idling while he packed my suitcase and cooler into the trunk of my Hyundai, still without raising his eyes to look at me at all. I was invisible to him now. Punished rather than rewarded, for the first time in my life, for acting like ... well, like I'd always acted. Like a spoiled, self-centered ... child of (formerly) narcissistic hippies.

I stood there helplessly, next to the door of the car, with my trembling hand on the handle, hoping he'd have a last-minute change of heart, hoping he'd at least take pity on me. Or at least look at me. See me. Acknowledge me.

He did not.

He got back in the truck, and without hesitation, he left me there.

Alone, in the dry and choking cloud of his dust.

ANGER MANAGEMENT

The next couple of weeks were a blur. Or at least they come back to me as a blur now, probably because I don't like to remember them too clearly. They sucked, basically. That's what I'm trying to say.

I'm not sure how I drove myself back to Albuquerque from the ranch. There was pastry involved. I stopped at a gas station in Capitan—or was it Carrizozo?—and bought something sweet and fattening to make myself feel better. I realized as I did so that whatever I was shoving into my mouth probably wouldn't actually make me feel better, but I did it anyway. Sweet rolls, I think. Little ones. With sweet coffee, vanilla. These things only made me feel worse, as palliative junk food always does. I hated gas stations. I hated driving. I *clearly* hated my pancreas. I hated the sky for being so bright and blue, and the sun for continuing to shine as though nothing were wrong, and the birds for singing. Didn't they know the weight of my loss? Didn't they care? Didn't they . . . I stopped thinking, and I ate. And cried. Lovely little me.

I remember crying almost the entire way home, feeling embarrassed when semi trucks passed me because I knew their drivers could see my puffy red face and tear-streaked cheeks. I beat myself up, mentally, replaying all the ways I'd blown it with the cowboy. I was extremely sad, almost sadder than I'd been when my marriage fell apart, which struck me as incredibly strange because I'd really only just met this man. But they say that when you meet The One, you just know it. I felt that I had met my One and then managed to scare him away, like a creepy bald man with clown shoes on might scare a group of savvy sixth graders at the basketball court.

I muddled through my life back home, trying to put on a brave face for my son, trying to get him to school and home again without revealing too much. My son, like most children with mirror neurons and a conscience, has always been very good at reading even the slightest changes in my facial expressions, however I am also notoriously sucky at poker. Therefore, he could tell that I was now depressed, and like most kids his age (ten) who are saddled with wackadoodle single moms who mope around the house with a fake smile shellacked across their aging faces, he worried it was somehow his fault and hoped he could fix me. He was very curious about my seeping sorrow and kept asking about it, and it was all that I could do to lie to him and say everything was fine. Finally, I felt bad about lying, because he could clearly tell that I was lying, and I didn't want him to grow up thinking I was untrustworthy. And so I simply told him that I was sad for my own reasons that didn't concern him and that it would pass and he shouldn't worry too much about it. I reassured him that it had nothing to do with him. He seemed satisfied with that but still mistrustful. "You need to take karate," he told me. "Karate helps you develop pain tolerance."

My father, upon seeing my mopeage, was another matter.

After my son was off to school, I basically came home and fell apart. Because my father had recently retired from years as a sociology professor, he was home puttering about in his garden. This is how he was aware of the dramatic manner in which I sobbed and sniffled. I dragged myself around the house with my shoulders sagging toward the floor, my eyes looking like I'd pried them out with a fork, dipped them in acid, and shoved them back in with a piece of charcoal. I was defeated and despondent, puffy and damp. My father saw this and asked if he could help. I told him what had happened, and he grew thoughtful and sad. We talked for hours about the past, about how he regretted having been brutal to me as a kid. He was sincere, and, I realized, he'd only been nineteen when my mother got pregnant with my older brother. He had been nothing but a kid, an abandoned kid himself, trying to make sense of a senseless world. He loved me and was sorry. I loved my dad. It helped to hear his words. It went a long way toward making me feel better.

After some consideration, I went against my ego and confessed to my dad that I had physically attacked the cowboy and that I was worried about my inability to control my own anger. My father agreed that it was a serious problem, one that he had even seen me turn against him on occasion. He also admitted that it likely had been handed down to me from him, and then told me that he had picked it up in much the same inadvertent manner from his own stepfather, whom he had often seen beating his mother. We wondered, musing aloud, how many generations this anger went back, and when it might stop being handed down like some chipped heirloom china that nobody wanted to eat off of anymore and that certainly would never be accommodated by a dishwasher.

"I know it hurts right now," he said, placing a soothing hand on my back. "But think of the good that can come from this moment. You're realizing something very important about yourself. In its own way, this short, intense relationship you've been through has been a gift to you because now you can begin to heal, and change these patterns so that you don't do it again."

It was a beautiful thing for my father to say, but it didn't make the pain go away. Every morning that came without the customary "good morning" email from the cowboy, on my BlackBerry, was a reminder that I had lost the best man to cross my path in my entire life. I'd stare at the screen of the smartphone, and I'd curse the spam that had shown up in the night. It should have been a love note from the cowboy. But it wasn't. It was a promise that someone somewhere could give me a pill to give me a bigger penis. I didn't want a bigger penis. I didn't want a penis at all. Well, not one of my own, anyway. Nor did I want to call my long-lost Nigerian prince of a relative who had a fat inheritance check for me.

I missed the cowboy terribly.

I hated myself for screwing it up so badly. And, being a slave to my emotions, I emailed him constantly to let him know just how unhappy and remorseful I was. Email, email, email. No impulse control whatsoever.

For more than a week, the cowboy totally ignored my sloppy flood of overwrought and emotionally unstable emails. I heard nothing back from him. When I tried to call him, the phone rang and rang and no answering machine picked up, as though he had simply disconnected the line when he saw my number. I grew increasingly desperate.

"Tell me what I can do," I wrote. "I'll do anything. I can't lose you. How can I assure you that this will never happen again?"

Finally, the cowboy wrote back. He told me to stop writing to him. He told me that he thought I needed professional help.

Now, let's stop for a moment and say that I was aware then, as I am now, that many men say this to women sometimes whenever there is a problem. This is probably because women tend, for whatever reason, to react to stress and conflict in more emotional ways than men do, which leads too many men to wrongly assume that women are simply crazy. I'd heard it before, from men I knew and also from men who'd said it to lots of my noncrazy female friends. It was almost a cliché. But this time, in this case, after this incident, it was different. I realized that the cowboy, a man who measured his words and opinions quite carefully, a man who was not given to hyperbole or insults, wasn't just saying I needed help because he couldn't think of anything else to say. He was saying it because, let's be frank here, it was true. In light of what had happened, and how I'd behaved, it was obvious that I did, in fact, need help.

"I'll get some," I promised. "I totally agree with you." Then I told him that it wasn't the first time I'd done something like this. I'd done it a couple of other times in my life. I told him where it came from, or at least where I thought it came from at the time. He responded by reiterating his wish that I seek professional help. I asked if he would consider seeing me again if I did. He said that he would never rule anything out but that right now he was not comfortable with continuing to date me.

Energized by the fact that he was communicating with me at all, I resolved to sincerely try to fix this anger management issue in myself. I got online and started doing some research. I found an anger management class in town, one that was meeting that very evening, as a matter of fact, and I signed up.

I told the cowboy, in an email.

"Good," he said. "I hope it helps you."

"I miss you," I wrote.

He did not respond. At first, this hurt me. But with the benefit of hindsight I now know that he, too, struggled with anger issues, and that his way of avoiding doing anything stupid was to withdraw from anything that might trigger him. He kept his distance, more to protect me than to protect himself. Meanwhile, I didn't have any tools for dealing with anger, except to blow up. It was time to fix that.

I can legitimately say that I had never wanted a man as much as

I wanted the cowboy. I had never wanted anyone badly enough, and had never been held accountable by them, to have to face what was wrong with me or lose them.

I left my son with my father that evening and drove to a seedy part of town to attend the class at a counseling center there. I walked into the somewhat dingy offices of the center, wearing relatively expensive clothes and carrying myself in a somewhat more confident and less criminal way than the other people I saw in the waiting room. I was also carrying a Vuitton bag that was leftover from the feast days of yesteryear.

I approached the receptionist, who was hidden behind bullet-proof glass along with her big gray pit-bull terrier.

"Hi. I'm here for the anger management class," I said.

The receptionist, a burly sort of butch woman, looked at me in open surprise. Even the dog seemed not to believe me. "Are you sure?" she asked.

"Yes."

She seemed to think I was out of my mind but handed me a clipboard with a pen chained to it and asked me to sign in. Then she directed me to a conference room down the hallway whose carpet was stained from cigarette burns and dotted with discarded chewing gum that had long ago been ground underfoot and deep into the fibers.

There were a few other people in the conference room already, all of them of the type who would not look out of place on *The Jerry Springer Show*. There were gold teeth, tattoos, shaved and lumpy homeboy heads, men in tank tops as their only shirts. There were women who looked dead inside, bored and cruel, staring at the wall and smacking their gum. I felt like a high school kid who had accidentally ended up in detention when she'd meant to find chess club.

The room soon filled up, all of us sitting around a large oval table. Then the instructors came in. There was a middle-aged woman in jeans and a T-shirt, and a younger man in slacks and a tie.

The woman, who had long blondish gray hair, was in charge. She affected a tough attitude and began joking around with the people who were there, people she already knew. None of them seemed to want to be there, and she knew it. The dynamic was beyond strange. She tried to pull them out of their shells, knowing they'd never come; they looked at her as though trying to figure out the best way to stab her on her way back to her car later on.

Then she zeroed in on me.

"Class, we have a new participant." She looked at the list. "Alisa Valdes, is that right?"

"Yes," I said, hoping to God no one here recognized my name as the same one that had just appeared in *Albuquerque The Magazine* for having been voted my city's "Best Writer" by its readers. That would have sucked for sure.

The woman told me her name, and then the young man introduced himself similarly. I will call her Meg, though that's not her real name. I will call him Tim. Meg suggested that we all go around the room and introduce ourselves and say why we were attending this group.

One by one my fellow angry people did as she asked. All of them were here because they had been ordered to be here by authorities, for beating their kids or threatening to kill people or, in some cases, actually getting arrested for assault or battery. None of them seemed to think they belonged there, because the kids or whomever they'd assaulted or beaten clearly deserved it. They all complained that whatever they had done either hadn't happened or had been totally justified because the person on the receiving end of their anger was an idiot.

My turn came, and I told them the story of what had happened at the ranch, and then I told them that I had a history of this kind of outburst and I was referring myself to the group. I said how deeply I regretted what I had done, and tearfully said I never wanted to end up in that place again. I was there to learn how to control myself, I said. I was sick of being a loose cannon. I never wanted to be that woman again.

Everyone in the room stared at me in shock, including the counselors. Especially Meg. Meg's eyes connected with mine, and the wall that she had up for the rest of the people in the room came sliding down. In me, I felt she saw a person she could actually help. It was pulling teeth to help these others, but here I was, a rotten and decaying tooth, falling out all by myself.

After the class, Meg took me aside. "Can I speak to you privately for a minute?" she asked.

I followed her to her office, and she closed the door behind us.

"You don't need to be in that group," she said.

"Yes, I do. I'm very angry. I promise."

"No, I know. I get that. What I'm saying is—well, maybe you noticed that most of the people in there are assholes."

I was shocked by how she'd spoken of her clients.

"They're not in this to change," she said. "They're here because they'd go to jail if they weren't. With all due respect to the program, I don't think you're going to benefit a lot from sitting in a room two hours a week with noncommunicative people so deeply in denial."

"Oh."

"So what I'd like to propose is that you come to me for individual therapy instead. We'll get a lot more done that way."

I perked up. "Okay," I said. "I just need to learn to get a handle on this stuff. I'm totally out of control."

Meg and I set a time later that week for me to return to see her privately. I went home and emailed the cowboy to tell him how it had gone. He wrote back that he was happy for me and hoped it would help. I asked how his day had gone and he didn't answer. I felt devastated. But I was learning to know better than to push this man to do anything he wasn't comfortable doing. If he was going to come around to loving me or being interested in me again, it was going to be on his own time.

MEG'S DIAGNOSIS OF ME

I sent the cowboy emails in the days leading up to my first visit with Meg, and he did not answer them at first. Then, one day, he sent a thoughtful email telling me he had been thinking a lot about my situation and that it seemed to him that while, yes, I had an anger management problem, there might be something bigger than that at work here.

"It seems to me from what you've told me that you have a pattern of impulsive behavior that is self-destructive," he wrote. "I'd venture to say you have impulse control issues, and that anger is just one facet of that delightful whole."

I remembered that the cowboy had told me he had studied child psychology in college. I remembered that he was very smart. I didn't like what he was saying, because it hurt, but I was able to recognize some bit of truth in it. I wrote back thanking him and said I missed him and loved him. He did not reply. I was undeterred, however. I would fix myself. I would get him back.

I went to my first appointment with Meg. I'd been to therapy a couple of times before in my life, once as a teenager (when the therapist told me my dad was a narcissist) and again when I was in my midtwenties for a couple of months. This felt different. I felt focused, with a goal, as though I'd caught a glimpse of what was actually wrong with me this time. I felt like I might figure something out.

Meg's office was cozy, with a comfortable sofa, pretty wall hangings, and a hook rug that would have been at home beneath a cat who might play with a ball of yarn while someone's bespectacled grandmother knit something warm and protective for someone. There were shelves of books about psychology and Buddhism. And there was Meg, in her chair, in jeans and a T-shirt, with intelligence and a weary sort of humor in her eyes.

"Come in," she said. "Have a seat. How are you?"

It seemed an odd question to ask a person who has come to you for psychological help with their monumental anger problems. I wasn't sure how to answer. If I said the usual "fine," it would be an obvious lie. So I settled for "Oh, you know. How are you?"

"I'm okay," she said with a shrug.

I took a seat on the sofa, on the end closest to the door. Meg seemed to notice this and a brief expression crossed her face that made me think there was some significance being ascribed to my having sat there. So I scooted a little more to the center of the couch. She seemed to notice and smiled.

"So, talk to me," she said. "Tell me what's been happening."

So I did. I told her. I told her about losing my temper, about drinking too much, and about how desperate I felt about losing this man. I told her about how, even though this sort of violent behavior wasn't common for me, I had done this kind of thing a couple of times before, with my ex-husband. I told her about this rage that I carried around in me, about how I felt it crippled and blinded me. Then I told her about the cowboy's assessment of me having impulse control issues and told her about other episodes in my life when I thought I was being cool or clever, when I thought I was fighting a good fight, but which turned out to be self-destructive in the end. Writing a thirty-four-hundred-word resignation letter to the *Los Angeles Times* that ended up leaked and published in a newspaper in Florida, in which I insulted several colleagues. Calling *The Boston Globe* a "racist institution" to a reporter from *The Washington Post*, and having that published, too. There were lots of instances of crap like that. Again and again, I'd "fought" injustice in the stupidest of ways, ways that made it all too easy for my opponents to squash me, or label me crazy, or discredit me in some other way.

Meg listened. She asked a few questions about my childhood. I told Meg about my difficulties in kidhood, difficulties that don't all need to be detailed here but which I can sum up.

I told her about how I had an older brother who dealt with our wacky home life by, oh, you know, dropping out of school and getting himself addicted to stuff. Bad stuff. For decades. I told her that this brother and I were completely estranged from each other. And then I explained that I had dealt with the difficulties in our home growing up quite differently, namely, by deciding to act like the perfect kid and hope no one noticed how messed up my parents were.

"I was a straight-A student," I told her. "I was freshman class president. I was freshman band president. I made it my mission to become a complete and total overachiever in life, to prove to my mom that she was wrong about life and about me."

I told her about how my mom moved to New Orleans when I was in high school and invited me to come live with her so I could attend the performing arts high school in that city, which I did.

"I was the first kid to ever get accepted to both the music and creative writing programs at the New Orleans Center for Creative Arts," I said. "Ellis Marsalis was my jazz teacher, and his son Wynton came to give a master class. I'll never forget that. It was amazing. Tom Whalen was my creative writing teacher. I loved him. He was great. We had to keep journals for class, and so I started writing in it about how my mom left me alone all the time, and how I heard gunshots at night, and how I had to take a part-time job as a fry cook at a neighborhood restaurant so that I had lunch money. I guess this alarmed Mr. Whalen because he called the state about it, and pretty soon there were a couple of nice social workers knocking on the door of our apartment."

I told her about how social services made me leave my mother's New Orleans home shortly thereafter because she was deemed "unfit" by the state after it was discovered that she was leaving me alone in a roach-infested tenement for weeks at a time while she hung out with her pothead boyfriend, Lamar, an Alabama good ol' boy who hated "niggers and spics," in Metairie.

I told her about how my dad threw me out shortly after I'd returned to New Mexico because I'd been fielding inappropriate advances from my thirty-one-year-old saxophone teacher in New Orleans, something that in retrospect seemed like an obvious cry for adult attention at the time.

"Well, duh," she said. "An aware parent would have seen that. They would have also reported the teacher to the police."

It was then that I realized just how antifeminist this move had been on my father's part, how so much of the "feminism" of my childhood home had actually been nothing but lip service.

"Yeah, well. No. My dad reacted like a typical father from Havana, I guess," I said. "Like I was a whore who'd dishonored the family name or something. He blamed me. He hit me, put all my stuff in green Glad trash bags, and threw me out," I told her.

"How old were you?"

"Sixteen."

"So you'd been told by the state you couldn't live with your mom, and then your dad threw you out on the streets?"

"Yeah. Pretty much. I remember calling the police while he was hitting me, and him cutting the phone line with a pair of scissors halfway through. But the cops came after that, and I was sitting there in the driveway with all my stuff in a trash bag, and I was crying. I remember the cop putting me in the car with him, and asking me what I'd done to make my dad so angry. He blamed me, too."

"What did you do then?"

"I asked the cop to take me to my best friend's house. I went to live with my best friend and her rich, religious family. They took me in like a charity case."

"How did that make you feel?" she asked.

I told her about how that was the first time I felt the rage and self-destructive impulses that took over even now, when I got sad or felt rejected. I told her about how I felt like my friend's family seemed to think it was their Christian duty to help me, but that they never *really* wanted me around. I told her about how pretty their house was, how big and nice and clean, and how I wished to God I had been raised in a family like that. I told her about how I studied them, the way they treated one another. They were conservative, from Texas, and very kind to one another. My father had always put conservatives down, painted them out to be these horrible people without souls or consciences, and yet here they were, these right-wing religious people, taking me in and giving me a home when my own father, who was supposedly all about protecting the underdog, had thrown me away like garbage.

"I pretty much felt alone in the world, like no one loved me."

"That must have sucked," said Meg.

"Yep."

Meg paused for a moment, and then she said, "Well, I'd say you had a pretty invalidating upbringing. One of the worst I've ever heard about in this office, actually. I'm amazed you turned out as well as you did. I'm amazed you never turned to drugs or alcohol, frankly." She paused. "What do you think set you on a different course? What made you a bestselling author with a master's degree from Columbia, while many if not most others in that kind of situation might have become self-destructive?"

I thought about this. "Anger," I said. "Righteous indignation, I guess."

"How so?"

"It made me angry to see how my dad treated my mom. It made me angry that they could talk about equality but never demonstrated it. I resolved to fight, to stick up for myself, to never get pushed around like she did. But it's almost like I was born with fight in me, too. I've always had this thing in me, where I'd protect myself, even when I was really little. Where I thought I deserved better. Where I'd fight injustice. Where I was not going to let anyone, not even my parents, destroy me, or take my dignity away. I think of it as a gift from the universe, or God, actually, as weird as that sounds."

Meg smiled at me. "Hmm. Anger and fighting, huh? Sound familiar?"

I thought about it.

Meg said, "Sometimes, Alisa, our biggest weakness, the thing that brings us the most suffering, can also be our biggest strength. You're here in my office right now because you fight. Because you defend yourself. You protect yourself. You get angry."

"Right."

"You came to me because of this fighting impulse, because it's harming you in your relationships. And we want to help give you better tools for dealing with your emotions."

"Right."

"But I want you to recognize that this same angry, fighting behavior served its purpose, for a time. It kept you from ending up like your brother. That's how I see it."

"Wow," I said, as her words sank in. "I guess you're right."

Then she asked me if I had any other self-destructive behaviors.

I told her I had been bulimic on and off for nearly twenty years. She nodded as though this made perfect sense.

"Okay," she said.

Meg thought for a bit and then told me there was good news. She agreed that I had anger issues, but she didn't agree that they made me a bad person. She was more nuanced about it than that. She thought anger could be a useful emotion but that it could also be a destructive one if not understood or controlled. She told me about a very effective treatment for teaching people to find new ways to handle old emotional patterns in their brains and nervous systems, a system designed by a Buddhist woman who realized that mindfulness and learning new ways to cope with emotional distress worked a lot better in curing people like me than, say, psychoanalysis. Instead of dwelling upon the "problems" that made us this way, this therapy taught us how to compensate for our disability and repro-gram our brains and nervous systems to behave in new and healthy ways.

"You already know what's wrong, and how you ended up like this," she said. "Traditional therapy is only going to have you rehash how you got here and maybe even make it worse. We don't need to do that. We're not saying to deny the past. We're just saying to focus instead on the present and move forward with new skills. What we need to do is give you new tools, new ways to interact with the world. Basically, we're finding that many patients can actually be cured by changing the way they behave. But you have to want to do it."

"I can be *cured*?" I asked.

"Yes. These inappropriate reactions are not something you were born with. It's something you developed as a coping mechanism a long time ago, when you were really young, and it was a survival skill then, and it worked—then. But it's not working anymore. It's hurt-ing you now. It is in your power to let it go."

Meg went to the shelf and produced a book on this therapy and gave it to me. She also gave me a CD recording by Clarissa Pinkola Estés called *How to Love a Woman* and another CD set by a woman named Pema Chödrön.

"You're a reader," she said. "Read through this. Listen to these CDs. See what you think. These are good starting points."

It was time for the session to end. I thanked Meg and went home and began to read the book she'd given me. I tried one of the mind-fulness techniques I learned there, wherein I stared at the lit wick of a candle for five straight minutes, trying to simply observe what it was doing and not think too hard about anything.

I did this candle exercise a few times, usually while I was agi-tated about having lost the cowboy, and to my great and pleasant surprise found that I felt better afterwards. Mindfulness, I learned, was nothing more than being able to shut down the overthinking mind for a bit in favor of just truly living in the moment, experiencing what was going on around you instead of what was going on inside you. This was amazing! I knew I wasn't cured, or even close to being cured, but I was truly excited to have this door opened for me, onto a new understanding of old habits, and new possibilities for overcoming whatever obstacles had been holding me back in all aspects of my life.

I read, and read, and read.

And I thought, and thought, and thought.

I thought a lot.

I took long hikes in the foothills of the Sandia Mountains, with my dog, Topaz, and I thought about the past. I realized that it wasn't just the personal family stuff that had made me like this.

It was bigger than that.

My interpretation of feminism had also led me to this anger that threatened to destroy my life.

For me, a woman who had actually been born with an innate personality that leaned more toward the neutral, peaceful, nurturing, and typically "feminine," having been raised in a home filled with contradictory ideas about gender roles and responsibilities had contributed to my decision later in life to reject my nature in the name of feminism. I had been given two choices as a child—be domineering like my father or be a dishrag like my mother—and without understanding that there were other options, I'd remade myself in my father's male image in order to avoid what I had come to believe was inevitable female subjugation. Feminism, combined with the dysfunction of my family of origin, had combined to make me defensive, prone to overreaction, and extremely angry. It turned me into an angry, unhappy, conflicted, combative, lost, and disconnected soul. A woman dissociated from her nature, completely imbalanced.

I suddenly understood why this traditional, masculine, rugged cowboy appealed so much to me, at a visceral level. *The hidden true self of me, the woman I was born to be, the spirit I'd been hiding for decades, had connected instantly with him at a subconscious level.*

With him, I was able to start to feel all those things that I'd condemned myself for feeling or wanting to feel all my life under the thumb of my parents' misguided and dogmatic interpretation of progressive feminism and their hypocritical adherence nonetheless to a patriarchal paradigm that harmed my mother, in the home. The cowboy was the perfect yang to my hidden and "shameful" yin. His true nature matched my true nature, perfectly. I didn't know how much of it was nature and how much of it was nurture; like most people, I figured, I was a big old tangled mess that combined both biology and psychology in ways that were difficult if not impossible to untangle. He was that incredible elusive masculine ideal—a strong man who was not domineering—and this allowed me to seek to be my feminine ideal—a caring, nurturing, flexible woman who was not subservient. We *worked.*

It was a huge aha moment for me, and my soul lit up as the giant lightbulb over my head turned on.

I loved the cowboy—and had fallen deep and hard and fast in love with him—because he matched the woman I was always meant to be but had been too afraid to be, all my life. He was in tune with his innate nature as a human male, and he was confident enough to cling to his traditional values and masculinity in spite of the pressures put on all men in our society to emasculate themselves. He was a full man in a world of the neutered half male. As such he drew out the full woman in me and gave her permission to own her ovaries.

I wrote to the cowboy to tell him all of this and to tell him I was entering into intensive therapy that held great promise to help me overcome anger and impulse control issues. I told him some of what I was learning and thinking, and the new ideas that were hatching in my brain. I told him how excited this made me, because for the first time in my life things were starting to make sense. For the first time in my life, I had hope that I might actually be able to become a somewhat normal person who didn't screw up every good thing that had ever happened to her.

"I don't know what's going to happen between us, if anything at all," I wrote. "But I do know this. If I hadn't met you, if I hadn't fallen so fast and hard for you, and if we hadn't had that stupid, ugly weekend, I would have continued to stumble through my life without a clue about what ailed me. I would never have learned what it was that plagued me. Now I know, and I am grateful to you for that. You have helped me to understand why I'm a mess, and now, with Meg's help, I can finally start to try to fix it. So, thank you."

The cowboy wrote back. "I'm glad to hear that you've recognized a problem and that you're more than willing to do what it takes to fix it. I'm just as happy to see that maybe we have a chance after all."

MEANWHILE, BACK AT THE RANCH

The next couple of weekends, I went down to the ranch again and our relationship grew exponentially. Our reconciliation was intense, often beautiful, and very satisfying. The cowboy seemed genuinely moved that I'd sought help, and impressed that I was so quickly—and in his estimation intelligently—diving into the work of fixing what was wrong. And I, for my part, was grateful to have another chance—not just with him, but with life in general. I was committed to never losing my temper to the extent that I shoved anyone, physically or verbally, again.

"One thing you'll learn about me," I told him one evening as we sat out on the porch watching a group of deer dart across the hills toward their sleeping place. "When I set my mind to something, once I actually understand what I'm doing, I'm usually pretty effective at getting it done."

"That's how I live my life, too," he said.

We talked for hours about things—about feminism, about politics, about psychology. We talked about biology, about masculinity and femininity. We talked about spirituality. We opened up to each other, and it was, in a word, healing. I wasn't sure where I was going, only that I was supposed to go there, and that this man would be a most comforting companion on the ride. I was changing. Little by little.

Together, we researched all these things. We came across fascinating information, most of it coming out of evolutionary biology and neuroscience. Everything we dug up only served to confirm the idea that his long-held instinctual views on sex differences, and my newfound acceptance of my own gut-level agreement with him, were founded in science. Science, in fact, was only now starting to prove that many of the differences intuited by the world's "traditional" views on the sexes were based in the realities of our bodies.

Examples? Whew. There are so many. Some of the ones that caught our attention were those that showed the ways men's chemistry and women's chemistry worked together like two parts of a whole—as in the fact that when a man is near a woman who is ovulating, his own testosterone levels rise measurably. Just from being near her! Or the way that women can pick out the man with the most testosterone in any group, through nothing more than sniffing the T-shirts of various men. The high-testosterone man, for whatever reason, will simply smell better to her nose. Men, meanwhile, can do the T-shirt sniff test and will invariably choose the shirt worn by an ovulating woman over the one worn by a nonfertile woman. There are studies that show how very different our brains are, how different our emotional wiring is. Again and again, these differences complement one another. We evolved like this. To be different. That did not, we agreed, give either group the right to subjugate the other. What it did, we decided, was give both men and women an obligation to care for one another, and to learn about and accept the very real differences between us.

For instance, communication. The cowboy had asked me a question. Something like, "Are you going to that place on Friday?"

It was a yes-or-no question. So, naturally, I answered along the lines of, "Well, I've got to make sure the sitter is going to be here on time, and I need to get my dress from the cleaners first. Did you know they said seventy-five people have already signed up to go? Omigosh, I better get the car detailed. No use getting a black dress cleaned if you're going to sit in dog hair. I'm so sick of that dog."

The cowboy's face grew mildly annoyed, and he repeated the question. "Are you going to that place on Friday? *Yes or no, dear.*"

I blinked across the room at him, failing to understand why he had *failed* to understand that, *yes, I was going.* Was he deaf? "Why would I be getting my dress from the cleaners if I weren't going?" I retorted. "Gosh, I hope they got that stain out. Mustard! Who the heck eats a hot dog in a cocktail dress? In front of the publisher? Me. That's who. Next time, I'll wear yellow, like the man in *Curious George*. Next time, I'll just dress like a banana and save us all a lot of trouble. I think Lady Gaga already did that, though. I *hate* Lady Gaga. I used to like her, when 'Just Dance' first came out and I didn't know she looked like the Crypt Keeper in drag. Then she started trying too hard, hatching out of eggs and so forth. I hate when entertainers try too hard. That's the main reason I can't stand Elton John. That, and 'Rocket Man.' Do you like that song?"

The cowboy sighed deeply through his nose, and turned his head ever so slightly to one side as though to crack his neck a bit. He closed his eyes slowly, to compose himself. "I'll say it one more time," he enunciated deliberately. "Are you going to that place Friday? Yes or no."

I started to answer, but he held up a hand to stop me. "Hang on," he said. "I don't want any other words. Just a yes or a no."

I frowned. "Yes," I said, at last.

"That's all I needed to know," he said. "What time do you need to be there?"

"Well, it starts at seven, but you don't always want to be exactly on time to these things. Right? You don't want to look desperate. You don't want to be too *early*, either. I mean, late is okay, but not *too* late because then they'll think you don't care about them. Which I do. I really like these people."

The cowboy sighed, and we began again. "Alisa? *What. Time. Do. You. Have. To. Be. There.* It's a number between one and twelve . . ."

Sound familiar?

Yeah, I know. We do this all the time, the cowboy and I.

At first I thought it was just because he wasn't listening. Then I read this brain study, showing that in women the part of the brain that deals with language is 17.8 percent bigger than it is in men. This leads to what scientists call "significant sexual dimorphism in verbal ability."

Behavioral scientists have said as much for a while now, but this is the first study to prove it anatomically. Another study shows that this brain difference influences the way males and females problem solve, too. Women are more abstract thinkers. Men are more spatial and literal. Which is all a roundabout (and very female) way for me to tell you this one simple thing: Women talk more than men and are better at it. This means we probably also write better. In your face, Shakespeare! Booya! (Cue: Literary touchdown dance.)

But back to the topic. What was the topic again? Oh, right. Thanks.

My point? Men, it seems, don't just *want* simple answers because they wish to *irritate* us—though, let's not fool ourselves, they can be spectacularly good at the latter. It's rather that men prefer clearly stated answers because their brains process language differently than ours do. This isn't to say we're smarter than they are, or they're smarter than we are. We're just different, in spite of the feminist mantra about us being equal in all things. Difference is good. Men and women evolved this way to complement one another. See? He gets me there on time. I make sure we've brought the right gift.

So, ladies, remember this the next time you're talking to a man. Keep it clear and direct. Not that the cowboy doesn't understand me when I go off on tangents. He does. He'd just rather not have to decipher. As he told me, "For clarification (again, mainly to facilitate better communication between us, a better understanding of where we're each coming from . . . not merely to critique), it's not really that you have to Keep It Simple, Stupid, when communicating with me. It's that I'd like the answer to my question first . . . *then* whatever further explanation you desire. When I ask a question, I'm trying to get information. Information I need to be able to facilitate the goal. The information I need to plan. In the scenario given, I could discern the answer to my question. But I remain firm because I'm trying to get you to give me a straight answer *on a regular basis*, create a habit . . . for when I don't have time to decipher your response. I'm being *consistent*, not obtuse."

One of the best moments during that first summer together came one afternoon, on a day when we'd discussed our thoughts on religion. The cowboy lay on the bed and invited me to get comfortable next him. He had a book in his hands and showed it to me. It was Mark Twain's *Letters from the Earth*.

"Twain was having a crisis of faith when he wrote this because he'd just lost the love of his life, his wife, and his favorite daughter," the cowboy told me. "The far Christian right has listed this as a Satanic writing, but the fact of the matter is, he's questioning his own faith because he was in pain. He kept it secret, never published it because he knew it'd be too controversial. I think it's genius. Mark Twain was a genius."

The cowboy began to read aloud to me. He was a wonderful reader, a natural actor. I thought back to when I'd been married. A couple of times, when I'd been very sick, I'd asked my ex-husband to read aloud to me. He'd refused, for whatever reason. Now here was a man who just . . . read to me. Beautifully. From a deep, thoughtful, funny, and incredibly well-written book by one of my favorite authors. I listened carefully, and we both laughed at the same parts. He'd pause in the passages to discuss ideas with me. We talked, and talked. This wasn't how love was supposed to look with a man from the conservative side of the divide, was it? But here it was. Beautiful, thoughtful, deep, and life changing. So much, I realized, of what I'd thought was true in my life simply . . . wasn't.

The sun was golden outside, the room bright and comforting. The cowboy's voice was fluid, soothing. His mind was agile. His values were very much in line with my own, and nothing like I had assumed so long ago when I had been reluctant to meet him.

"I'm so glad I found you," I told him when he finished reading. Tears misted my eyes. I hugged him.

"Darlin', no disrespect, but I'm pretty sure I was the one who found you."

"Yes," I said, giddy. "You did. In more ways than one."

It was during this time that the cowboy began to show me bits and pieces of his world. He took me out on the big, burly all-terrain vehicle, for instance. For all you city folks out there, an ATV is like a motorcycle with four wheels that can chew its way over just about any kind of surface. I had never been on such a contraption in my life and had, in fact, on occasion mocked those people in Albuquerque whose children always seemed to have rat-tail hairdos, who always seemed to be gunning such machines up and down the arroyos of the valley. The ranch ATV was camouflage too, with a rifle rack on the front. I felt kinda strange, at first, getting onto the thing behind the cowboy, who in addition to the rifle also had a pistol full of snake shot in a holster around his waist. I took a photo of the ATV and posted it to Facebook with a caption about feeling very Sarah Palin, minus the being-an-idiot part.

"This feels very Yosemite Sam to me," I muttered as I straddled him and settled onto the seat.

"You're a dork," he told me as he started the engine.

"Tell me something I don't already know," I called out.

"I'll do better than that," he called back over the roar of the motor, backing the thing out of its parking spot by the toolshed. "I'll show you things you've never *seen* before."

Off we went, me with my arms wrapped around the cowboy's solid torso as he masterfully maneuvered the loud and powerful machine along the ranch's many miles of rough dirt roads. Talk about a core workout! My abs worked overtime just to keep me upright. Up rocky hills we went, down into beautiful valleys. The three dogs ran alongside us, excited to be working.

It was, I realized, incredibly . . . fun.

Then we came to a group of black cows. The cowboy drove the four-wheeler right up next to the group. I was terrified. I'd never been that close to cows before. They were beautiful and completely massive. Their eyes were so pretty and dark. But they were also huge, and this scared me. There were maybe twenty of them, all females except for one bull. In spite of their being so much bigger than we were, the cows were afraid of us. They were also afraid of the dogs, who circled them and barked and barked.

"Ksksksksks," said the cowboy to his dogs. "Git 'em git 'em git 'em!"

The dogs got fired up and obeyed. I watched as they circled the cows, bunching them tightly together.

"Look," said the cowboy. "You may be familiar with Australian shepherds or blue heelers or border collies. Those dogs work from the back; they push livestock. These dogs contain livestock because in rough country, cattle get wild; they tend to want to take off when they see you. These dogs circle an animal; basically they're triggering the natural defense mechanism of a cow, which is to bunch them in a tight group. That way, you come up on a horse, you don't have to go chase in twenty different directions to gather your cattle. Can you imagine being by yourself on a horse in this country? There's no way you can gather them without dogs like this."

I looked, and sure enough the cows were tightly together in a nervous, mooing, drooling bunch. This made me sad. I felt sorry for the cows. The cowboy was grinning from ear to ear, enjoying the show. He lived for this, I realized. He could have been a famous model or an actor, a millionaire stockbroker, and yet he'd chosen . . . this.

Cows.

"They're learning to bunch 'em up real good," he told me excitedly. He explained to me that the instinct to bunch cows was innate to Catahoulas. "They're gettin' real cowy," he said. I had no idea what that meant.

I was able to suspend my hypocritical steak-eating liberal impulse to pity the cows enough to appreciate what was happening here. It fascinated me. Man and dog, working together to raise cattle. It was an ancient set of relationships, one that I had long reaped the benefits of without ever having to actually participate in.

Still, I felt terrible for the cows. A couple of them were mamas, with babies that they tried valiantly to protect from the dogs and us. The cowboy seemed hardened to this reality, to the terror these animals obviously felt. I tried to understand it all, to reconcile my empathy and compassion with the realistic world this man inhabited. It wasn't easy.

On we went, across the ranch. The cowboy took me on a tour of the entire thing. The sun was so warm, and the feel of the wind on my face as I held on to this strong, sexy man was intoxicating. I was happy.

Then a crisis arose. The dogs were ahead of us on the trail, and suddenly we heard barking. The cowboy zoomed the four-wheeler toward the commotion, and there we saw what the dogs were circling: a weak, scrawny little bull calf struggling to his feet, all by himself, half blind from neglect, exhausted and struggling to survive, hiding under a juniper bush from the harsh, hot sun.

"Jesus Christ," said the cowboy, slowing the ATV to a stop.

He'd told me earlier that a calf had gotten separated from its mother from an adjoining ranch and was lost somewhere on his side of the fence now. He'd called that ranch's manager several times to tell them that the calf was here, on this ranch, and requested that they come and get it.

"Why haven't they come to get it?" I asked, horrified by the sight of this sickly animal. My heart went out to it, and I felt horrible and helpless.

"I don't know," he said.

The cowboy turned off the engine of the four-wheeler and got off to approach the calf. The cowboy looked pained, as though he were every bit as bothered by the specter as I was.

"He's dying," he told me.

"That's awful," I said. The tears sprouted in my eyes now, and poured out. I hated to see anything suffer. Up close now, it was obvious that this little black bull was starving. "Can't we save him?"

"Too late."

"But he's still here," I whined. "There has to be something we can do!"

"I know you think what I do is brutal," he told me, "but the truth is, baby, I don't like to see any animal suffer. I take my job seriously, to give these animals the best life they can have, for the time that they're here. Unfortunately, not everybody feels that way."

"Poor thing," I said of the bull calf.

The dogs were frenzied, circling the calf now, biting and latching onto it. They were trying to do their job, but because the calf wasn't moving—it couldn't—the dogs grew more excited and demanding. The bull calf, terribly weakened from hunger and thirst, hardly able to see them through its blinded eyes, tried valiantly to defend itself with the little strength it had left.

It was terrified.

I was heartbroken.

The cowboy grew very loud when the dogs failed to heed his call to stop. They sensed weakness, it seemed, and like most things in nature, had no problem taking advantage of it.

"No!" he shouted.

The dogs ignored him.

"Taz! Effie! Beau! No!" he shouted.

The dogs ignored him.

"Goddamn it! No!" he shouted.

They ignored him some more.

The cowboy seemed furious and yelled at them in an incredibly harsh tone I'd never heard him use with them, but they were focused on the calf.

The dogs ignored him.

Finally, the cowboy removed his .22 pistol loaded with snake shot and shot it toward the dogs. Not at them, but near enough. A pellet ricocheted off something and seemed to have caught Effie in the foot. She yelped and started limping.

I screamed, terrified. I'd never been around a gun going off. I'd never seen a bull calf dying. I'd never witnessed dogs so callously attacking something so weak. I'd never done anything like this, and I hated it.

The dogs scattered, the shots finally pulling them out of their single-minded focus. The bull calf staggered in fear and fell to its knees, weak.

"I hate this!" I cried. "I want to go home!"

"Baby," the cowboy said, coming to the rifle rack. "I know you're not going to like this, but I have to put it out of its misery. It's the humane thing to do. Turn away."

I was very shaken up by now, by everything I'd seen that day.

The thought of watching the cowboy kill the bull calf was almost too much for me then.

"Please don't," I pleaded with him. "Not with me here. I can't handle it. I'm sorry, but I just can't. I'm not like you."

The cowboy seemed annoyed but put the rifle back.

"Fine," he said. "Then let's get you back to the house; I'll put the dogs up; then I'll come back and take care of it."

And that's exactly what he did.

I heard the rifle shot from the house and was heartbroken. I knew I loved this man, and I understood very well why he had to do what he'd done, but I was also incredibly conflicted, trying to understand how I might one day be able to integrate my life into his, and vice versa.

Later that night, over dinner, I brought this up.

"We are so different from one another," I said. I told him that I pitied the cows. That it hurt me to watch them get so scared. That I didn't know whether I could handle the heartbreak of seeing him kill things. That I hated that he'd hurt his dog with the snake shot.

"It's like a BB," he said. "She's not even limping anymore. Barely nicked her."

"Still. I hate it."

"People in the city are so sheltered," he said. "Life and death are all around us, all the time. It's how the world works, darlin'. You guys in the city just like to sanitize it."

"I know."

"You people have no idea where meat comes from."

"I know."

"When you see life and death every day, like I do, you understand it. That doesn't mean I like it any more than you do. I'm not desensitized to it. I just accept it. You learn to appreciate life more. You understand the cycles, that death is just part of the whole thing."

I started to cry. "I get it. I just—it's hard. Those poor cows. They were so scared."

"Oh, baby," he said in mild annoyance. "You think they're scared, but the fact of the matter is that a cow doesn't think like a human being, so to equate a human emotional reaction to a cow is inaccurate. Pretty much all they think about is one of two things, ass or grass." He said the last bit to try to lighten the situation.

"Still," I said. "Even if that's true, is being stupid a good reason to eat something? I mean, if that were the case, then we'd be justified in eating mentally retarded people, too. But we don't. We have compassion for them. We think of it as our duty to protect them."

The cowboy shook his head, having heard this type of argument before. "Darlin'," he said. "If we didn't raise them for food, these cows you feel so sorry for right now wouldn't even be here. The whole reason they exist, the whole reason they're alive in the first place, is because we breed them for consumption."

I considered this. There was truth in what he said. But there was truth in what I said, too.

We were both right, even though our views completely contradicted each other.

"Wouldn't you be happier with someone more like you?" I asked him. "A cowgirl?"

The cowboy laughed. "I don't necessarily want to date someone just like me. I don't need a clone. I like you. I like the way you are. I don't always have to agree with you to like you and respect you."

"Poor cows," I said, frowning.

He looked at me with compassion in his eyes. "This is why I always tell my friends, you know, they always ask me how I can stand to date a liberal, and I tell them that I like liberals. You keep us from getting too hard, too cold. We need liberals to keep us human, just like you guys need conservatives."

"We do?"

He smiled. "We're the ones who make the hard decisions that you guys are too empathetic to make. Like going to war, when it's necessary to go to war. Or raising food animals. I don't ever want to see liberals disappear off the face of the earth, because we need the balance. We need you, you need us."

"I need you," I said. "I know that much."

The cowboy took the napkin out of his lap then, and put it on his plate. Then he stood up, smiling, and came to where I sat. He held his hand out.

"What?" I asked.

"Come on," he said.

I put my hand in his, and he helped me up out of my chair. Then he began to lead me across the kitchen, toward the hall.

"Where are we going?" I asked.

He led me down the hall, toward his bedroom.

"I just got this urge to show you just how much I like liberals," he said over his shoulder, with a mischievous grin. "Well, one liberal in particular."

He led me into the bedroom, closed the door behind us, and then engaged me in one of the most extraordinarily selfless acts of diplomacy ever committed across party lines.

THE B WORD (BOYFRIEND)

I went back to the city on a mission. I was going to start researching biology, psychology, history, and evolution and try, the way that an academic's daughter and a recovering journalist *usually* tried, to understand what was happening to me from a sound scientific place. I guess that even though I was happy with the relationship, I was still wondering whether it was okay to be happy with a man who was so clearly not what everyone I had ever known might want for me.

What I found floored me.

The cowboy had been right about men being able to see motion better. Studies showed that men had better vision in lighted environments than women did. Men were also better than women at perceiving depth and motion. Women, meanwhile, were better at seeing at night and better at differentiating between colors, and especially better at telling the difference between subtle color shadings. Women were better at seeing things in the red end of the color spectrum and tended to have a better visual memory than men.

Men, meanwhile, are seventeen times more likely to be color-blind than women. Why, you might ask, would this be an advantage? Well, it turns out that people who are color-blind have an easier time seeing through camouflage. And when, you might ask, would people need to be able to do such a thing? Well, how about when they are hunting?

And it wasn't just color blindness; there were all sorts of ways male eyes saw differently than female eyes did, most of them linked to historical advantages in hunting.

I thought about the way the cowboy was always able to see deer or sheep on the ranch, when I couldn't find them to save my life. "They're right there," he'd say, pointing. I'd squint and squint and still see nothing. "Right there, next to that tree," he'd say. He was forever seeing animals where I did not.

I thought about why these differences might be. There were theories about it. If women were better at seeing subtle differences in the red end of the spectrum, might that mean we would be better able to tell whether our child was overheated, or ill? I could think of many times during my marriage when I'd noticed our son was sick long before his father had been aware of anything different about the kid. As for seeing better at night—could this have evolved to go along with women's better ability to hear high-pitched frequencies and our tendency to be the first to wake up when the baby cried in the night? Could it be that in spite of the annoyingness of it, men had been sleeping through the night for millennia, while we women got up to soothe the baby back to sleep? Considering that we were the ones with the mammary glands, it only made sense.

It wasn't fair. But it was true.

I read on.

Men were bigger and stronger than women, all over the world. Period. On average, men were 30 percent stronger than women. Their muscles were composed differently than ours were.

It wasn't fair. But it was true.

Women had better hearing than men, across the board. Period. That didn't mean we were better listeners, though that often seemed to be true as well.

It wasn't fair. But it was true.

Women had a higher percentage of body fat, the world over, no matter what we ate or didn't eat. This made our bodies better suited to having children.

It wasn't fair. But it was true.

Women were better at remembering faces, outfits, and people in general than men were. A study on interpersonal sensitivity at the University of Ohio concluded that women were just better with other people than men were, at least in the ways that were valued by society, such as empathy and compassion. Slightly better. That didn't mean men couldn't overcome this biological disadvantage, but it would take work. A study out of the University of Iowa found that the part of the brain responsible for social cognition was significantly larger in women than it was in men, and that size mattered; people with a bigger straight gyrus (that's the part of the brain we're talking about) were better at social skills. Period.

It wasn't fair. But it was true.

Of course, I also found no shortage of studies that said things like "Yes, there are differences, but they don't really matter."

I found this strange.

Why was it that so many people in modern American society pretended that the differences between men and women were nothing but skin-deep? We could look at our bodies, side by side, and understand that we were different. Males and females were not the same. But as soon as a scientist tried to demonstrate that these differences extended pretty much to every facet of our beings, into everything from decision making to language learning to impulsivity, a chorus of feminists stood up to cry foul. Even when presented with irrefutable scientific evidence, the feminists were quick to say that socialization could change all of that.

I knew very well this sort of tactic, having engaged in it myself most of my life. But I also knew, deep down inside, that it was nonsense to try to explain away or deny sex differences between men and women. The fastest person in the world would likely always be a man, I realized. While there were certainly many women who were faster than many men, this did not negate the fact that men and women were built differently and men had the speed advantage on the whole. Clearly, if a man sat around eating bonbons and watching *SportsCenter* all day and night, he'd be slow and soft. Socialization comes into play. But it does not change basic genetic facts.

This was all very interesting to me and started to open doors for me. I was starting to understand myself better. I was starting to understand why it was that I was so incredibly attracted to the cowboy. It was hardwired in me. I had been *socialized* not to like this about myself. I had been *socialized* to want to be the fastest person in the world, in spite of my biological limitations. But the facts of my biology remained what they were. I was a woman, descended from a long, long, long line of women, most of whom had benefited in one way or another from having an alpha man around. It didn't have to make sense in the modern context for it to be true.

It didn't *have* to be *fair*.

Turned out that women were better at language than men, too. Girls and boys learned language differently, using different parts of the brain, and females had better communication between the left and right hemisphere than men did.

Didn't have to be fair to be true.

Then there was the touchy issue of PMS. I'd had a mild version of it since I started menstruating. You could not deny that many women were drugged by their own bodies throughout each month. We were more amorous when we ovulated. We were nasty and mean when it might be time for a fertilized egg to implant in the womb, meaning we were most likely to keep men away during that crucial time and thereby increase the likelihood that the embryo would be off to a good start. There were sound biological reasons for all of these differences, reasons that had contributed mightily to each and every one of us being here, walking around, able to formulate ambitious, academic, nonsensical arguments *against* them.

It wasn't fair. But it was.

It just . . . *was.*

I was so excited by all of this. I wrote emails to the cowboy about what I was figuring out. About how things were starting to make sense to me. About how I was shocked and strangely liberated by the fact that many of my new ideas were actually in contradiction to the canon within which I had been raised.

Feminism, I told him, was valuable. It was certainly very valuable. But it had gone too far. It had gotten to the point that the reaction had become the identity for many women, meaning that without patriarchy to rail against, there would be nothing to them at all. The irony of it was astonishing. The very thing these women had arranged their lives around fighting actually defined them, in some strange way. Without the enemy, they could not exist at all.

People living solely in reaction to an injustice were every bit as much a part of that injustice as those who perpetuated it, I told him.

A life in reaction was no life at all. Life, I reasoned, had to be about action, not reaction, and it had to be sincere, and suited to each person.

The cowboy supported me, and we had good conversations.

I went to see Meg. I told her about what I was learning, too. Meg told me that she was a lesbian but that she totally understood where I was coming from. Meg said that she agreed with the cowboy that every relationship required someone to be the alpha. And sometimes that job shifted from one partner to the other, in an area that they were better at, she said. It didn't work if both were trying to be the alpha at the same time. I was shocked that she'd agree with me. I told her that I felt suddenly more in tune with my true self than I'd ever felt before, and how much that scared me.

"I dated someone who ran a ranch for a while," she told me. "They're just much more in touch with nature. With reality. That's what you're feeling. I'd say this man is just what you need. You are prone to impulsiveness and a lack of self-control, and he's a very controlled and controlling person. I think it's a very good match, actually."

"But my friends and family won't agree."

"Who cares?" said my therapist. "You have to do what feels right to you. That's called growing up."

I wrote to tell this all to the cowboy. I called him my boyfriend on the phone, and he was fine with that. It was exciting, and strange, and it all made me feel so balanced in a way I'd never felt balanced before. Safe. Safe and balanced.

The cowboy was pleased by my new insights. He was also funny. He often met my eureka moments with something jokey, like "And you're just figuring this out *now*? I thought you said you were smart." He'd known this stuff already. Life had taught it to him. He was an astute observer. And a traditionalist.

A cowboy.

I was happy to be sharing with him. I was energized and found all of this new input empowering. Feminism had thought the problem was acknowledging the innate inequalities of the sexes. We were all equal, it taught us. But that wasn't true. At all. We weren't equal. We should have equal rights, and equal value, but we ourselves were not equal, so far as equal meant the same. Men were better at some things. Women were better at others. That was fact. The solution to the subjugation of women wasn't to insist against science and evidence that we were all the same; it was to embrace all of our differences and to celebrate them.

"We must *all* have equal rights," I wrote to the cowboy, "but we *must* stop insisting that we are the same. We're not. My anger about this fact nearly ruined my life!"

We went back and forth like this a while. And then, one morning, the cowboy failed to write to me.

No good morning.

Nothing.

I sent a good-morning greeting to him.

He did not answer.

I wrote to ask if I'd done something to offend or upset him.

No reply.

I called him.

He did not answer the phone.

I started to get panicky. It wasn't like him. He'd been very consistent for almost three months, writing to me each morning, and throughout the day, at even intervals, as predictable as Swiss clockwork.

The day crept on, slowly, agonizingly, with no communication from him.

What had I done? I wondered. And then, when night came and the cowboy did not send a good-night message, and did not answer his phone, I began to worry.

I thought about how alone he was out there on those ten thousand acres. I thought about the windmills, and what might happen if a man fell from one of them and hurt himself. There was no cell phone service on the ranch, and the cowboy didn't have a satellite phone. If he got hurt somehow, he'd have no way to get help. I thought about how he told me he'd rolled the ATV once, how it had thrown him into a cactus and knocked him out. How he'd regained consciousness and realized the ATV was on top of him. It wasn't safe out there.

I emailed and called. Nothing. No response. I went through everything we'd talked about in the days leading up to this silence. We hadn't fought. There hadn't been any disagreements. In fact, we'd been getting along better than ever.

It made no sense.

Worried, I decided to go to the ranch to see what was going on.

The next morning, I arranged for care for my son and I got in the Hyundai, and I started driving south and east. I was trembling with worry. I kept calling from my cell phone, leaving messages on the cowboy's home and cell phones. I told him I was sorry if I was being overly cautious and mother-hen-like, and that if he was fine I hoped he'd forgive me for overreacting, but I was coming down to make sure he hadn't been hurt.

I made it to the town near the ranch. I went into the post office and asked if anyone had heard anything about the ranch, or the cowboy, and whether or not he was okay. They looked at me like I was crazy. I drove on, hoping to make it to the neighbor's house where I parked when I went to visit. That's when I got the text from the cowboy at last, from his cell phone, as I was pulling into the neighbor's driveway. It said he was fine. It said the wind had kicked up something fierce at the ranch and that the phone and power lines were down. He said he was "up on the hill" where he could get a cell signal, and that he was busily working to resolve the problem. He said he was sorry for not being in touch and said he appreciated my concern. He said his cell battery was almost dead so if I didn't hear from him again that was why. I asked if he could come to the road to meet me, seeing as I was close to his place now and would like to see him. There was no answer.

I turned around and drove back to Albuquerque, relieved and still very much in love. I was so happy he hadn't been angry with me. Cowboys, being extremely independent and self-sufficient, seemed like the type that might find simple worry to be a declaration of lack of confidence in their abilities. I felt so foolish for having driven all the way down there. I just didn't understand life on a ranch, I realized. But I was learning.

There was so much I was learning.

And so much more to learn.

Unfortunately, not all of it would be good. And not all of it would be true.

And Mary Pickle had not disappeared.

At all.

THE ANSWERING MACHINE DOESN'T LIE

The following weekend, I went down to the ranch again, to see the cowboy, armed with all the new information I was gathering, as well as with all the new emotional regulation skills I was practicing. I listened to the Pema Chödrön CD in the car as I drove and felt enlightened and uplifted by it. Pema was amazing. She understood what life and love were all about. She was a Buddhist with a sense of humor. I loved her. Several times during the drive, I found my arms covered with goose bumps because the epiphany I'd just experienced was so large as to be exploding out of my pores in a bright white light.

I was in love. I was growing as a person. I was at peace with so many things I had never understood before. I was becoming a better person, all for having known this cowboy.

The drill went pretty much as before. I met him at the road and parked at the neighbor's, and together we went in the cowboy's pickup along the hour of rocky dirt road to the ranch. We kissed at the gates. We talked and talked and talked. He was gorgeous enough to take my breath away. He was filled with compliments for me. I loved him and told him so; he thanked me but did not return that particular sentiment. I was okay with that. He'd come around.

We got to the camp, and the houses and the barn. As he'd done before, the cowboy suggested I wait for him in the house while he went to "release the hounds" from their pens. I obliged him, going in to freshen up.

I waited for the cowboy in the living room, next to the end table at the elbow between the love seat and the sofa. The phone rang. I wondered if he heard it. I considered answering it for him but reasoned that I didn't know him well enough yet to take that sort of liberty. I looked at the caller ID because my son's father had the ranch number and had been instructed to call me here if there was anything that came up involving our child. It wasn't my son, or his father, however.

It was Mary Pickle.

Yes, that's right. Mary Pickle, the fake name that I am using instead of the real name of the woman who'd sent the cowboy that greeting card all those months before, with the pink envelope. I felt my blood run cold at the sight of the name but tried to remain open-minded. Perhaps Mary Pickle was just a friend, or a relative.

And then the cowboy's greeting came on. And after that, the beep. And then Mary Pickle's voice.

"Hi, it's me," she said in a voice like a slippery little purr. "I just got home from a run, and I'm about to get in the shower and was thinking how much I wish you were here to join me. Anyway, call me when you get in. Miss you."

Click.

I sat there, frozen with a feeling that I can only describe as terror. It was that same sick feeling in the gut, that same impulse to flee, that same breathless anguish. He'd told me he'd take care of the other women he'd been seeing. And he'd said that weeks ago. More than a month ago. He'd let me call him my boyfriend. He'd been in touch with me pretty much every day. Every day, several times a day. He'd been attentive and loving and wonderful. And yet . . .

The door opened, and in walked the cowboy, still wearing the happy attitude he'd had since he had picked me up at the road. He made a comment about the dogs, something about how energetic they were. I tried to calm my mind. I thought of all the emotional regulation training and counseling I was getting, and I tried to understand what a normal person without emotional dysregulation issues would do in a similar situation. *Keep calm*, I told myself. *Keep an open mind. Don't jump to conclusions. Don't lose your cool.*

The cowboy came to me, where I sat, and leaned down to give me a kiss. I kissed him back, but he noticed the difference, I guess. I was not open to him as I usually was. I was trying to control myself, but my discomfort showed in my body language and, when he backed up to get a better look at my eyes, in my face.

"What's wrong?" he asked.

"I'm not feeling that well," I said.

He did not have a clue as to why I might not have been feeling well and seemed concerned. "Do you want an aspirin or something?"

"No," I said.

This is when he noticed the red blinking light on the answering machine. "Huh," he said casually. "Musta gotten a message while we were out."

He went to the machine and pressed Play.

"Hi, it's me," began the message. I watched the cowboy's face very carefully. He revealed nothing. But as soon as he heard those first three words, he pressed Delete. I kept watching. He smiled at me like nothing was wrong and told me that it had been the woman who ran the post office calling.

"She's a real sweet lady, married to a guy who owns a ranch out here. She calls me every time I have a package in. That's one great thing about living in a rural community like this, the way everybody looks out for everybody else."

I stared at him as my pulse thundered in my ears. He was lying, boldly, to my face. And he didn't reveal so much as a twitch. He wasn't just a good liar. Oh, no. He was a world-class liar.

"You must be really good at poker," I said. I forced my breathing to stay slow. I concentrated on the memory of the candle flame as I watched it during my meditation exercises.

The cowboy stopped and looked at me with his smile sort of frozen on his face. "Poker?"

"Yeah," I said, feeling the defensiveness rising in my belly, the urge to eviscerate, to fight, to go back to that place I swore I'd never go to again, no matter what. I fought my impulse to slap his face, to throw things. I forced myself to calm down and handle this like a grown-up.

"What do you mean, dear?" he asked, affecting a cheerful face now and sifting casually through a stack of mail he'd found on the mantel.

"Well, that message you just deleted without listening to?"

"Uh-huh," he said distractedly, looking at the bills in his hands.

"It came in just now, while you were letting the dogs out. I was sitting right here. I heard the whole thing. I didn't want to, believe me. But I couldn't help it."

He gulped and looked up at me now.

"And unless the postmistress is cheating on her husband with you, and unless her name is Mary Pickle instead of the name you just gave me, and unless you are in the habit of taking showers with the married woman who runs the post office, and unless she inexplicably has an Albuquerque phone number, I'd say you just looked me in the eye and told me one of the clearest, calmest, and most convincing lies I've ever heard."

The cowboy's face fell. I braced for whatever might come next. I'd never confronted him with his own misdeeds before, because there'd never been any. Was he the kind of man who would handle it with grace? Or was he the kind who'd grow belligerent and blame me?

"Baby," he said, all salesman now. He put the mail back down on the mantel and walked toward me. I got up and moved away from him, going to sit in the armchair on the other side of the room.

"Alisa," he said. "Don't do this. Listen to me. It's not what you think."

"How do you know what I think?" I asked.

The cowboy stunned me now, by dropping to his knees in front of me. He put his hands on my thighs. I felt tears in my eyes and looked away. I couldn't look at him. I didn't want to look at him.

"Hey," he said. "Alisa. Please. Look at me."

"No," I whined.

"It's not what you think."

"Then why'd you lie about it? Why'd you delete it as soon as you heard her voice?"

"It's not what you think," he repeated.

"Right. A woman just called to tell you she was home from a run and getting in the shower and wished you were there to join her," I said. "How is that *not* what I think?"

The cowboy sighed heavily, knowing he was caught and not liking it very much.

"Okay," he conceded. "Fine. You're right."

I felt like throwing up.

"You told me you'd take care of it," I said, finally looking at him. I was proud of myself for not flipping out, even though every fiber of my being wanted to. I'd never been faced with anything this painful or difficult in a relationship before without completely losing it. Though my ex-husband had lied to me a lot and cheated on me, I had never felt a depth of love, attraction, dependency, or connection to him like I felt for the cowboy. It was much more devastating this time around.

"I know. I did. I told you that. And I have been. I've been taking care of it. I took care of all the other ones."

I laughed bitterly. "Is that supposed to reassure me? That there were enough of us to call 'all the other ones'? Wow. Thanks, Casanova."

"Baby, listen to me."

The cowboy tried to hold my hands, but I pulled them away and crossed my arms over my chest. I tucked my hands safely in my armpits.

"Damn it, baby. Listen to me."

"I'm listening," I said.

"I told you, you're the only one I want. But after that one in Las Cruces chewed my ass out for not breaking up with her in person, I thought it would be best for me to do it in person with all of them. Mary's the only one left. I haven't had a chance to see her yet. I was planning to do it next week."

I considered this. I so wanted it to be true. But I had been lied to so many times by men in the past. It just felt too familiar. It was like I was wearing a big sign on my back, but instead of KICK ME, it said LIE TO ME.

"Really?" I asked.

He looked at me imploringly and seemed so sincere. "Yes. Really. Baby, you're the one I want. You're my girlfriend. Not Mary Pickle. She's a nice gal. There's nothing wrong with her. But she's not you. You're the one I want."

"So call her right now and tell her that, in front of me," I suggested. "That would help."

"Baby," he said.

"What?"

"I can't do that. You don't understand what she's been through. It'd devastate her."

I felt sick. "Well, as long as she's happy, I guess it's all good," I said sarcastically.

"I have to do this my way," he said. "You can either trust me or you can't. It's up to you."

"I hate this," I said, the tears pouring down my cheeks now.

"I know, baby. I'm so sorry. I should have taken care of it by now, but I didn't. I'm sorry. I've just been sort of avoiding her. I don't like to hurt people."

I laughed bitterly again. "Um, hello? Are you not seeing me here, crying? You've hurt *me*."

"Yes. I know. I'm sorry."

"Do you not understand that by avoiding hurting her you're actually hurting me? And us?"

"I know. It was stupid. I know. I'm so sorry."

"I don't know what to do. I only just got here. I don't feel like getting on that road again."

I felt so sad, so scared, but his face was so open and so sincere. He looked as I'd never seen him before, as though he were genuinely afraid to lose me. Then again, we knew he was a good actor. As good as they came.

"Please don't do this," he said. "It's not what you think. I want you. And only you. I swear that to you."

"I wish I could believe you," I said. "But it's kind of hard right now."

"I know. It's my fault. I admit it. I'll fix it. I'll make this right. I'm going to prove it to you, how much I want you."

I looked at him, and he was absolutely beautiful. I loved this man. It hurt, but I loved him. I sat there looking at him and weighing the options. It would hurt to stay with him now. That was guaranteed. It would be very hard, and it would hurt like hell, and I'd have this ongoing struggle with trust where he was concerned. But it would hurt to lose him, too.

Which would hurt less? I wondered.

Losing him. Hands down, that would hurt more.

He stroked my cheek gently with his fingertips. "Hey," he said softly, coming close as though wanting to kiss me. He seemed so sorry. So apologetic. So convincing. "Listen to me. I want *you*. Only *you*. This is it for me. I found you. You're everything I've been looking for, all my life. You're the one I've been waiting for."

I looked at him and tried to understand. Was he full of it? Did he mean it? He seemed to mean it. People, I told myself, made mistakes. And what he was saying was entirely plausible. He hadn't denied being involved with Mary Pickle. In fact, he had told me about her, or at least about "the others," before. He'd mentioned the thing about getting in trouble for breaking up with one of them over the phone. It made perfect sense.

But it still hurt.

And he'd still lied to me. Big time.

"I don't know what to do," I said.

The cowboy stood up, knowing, as I did, that he'd broken through my meager, flimsy attempt at a wall. *Gravity*, I thought. It was all about gravity. I could not resist staying in this man's orbit, even if I wanted to. He was too big, too beautiful, too sexy, too intelligent, too . . . everything I wanted. He knew this. It gave him such an advantage over me. He was completely in control of me, and he knew it.

He reached into my armpit and took my hand out of it and squeezed it.

"Whatever you need me to do to prove to you how much I want you, I'll do it," he said, gently pulling me up out of the chair, to standing.

I looked at the floor. He raised my face, with his fingers gently under my chin. And then he kissed me. I hated him. I loved him. I was hurt. I wanted him. I was the one who was here, right? Not Mary Pickle. Me. I was here with him, and he was touching me, not her. Me. I was winning, wasn't I?

He pulled me into him and held me.

"I want *you*," he whispered. "Only *you*."

As he'd done before, he led me to his room. I was weak, confused, excited, in love. And extremely turned on. This was terrible to me. How could I be faced with a cheater and a liar, and yet still want him so badly? Was he even cheating? It certainly seemed like it. But his story was plausible. Maybe he wasn't. But the question remained: Why did any of this turn me on?

Later, after I'd gone back to the city, I'd Google this and come across research that showed that women were biologically programmed to find cheating mates more attractive. There were theories about why that was. Something about competition with other females. Also, men who were more attractive than their mates were more likely to cheat, according to studies. The less attractive partner was the least likely to cheat, apparently. And confident or high-status men cheated more, probably because the opportunity to do so presented itself more often. Basically, women were screwed. We were programmed to want men who'd maybe be wanted by lots of other women.

I didn't know this then, however. I only knew that this new and psychologically painful information had had a profound and annoying physical reaction in my body. I was hurt, sad, and turned on. All at once. It was strange. It wasn't fair. It just . . . was.

We stood at the side of the bed, and he began to unbuckle his belt.

"How do I know you're telling me the truth?" I asked, weakly.

His eyes met mine, and he said, "I want you. Only you."

"But you just lied to me and there was no sign at all that you were lying."

He took my hand and kissed it.

"The way I see it, you have two choices, Alisa."

His eyes bored straight through me, unflinching, powerful, seductive, thrilling.

"You can either believe me and stay with me and have a great weekend, or not, and we leave, and you go home and I never see you again. It's up to you."

He released my hand and looked at me, hard.

"Which will it be?" he asked.

Against my better judgment, I threw my arms around his neck. Seconds later, he threw me down on the bed.

"Good choice," he said with a grin.

The tears sprang from my eyes, as I understood a hard and painful truth that would have been unthinkable to the woman I'd been before meeting this man. I thought back to all of the traditional Cuban women I'd known, older women, who said things to women in my generation that had never made sense to me when I was younger. Things like "you have to fight for your man," or "if he strays, it's your fault," or "it's in man's nature to be with more than one woman," and I wondered if this was all about biology, too.

I calmed my mind and listened to my heart. Did I still love him? Yes. More than before. Something competitive and ancient was stirring inside me. I was in this to win this. And how was I going to win this? I wondered. Not by forcing this man to do what I wanted. Never through force. He would meet force with force, and he would obliterate me. I'd win this game through softness. Through relenting. Through yielding. By giving, and giving, and giving until it hurt.

I was physically turned on by this situation because there was something intoxicating about a man whom other women wanted, and that man wanting *you*. This was why women always seemed to like the challenge of seducing men with wedding rings. We were competitive by nature, with one another.

Biology.

"I'm sorry," he whispered.

"I love you enough to share you if I have to," I whispered back, tenderly.

Now, I know that this last bit is going to make a lot of you sick. You will think me stupid. I know the reaction, because for the longest time it would have been mine, too. I understand. But I ask you to keep an open mind.

The old me was horrified by this unexpected visceral reaction from me, but the new me, the ancient me, the genetically female me, knew that it was true. I *would* share him, if I had to. For now. I'd share him if I had to, until I couldn't anymore.

"I won't like it, and I don't think I could do it forever, but I love you enough to want you to be happy, even if that means sharing you for now. I wouldn't like it, but I'd like it less if I lost you completely."

The cowboy stared at me in shock, and with a painful sort of respect crossing his face. He kissed me tenderly, with an agonizing remorse blazing in his eyes.

In the face of my anguished submission, he'd changed.

Something deep inside him *changed*.

I saw it.

I felt it.

Something he could not lie about, even if he'd wanted to.

I knew then that my submission to him on this, my acceptance of my own pain in exchange for his love, moved him, but also that it excited him deeply and made him want me even more. Oddly, it made him protective of me. Passionately so. He was committed to protecting me . . . from himself.

It wasn't fair.

But it was.

"Baby, you don't have to share me," he said, kissing my neck hungrily. "I'm all yours, and only yours. I promise."

I don't know why, but I believed him. If I'd fought him, or demanded that he be true, or screamed at him, he would not have wanted to protect me at all. He'd have wanted to be rid of me. But I'd submitted. I'd accepted. I'd chosen the pain of loving him over the pain of losing him, and he realized, with a shock, just how much strength that took for me. He understood then and there that he could trust me to love him, foibles and all.

"It will never happen again," he said, the tiniest hint of a tear glimmering in the corner of his eye.

And I knew. I just knew. I knew without a doubt that he meant it.

IMPULSE CONTROL FAIL

The weekend was good, or as good as possible under the circumstances, but hard. I pushed down my reactive panic, my well-practiced fear response, my own seemingly natural dread and anguish that I now understood were actually myths that my emotional system played out every time a situation seemed or felt familiar to past trauma. I did my mindfulness exercises. I wasn't being abandoned or rejected or ignored or neglected, and yet my body and mind were so used to snapping to those assumptions that I had to literally fight myself out of feeling terrible. I had to will myself sane. I worked harder than I'd ever worked in my life at being healthy. At getting through this episode. At honoring my feelings of love and devotion to this man, even if they didn't seem to make sense. Even if what I had to endure wasn't fair.

But I'd be lying if I said I was totally *fine* with the situation. I wasn't entirely fine. Not by a long shot. In fact, I had committed Mary Pickle's phone number to memory and had it in the back of my mind that I would call her on the drive back to Albuquerque, in order to see whether the story he had told me about her matched up to whatever her version of the cowboy was. If it did, great. If it didn't . . . well. I didn't know. I didn't know what I'd do. I probably should have thought about that. But this sort of spy work was what had helped me to finally escape a marriage that was bad for me, and it had brought me so much positive reinforcement that it was almost second nature now.

The cowboy left me at my car at the end of the weekend, still extremely tender with me, still working overtime to win my trust back. I got in the Hyundai and drove away. There was no cell service until I got to the town of Carrizozo, or at least none that was strong or reliable enough for me to sustain a conversation with Mary Pickle. I didn't really want to talk to her, but my pulse kept racing; adrenaline kept surging through my body. I was afraid. Very afraid to end up in the same situation I'd been in with my marriage, where I was in love with a liar, where my entire life was built around the flimsy foundation of a house of cards. In the throes of my fear, I caved and gave in to my impulses.

I pulled over to the side of the road just outside the small town and turned the car off. The sun was hot, beating down on the car, so I rolled the window down. The dried yellow grasses of the plains stretched on forever, and the sky was bright and cheerfully blue.

I took a couple of deep breaths. I'd survive this. I would. I would.

I got my BlackBerry out and Googled her name, Mary Pickle, along with the city of Albuquerque. Some listings came up. I found her. It could be no one else. She was a licensed social worker, a therapist specializing in autism. She worked with children, owned her own company, made a lot of money. This annoyed me because my own son had been *misdiagnosed* with the trendy "disorder" once before, and it had been heartbreaking and painful to go through such sloppy medical work. In my mind, I blamed Mary Pickle and all the others like her, the ones who grew rich off the autism epidemic that I suspected was created in part by drug companies who were growing rich off medicating our kids. It was unfair of me to put the weight of all this conjecture upon the delicate shoulders of Mary Pickle, but when you're jealous and frightened, fair doesn't come into play. In all fairness, she was probably a nice person, doing good and important work. But I hated her.

There was a photo, but only one. Who had only one photo of themselves on the Internet? In it she had a strangely insincere smile, no lips to speak of, pretty bright blue eyes and shiny blond hair cut in a shoulder-length bob, bouncy and clean. Her face wasn't very pretty, though, at least not to me, but I could see how some men might think she was attractive because she was perky looking and blond. Sometimes, for the unimaginative, that was enough. Her face was shaped a bit like mine, sort of heart shaped, and her nose was kind of like mine. She looked like a blond, blue-eyed version of me. I felt sick.

I knew, deep down inside, that I should not call her. I *knew* this. But I ignored that little voice of sanity inside me, and I dialed her number anyway. I'm not sure why, or what I was expecting. Control. It all boiled down to bunnies. No, wait. To control. To needing to control everything and everyone. I needed to find out what was actually going on in my life with the cowboy. I needed to wrestle control back. I'd given it all away, and now I was in a complete panic.

Ring. Ring.

My heart raced. I felt sick, sweaty, panicked. What would I say? How was I going to play this?

"Hello?" The voice was cheerful, with a slight southern accent. Mississippi, I thought. Or something like that. Her voice was pleasant and measured and medium, and not high-pitched like mine. I was already jealous.

"Um, hi," I said. "May I please speak to Mary Pickle?"

"Speaking."

Oh God. Think, Alisa, think. What now?

"Hi, Mary. Um. My name is Alisa. You don't know me, and I'm sorry to be calling like this, but I, um, I think you and I might be dating the same man."

There was a silence, and then Mary Pickle took a deep breath. "Really?"

"Yes." I gave her his name and description, and her skepticism vanished.

"Oh my God," she said, miserably. "Yes. I'm dating him. How did you get my number?"

I told Mary Pickle about the weekend, and her phone message, and how I'd been sitting politely at the ranch on the sofa waiting for the cowboy to come inside when it came through.

"I didn't go looking for you," I clarified to her. "You just sort of made yourself known to me, without knowing it. Hope you had a good shower. Good for you for jogging. Good for the heart."

"Oh my God," she said again.

I then told Mary Pickle what the cowboy had told me, about not having seen her since he and I started dating months ago, and about how he was planning to break up with her next week in person, and about how he'd been avoiding her.

"I just got off the phone with him," she told me. "He called and said we needed to talk."

This was good, I thought.

"I was planning to get in the car to come down there today," she said.

This was not good, I thought.

"Really? I'm just leaving the ranch now."

"Oh my God," said Mary Pickle. "Well, I was supposed to come down today, but he told me not to last week. Guess I know why now."

"Yeah. That could have been awkward. Don't think we could have all three fit in the shower."

"Oh my God," she muttered again, not finding nearly the humor in the situation that I saw there. Or not having the jackass smart-ass coping mechanism that I did to stressful soul-sucking sickening situations.

She asked me how long I'd been seeing him, and I told her the exact date that I'd met him, March 25, 2011.

"Oh my God," she said. She asked me to hang on and went to fetch her calendar. "He stayed at my house that night. He was with me here in Albuquerque that whole weekend."

"He was?" I said, surprised.

"Yes."

"We had lunch that Friday."

"He had lunch with you and then came right to my house?" she cried. "What an ass."

"He told me he was getting together with some guy friends to play golf in Albuquerque that weekend," I told her. "He said his guy friend had a house in Tanoan." The last word was the name of the upscale gated golfing development in Albuquerque.

She laughed bitterly. "No. He played golf with me. I'm the golfing buddy. I have a house in Tanoan."

"Oh my God," I said.

"Oh my God," she said.

"This sucks!" I cried.

"Yeah."

"Was that the last time you saw him?" I asked.

"No."

She then told me that he had spent another weekend with her at her house quite recently—the weekend that I got worried enough about his lack of response to get into my car and head down to the ranch to see if he was okay. I told her about this.

"He was here, with me," she said. "I noticed he turned his cell phone off. Now we know why."

"That asshole," I said.

"Yeah."

Mary Pickle told me that the weekend I had my first date with the cowboy, he'd had dinner with her closest friends at her house. She'd thought it was getting very serious because he'd agreed to meet them. They'd thought he was great and told her she had finally found someone worthy of her. "I was very in love with him," she said. "And he said he was very in love with me, too. He ran baths for me, real romantic stuff, with candles burning. I felt so special."

I was devastated.

I told her that he had told me he was dating others, too, "not just the two of us morons."

"What?" she said. "He said we were exclusive."

"He did?" I asked.

"Yes. Did he tell you that you guys were exclusive, too?"

"Sort of," I said. "He admitted that there were other women around but said he'd take care of the problem soon, that all he wanted was me."

"He said all he wanted was me," she said.

"Oh my God," we said in unison.

It was then that she told me all the beautiful things he'd told her. That he wasn't looking for the next one, he was looking for the last one. Etcetera, yadda yadda yadda. It was all eerily familiar. Too damn familiar. As in *verbatim* familiar.

"Told me that, too," I said. I asked her if he sent her texts and emails every morning and every night.

"Yes," she said.

"At about seven in the morning?" I asked.

"Between seven and eight, maybe earlier some mornings, but yes. 'Good morning, love,' that kind of thing."

"I felt like I was so important to him." I sighed.

"Me, too."

"What an ass," I reiterated.

"A complete ass," she said.

I asked if he sent her texts asking her if she wanted to wrestle.

She said yes. "Wanna wrestle? Right?"

I read her some of the racier texts he'd sent me, and sure enough, he'd also sent them to her, verbatim. Descriptions of us (or insert random woman here, I supposed) in a business suit, bent over a conference table . . . etcetera. What was it, I wondered, about men wanting to take women in business suits in the women's offices? Something visceral and ancient, about wanting to make sure we could still be put in our proper places, perhaps.

"Oh my God," I said.

"Oh my God," said Mary Pickle.

I suggested Mary Pickle meet me in Carrizozo and we both confront the cowboy later that day. I had visions of us going all Thelma and Louise on his ass, throwing him off a cliff. Then I remembered that it was Thelma and Louise whose asses ended up over the cliff. Right.

She, ever the southern gentlewoman, declined, saying that it was her opinion that it would be best to never speak to the man again. She said she was happy that he had revealed his true nature to her this early on—she had been dating him about three months longer than I had by then—and that, in her words, this was a blessing and she would be dodging a bullet to never see him again.

"He knows that I'm not the type to ever talk to him again once you do something like this to me," she said.

"I wish I were as strong as you are," I told her. "Because the truth is, I love this man like I've never loved anyone before. I'd love to say I won't take it, but I can't. I can't believe that everything was fake. I saw his eyes. I know he meant what he said a lot of the time. There's something there."

"That's foolish," she said.

"Maybe. But I can't let go. Not yet."

"Wow," she said. "That's sad."

"Maybe so."

She agreed that he was astoundingly handsome and charming

and smart. No one who ever met the cowboy would walk away with a different opinion of him. It simply wasn't possible.

We kept talking, and there were a few things that told me he might have been somewhat truthful with me about her, if not entirely truthful. He'd never told her he loved her hands and feet, and other assorted body parts, which he often told me. He'd never told her quite a few of the things he told me. And he'd seen me many more times in the past three months than he'd seen her.

"That might just be because you're willing to make it easy for him by going to him," she told me. "I'm old-fashioned and think the man should have to come to me."

She was probably right.

"He's got it good with you," she said. "You don't sound like you'll make him accountable for much."

I began to cry. I thanked her for being honest. She thanked me for calling her.

"Don't call him," she said. "I think we should both just treat the bastard like he fell off the face of the earth. We both deserve better."

I wished her well and hung up.

I was perspiring now, beads of sweat dripping down my neck and back. It was hot, and bright, and I was extremely sad. Sadder than I'd been the last time I'd had to drive home from here thinking it was over with this man. I was, to put it simply, devastated. I knew I shouldn't call him, but I had zero control of my impulses now. I was spinning out of control again.

I dialed his number.

He answered cheerfully.

"Hi, puppy dog," he said, sounding very happy to hear from me. "How's the drive going?"

I told him that I'd just gotten off the phone with Mary Pickle, and then I shared with him all that had been discussed. He listened in silence. Caught.

Again.

"Well?" I asked, finally. "What do you have to say for yourself?"

"What do you want to do now?" he asked me.

"I want to know why you lied to me," I said. "I want to know the truth. I want to know what's really going on here."

He amended the story he'd told me before, about Mary Pickle. He admitted to having been at Mary Pickle's Tanoan home that weekend that I feared he'd fallen off a windmill and died.

"You came to Albuquerque and never called me? You just ignored me? You'd come up here to see her but never came up to see me after that first date? Wow. She must be pretty great to get that kind of effort from you."

"Baby, I'd agreed to come up a long time before I met you. She had plans with her friends. I planned to break it off with her that weekend. That's the whole reason I went up there, but she seemed so fragile. Her ex had cheated on her and really hurt her. I didn't want to hurt her again."

I was furious and told him so. He told me that he'd liked her initially but that in the end she was "too brassy" for his tastes and that he'd started looking to meet new people, then met me and really liked me.

"The truth of the matter is, dear," he said, "that if I'd liked her that much, I wouldn't have wanted to meet you in the first place. I was already looking for a way to get out of that deal by the time you and I had our first date. I just don't like hurting people."

He said she was getting pushy, demanding that he go on business trips with her, wanting to buy him a car, and suggesting he come and work for her.

"Yeah, that sounds just terrible," I said. "A house in Tanoan, a rich blond former cheerleader of a girlfriend with that southern drawl you say you love, taking you on trips around the country. Giving you money and cars. Compared to me, living with my Marxist dad and broke, that's all just totally repulsive."

"Mary came down to the ranch once," he said. "And she didn't like it. My lifestyle and hers weren't compatible. I tried to ask myself if I could adjust to living in the city, to her lifestyle, just, you know, going to the gym and playing golf. She told me over and over that I'd be perfect for managing her company. It isn't a bad life, but you know what? It's not me. And she was never going to adjust to my lifestyle."

"But you kept it going," I insisted. "And you lied to me about it."

"I admit I handled this badly. Very badly."

"Yes, you did. I wish I could believe you."

"What can I do to prove to you that I only want *you*?" he asked. Then he told me he'd called her as soon as I left to try to arrange a time as soon as possible to talk to her about breaking it off.

"She said you'd just talked to her," I conceded.

"See?" he asked. "That's true. When you left here I was so high on us, so excited about the potential of us, I was ready to just cut it off with her. If you hadn't called her, that's exactly what would have happened, and you would have had everything you wanted, without all this drama."

"Do *not* blame me for this," I warned him.

"I'm to blame," he said. "I accept full responsibility. But your impulse control issues are not doing us any favors right now, either. You did not need to call Mary."

"Yes, I did. She said she was about to get in the car to come down to your place this weekend," I said.

"That's a lie," he countered. "Well, okay, wait. We had plans for her to come down this weekend, a while back, but I asked her not to because I wanted you here instead."

"Yeah, I guess that would have been awkward, you having us both down at the same time. I mean, who would you have run the bath for and lit the candles for?"

"What? Bath? And candles? What are you talking about?"

"She said you ran baths for her, and lit candles. She said you told her you loved her. That you told her she was the one you'd been waiting for."

"Bullshit," he shouted, growing angry. "I never did any of that. I don't love her. I never told her that. She's lying."

"Why would she do that?"

"To mess with you. To try to win. Because she's hurt. Have you ever done anything stupid that you regret when your feelings were hurt?" He didn't say what he meant, but I surmised he was referring to me shoving him into the wall.

"Whatever," I said.

I didn't know what to believe anymore. I just broke down, crying.

"Baby," he pleaded. "Please. I want *you*. If you hadn't called her, it would have all happened exactly the way you wanted it to. I'd called her today so that we could set the time to actually end it face-to-face. After how understanding and loving you were this weekend, I was ready to commit to you, completely. We had never had a conversation about committing, by the way."

"It was unspoken," I said.

"That sort of thing is *never* unspoken," he said. "Not in my book. We weren't quite there yet, but we were getting there." He paused while I sobbed into the phone; then he said, "You shouldn't have called her. This complicates things now."

"I had to! You hadn't told me everything. I needed to know what was really going on."

"Baby, I was taking care of it. You didn't trust me."

"Exactly! How could I?"

He asked again what he could do.

"I wear a size seven ring," I told him. "Beyond that, I don't know what to tell you."

"Baby."

"I need to focus on the road and drive home," I told him.

"Okay," he said. "But I promise you, I'll prove to you that this isn't who I am. I've never cheated on anyone in my life. I am a one-woman man and I always have been. This is very out of character for me. This was just a sloppy, stupid thing I did, and I am very sorry. I was just in dating mode for so long, and I wasn't in relationship mode, but then I met you and you were what I wanted. I just didn't want to hurt Mary. She's not a bad person. She just wasn't the one for me, but she'd never done anything to deserve to be hurt by me. I was trying to figure out a graceful way out of it. Honestly, I was kind of hoping she'd figure out that I wasn't very interested in her and just move on, on her own."

"That's very brave of you."

"I understand. I handled it badly. I am sorry."

"Okay," I said.

"I swear to you, you can ask anyone who's ever known me, any of my exes, I'm not a cheater. I'm not that kind of guy. I hate that you might even think that I am."

"Well, you kind of did cheat. So you kind of are that kind of guy."

"It wasn't my intention. I'm not a player."

I wanted so much to believe him. "Okay."

I said good-bye, and I hung up on him. And I started to drive. I drove in tears and tried to hold it together. I tried to tell myself that I was better off, that it was good to find out now.

By the time I got to the town of Socorro, an email came through on the BlackBerry, from the cowboy.

I pulled over at a gas station and read it. It was a copy of an email he had sent to Mary Pickle. In it, he broke up with her and apologized to her for having to do it in email, saying he had intended to do it in person later that week but that things had gotten urgent now that she and I had talked. He told her that he'd been meaning to break it off with her but that he had not wanted to hurt her after all she'd been through in her previous relationship. He told her she was a nice person, that he hadn't meant for any of this to happen. He told her that when he met me he knew that it was different, that I was one of a kind, that I was what he was waiting for. He said that he had fallen for me and that he was miserable now that he had ruined it with me.

He was very clear, direct, and told her everything he had told me about the situation. He said that he wished he could go back in time and make it better with me, fix it with me. He wished Mary Pickle well and said she was a great person but that their lifestyles just weren't compatible. He was never going to move to the city and she was never going to move to the country. It just didn't work, he told her. He wished her well and said that for the sake of my relationship with him that he could never see her or talk to her again.

I read it five or six times, tears rolling down my cheeks. I didn't know what to do. Then I decided precisely what I'd do. I couldn't stand to lose him, even after all of this. I decided to believe him. Completely. You couldn't move forward from something like this without making that decision to trust someone against all your fears. You either trusted and stayed, or you left.

I would stay.

Mary Pickle called me almost immediately.

"Alisa?" she asked.

"Yes."

She talked over me. "I just got an email from him."

"I know. He copied me on it."

"See? Exactly! You know he only wrote that for your benefit," she told me.

"You think?"

"Of course. He knows that of the two of us, I'm the only one strong enough to actually walk away. He's hedging his bets and going with you because you're obviously the type who will just sit there and take it. No offense, but you're the weaker of the two of us."

"You think?"

"Obviously."

"Maybe so," I said. "But maybe weakness in these situations is a kind of strength. Everyone makes mistakes. I've made mistakes. I think sometimes it takes a lot more strength to forgive someone than it does to walk away. Plus, it's not like we were married, and honestly we'd never really had a commitment talk. We've only been dating a couple of months."

Then Mary Pickle started to propose all kinds of things I'd never thought about. Why, she asked, did this man live in the middle of nowhere? Why was there nothing on Google about him? Why was he estranged from everyone in his family? Why did it seem like he was on the run from something? Maybe, she posited, he wasn't who he said he was. Maybe he was dangerous. Maybe he was a murderer.

I listened.

"Think about it," she said. "His whole life doesn't make any sense. I mean, what the hell does he do down there all day? You've been there! You've seen that place. There's nothing to do there. He's probably into some kind of crime."

I didn't want to listen to this, so I said good-bye and hung up.

I texted the cowboy that I'd gotten his email and that I appreciated the effort and hoped we would be able to get through this. I told him I loved him. He did not respond in kind, but he did write to say he was glad I was willing to give him another chance.

"I wear a size seven ring," I typed.

"Um . . . okay. I'll keep that in mind," he wrote back. "Might come in handy someday."

"You're going to have to work very hard to win me back," I wrote. It wasn't exactly true. In truth, I knew that he had me hooked and that it would take a lot more than this to send me away. He knew it, too.

"I'll do whatever it takes."

"You better."

"I want *you*, Miz Valdes. No one else."

"Prove it."

"Just do me a favor," he wrote.

"What?"

"Don't call Mary anymore. Don't text her. Just let it go. Please."

"Okay. I will."

"I want *you*. She's gone. She's history. Let's focus on us."

"Okay."

"Wanna wrestle?" he wrote back.

"Unfortunately for me," I replied, "yes."

Even if I got pinned, and pummeled, and lost everything in the fight. I was, like so many generations of women before me, going to fight for this intoxicating alpha man because I was finally starting to understand, in my forties, that life and love were messier and more complicated than you liked to think they were when you were in your twenties or thirties. Nobody was perfect. Nobody. People made mistakes. Men could be interested in more than one woman at a time, particularly early on in the dating process. There were lots of good and attractive women in the world, and it was silly to think the cowboy wasn't going to run across a few of them now and then. There was plenty of competition, especially when the prize was as amazing as he was.

I was determined, however, to win—not by being a doormat, but by being the most incredible, beautiful, loving, and confident version of me that I had ever been.

This thinking was new for me. In the past, I would have done what any self-respecting independent and demanding woman would have done, and I'd have walked away, convinced that the problem was all his fault, certain that the solution was to keep looking for another man, preferably one who didn't feel or act anything like, well . . . a man.

I thought about how that approach had worked out for me so far. It hadn't. It had left me angry, bitter, and alone.

I was going to give this time. And then give some more. And see what happened.

YOU WON'T LIKE IT

By the time I got home—or to my dad's house, which was serving as home at the time—I was relieved, happy, and a bit confused. I was filled with mixed emotions, but mostly I felt triumphant. He'd picked me.

I sat on the steps leading from the house to the backyard and watched my son play. He was beautiful to behold, my child. I felt so incredibly blessed by life. I had a great kid, a kind and loving father, and a boyfriend—yes, that's what he finally was, officially—who, while he was far from perfect, was good for me. I was learning a lot about myself. Learning to stretch the boundaries of what I thought myself capable of accepting and understanding. I felt, in truth, like I was finally becoming a grown-up.

Then my cell phone rang.

It was the egg sucker, Mary Pickle.

I answered, curiosity getting the better of me. My pulse raced and adrenaline poisoned my blood. Fight or flight. In retrospect, I should not have given in to that impulse. I should have let it go. But I didn't.

She wanted to ask me some more questions about my relationship with the cowboy. I obliged. Then she wanted to tell me about how stupid I was being for taking him back, because if he was truly a dangerous criminal, as she suspected, then I would be putting my son in grave danger.

"They've never met," I told her. "I'm pretty protective of my son. He will not meet any boyfriend of mine until I'm pretty sure it's a forever thing."

"I work with children," she said in a tone that sounded just a tiny bit boastful. "I am telling you, you need to be careful."

"With all due respect, I don't need your advice right now," I told her. I hung up, proud of myself for sticking to my guns about this. I called the cowboy to tell him how well I'd handled her call.

He surprised me by growing angry with me. He raised his voice. "You told me you weren't going to call her anymore," he said. "Now you're lying to me."

"What? No! I didn't call her. She called me!"

"You know what I meant with that. You shouldn't talk to her anymore. At all."

"Why not?"

"Because. It doesn't help anything. It's over. We need to move on."

"I didn't want to be rude," I said.

"I can't do this," he said.

My blood ran cold.

"Can't do what?" I asked.

"This. Us."

"What? Why? Why not?"

"Your impulse control issues are out of control," he said. "Red flag."

He then told me that even though he knew he'd done wrong with me and Mary, he had been thinking about how I'd handled the situation and was increasingly disappointed the more he thought about it.

"You have serious anger and impulse control issues," he said. "And frankly, even though I was willing to give it another try, after hearing that you've been talking to Mary even after you told me you weren't going to do that anymore, I'm starting to think you'll never be able to get a handle on it."

I sat there with my jaw dropped. Night was falling, and my son was on the tree swing. I remember the moment so clearly. The suddenness with which the earth was pulled out from beneath my feet. I'd thought we were fine. I'd thought we were over it, that we were moving on, that he was finally mine and only mine, and here he was, breaking up with me. I had worked so hard not to dissolve into despair during this whole ordeal, to be strong and endure, to be patient and loving and accepting. And now . . . he was ending it with me?

"We're over?" I asked.

"Yeah." He sighed. "I think we are. I'd say we've gone about as far as we can go."

I began to cry and took the call inside so that my son wouldn't hear or see me. I asked the cowboy how he could have been so apologetic and full of promises earlier that day but now wanted to end it. He reiterated his concerns about my snooping nature and the way I'd played detective and infiltrated his privacy.

"But I love you," I told him.

"I understand. This has nothing to do with love. It has to do with trust. And every bit as much as you might not be able to trust me now, I don't think I can trust you not to give in to every crazy-ass impulse that comes across your mind. It's not good. It's going nowhere."

"Please don't," I cried.

He said it was over. He wished me well. He said good-bye. And then he hung up.

I was shocked. I'd given so much! I'd been so forgiving, forgiving beyond the point that I had ever been forgiving before. And yet he'd still found a reason to be rid of me! It made no sense!

I called my therapist, Meg.

To my astonishment, she agreed with the cowboy.

She said I had been out of line to call Mary Pickle. I should not be taking her calls either, unless, she said, I intended to break up with the cowboy. If I wanted to move forward and carry on a relationship with him, I had to trust him. And if I didn't quite trust him yet, I'd have to live with him as though I trusted him, faking it until such time as he actually gained my trust again. But this sneaky talking about him behind his back with the other woman was going to get me nowhere, she said.

I went through the motions of evening, making dinner and help-ing my son with his homework. I tried to seem cheerful, all the while feeling like everything inside me was breaking apart like a supernova. My son and I worked on a jigsaw puzzle. We played cards. He took his bath, and then I tucked him in. I was waiting, in a holding pattern, for him to fall asleep so that I could dive back into my misery fully.

Around ten P.M. I settled myself in at my computer in my bed-room. It was a very large, very beautiful room, with a kiva fireplace in one corner and a wall of windows that looked out over the backyard. The computer was a very big iMac. I called up my email account and started to write to the cowboy. I told him that I was sorry, that he was right, that my therapist had agreed with him, that I thought I had serious impulse control issues and a personality disorder that I wasn't always in control of yet, that I was willing to work on it, that I wanted him back, that I would do anything, whatever I could. I also grew defensive and tried, in the midst of what basically amounted to shame-less begging, to try and crucify him again for what he'd done to me with Mary Pickle.

The cowboy did not write back.

I called him.

He did not answer his phone. It rang and rang and rang as though he'd disconnected it when he saw that it was me calling.

I emailed him again, three or four more times, begging, desper-ate. Not one of my finer moments. But it was what I had always done when feelings got too great for me to endure. I'd written them out. Written it all down. Tried to "fix" the problem instantly.

That was the first time it occurred to me that my emotional intensity and my career were two sides of the same coin. My passion and incredible focus made me a good writer; they also made me a crappy girlfriend.

I cried myself to sleep and awoke with a knot in my belly. Had he written back? It was the first thing I wanted to know. I took my

BlackBerry from the nightstand and checked it. There was nothing. It was seven in the morning, hours since the cowboy had risen to feed his horses and tend to the dogs and cats. He had already had his coffee and logged on to read the news. Surely he'd read my emails. And he had chosen to not respond.

He was done with me.

I gave in to the tears and cried into my pillow for exactly five minutes. After that, I told myself, I'd have to pull it together and get my kid off to school as though it were a normal day like any other. And that's exactly what I did. The old me, the me before I'd met the cowboy and gone to therapy, would have probably tried to engage my poor son, all of ten years old, in a conversation about why Mommy was sad. I'd not have been able to control my impulses or actions, and now I could. If nothing else, I realized, I was an improved person for having gone through this hell.

It was then, after dropping my son off, and as I drove away from the school and toward the food co-op in Nob Hill, that I realized just how crazy I'd been. I'd been so self-centered. So controlling. Toward everyone and everything. I realized that what I needed was to learn to let go of the need to make things happen the way I thought they should happen. I needed to learn how to trust. I'd never trusted anyone, not fully.

Least of all myself, to be deserving of people I could trust.

I went to the co-op with a strange new impulse to reach out to men I'd dated before and to my ex-husband. I knew enough about myself by now to recognize this as the desperate attempts of a woman who derived most of her sense of self from the approval and attention of the men in her life to find a quick substitute for the missing cowboy. I knew, logically, rationally, that I was simply regressing to that state, way back when, when I'd been invalidated so much that I needed someone, anyone, to give me an identity, to make me feel like I existed.

I fought the impulses.

I failed.

I texted my ex-husband. The one with the slippery relationship with the truth. I asked him if I could talk to him as a friend, about what had happened with the cowboy. He said I could. We spoke on the phone, and he was supportive. I told him all of the ways I thought I might have poisoned our marriage, and he listened and said he was glad I was experiencing some personal growth. Then he told me that he did not think it was actually over with the cowboy.

"It sounds like you two are probably good for each other," he told me. "I bet you anything he'll be back. Just be patient."

"Really?" I asked.

"Alisa," he said. "You just said yourself that you try to control everything. You did that when we were married, and I can tell you from experience from being on the other side of that, that it's a man's natural reaction to pull away when a woman starts trying to control him."

"Is that what happened with us?"

"Yes," he said.

"What would have happened if I just ignored you when we were having problems?" I asked him.

"I would have come back, groveling," he said. "But that would have taken you waiting longer than you're able to."

"So I should just wait now?"

"Yes. I think it takes guys longer to cool down than it takes women sometimes. You guys always just want to talk it out immediately. Guys need space."

"And he'll come back?" I asked, incredulously.

"Yes. It's not the end of the world. Stop acting like it is. That'll scare him off even more. Just relax, live your life, be happy, and you'll see. I guarantee it."

I was very appreciative of my ex-husband at that moment, and impressed with myself for being able to stand back enough from the pain of that failed marriage to finally admit that I had some role in how badly things had gone. I owed this to the cowboy, too. If I hadn't met him, I would have continued to blame everyone else and everything else in my life for all of my problems.

I told my ex as much.

"He sounds like a great guy," he said of the cowboy. "He's saying things I would have loved to say to you, but I was too scared. Probably every guy you've ever been with has wanted to tell you the stuff he's saying, but you're intimidating. You're controlling, and you can be mean. This guy's got the balls to say it. For your sake I hope things work out with him. Sounds like he might actually tame you."

I then asked my ex if he was bothered by the fact that the cowboy was politically conservative.

"Why would I care?" he asked.

"Because the two of us are raging liberals, and our son might end up spending time with him if it works out like you say it will."

"My parents are conservatives," he reminded me. "And they were good parents. Unlike your family, I'm not someone who thinks that being a conservative makes you the devil."

I thanked him, and he reassured me that it would all be okay. I hung up and sat there looking at the bright green tree I'd parked next to. It was such a beautiful day, one of those incredibly invigorating New Mexico spring days that feels like summer. No breeze. Warm sun. Bright blue sky. It felt good to be alive. There was a sadness in me, and a doubt that the cowboy would ever reach out again, but there was a peace that washed over me now, knowing that if nothing else, my ex and I would be able to move forward as respectful co-parents, and maybe even as friends. I'd never thought that would happen. Not after what we'd been through. But people made mistakes. I forgave my ex and began to understand how much my having been a controlling, ball-breaking bitch had played into the problems between us.

Then, almost as though by magic, the BlackBerry pinged to alert me to a new email coming through. I glanced at it, not expecting anything important. Probably junk mail.

The message was from the cowboy.

The cowboy I'd never expected to hear from again. He'd done just what my ex said he would. Or at least he'd responded. That was something.

I clicked the email open and read it with my heart pounding. I was extremely anxious, overwhelmed with emotion. What was he going to say? How was I going to handle it? I knew that no matter what I did, I needed to be more cautious and thoughtful than I'd ever been before. I was no longer going to be able to get away with impulsive, careless responses to things in my life.

The email began: "I have read your emails and thought about them, and here's what I have to say. Yes, I think there is a chance we might be able to work this out. But you're going to have to stretch the limits of what you're comfortable with, and you're going to have to do things my way from now on, no argument, no deviation. You're not going to like it, and fairness isn't going to be part of the equation."

I stopped reading then because my heart was about to explode in a thunder of sickness and fear. What could possibly come next? This was such a blatant challenge. I was going to have to do things his way? What did that even mean?

The cowboy went on to explain that he was finished "screwing around" and that if we were going to make a go of this thing it would first require that we have "a come-to-Jesus meeting," where he laid down the law of what he would expect and accept from me, and what he would not tolerate. At all.

If I wanted him, I could have him, but only if I was ready and willing, he said, to submit to him as the leader of this relationship. That was the only way it was going to work. He didn't say it exactly like that. More like "We'll do things my way, and there will be no questions asked, no attitude, no argument."

I read the message two or three times and felt nauseated and battle ready. I talked myself down from the impulse to fire back a message to the effect of "go fuck yourself, you disturbed caveman," which was the first instinct I had. I was angry. I wanted to fight. I even typed up a nasty, angry response, on the tiny keys of my Black-Berry, but I deleted it, and then I turned the phone off and stuffed it into the glove box. I forced myself to drive home with the grocer-ies and made myself promise to wait at least a day before responding to the email from him. *Let the feelings fade*, I told myself. *Think hard about it.*

I called an old friend then, a guy I'd gone to Columbia with, the one who trained wolves and knew how to shoot a gun, a man I deeply wished I was attracted to but wasn't, a man who, if I could have felt that sort of heat for him, might have been a really good partner for me. As it stood, however, he was a dear friend instead. I read the cowboy's email to him and asked him if my initial reaction of anger and outrage was warranted. He listened thoughtfully, asked about the situation leading up to this, and then surprised me.

"I think he's right on target," he said.

"What?"

"I think he's just exhibiting leadership at a time when you're threatening to spin out of control and bring the whole thing crash-ing to the ground. Don't know if you've noticed, Alisa, but you have a tendency to do that shit. A lot."

"Really?"

"Yep. I like this guy."

I was stunned.

So then I read the cowboy's email to my father and asked his opin-ion. My father listened, his scowl growing deeper as time wore on.

"What do you think?" I asked him. "This man has been so good for me, in so many ways. What do you make of this demand to do things his way or no way at all?"

My father took a deep breath and exhaled slowly before saying, "I think that message is fucking brutal. That's not how you speak to someone you love. I'd never even speak that way to my worst enemy."

"Really?" I asked, confounded by this. I trusted my father's opinion, a lot, but wasn't sure I agreed with it now.

"Alisa, this man is a recluse. He needs to control everyone and everything. You are a strong and independent woman. I am surprised you haven't bitten his head off for that by now."

I explained to my father that part of me liked the note.

"You have a masochistic streak, Alisa. A self-destructive streak. My suggestion to you is that you let this one go. It's not going to work."

I retreated to my room and thought, and thought, and thought. I meditated and watched candle flames flicker. I went for a jog around the north university golf course with my dog. Exercising in the outdoors has always helped to clear my mind.

And then I went to pick up my son. We had a normal afternoon. And evening.

By bedtime, I got another email from the cowboy, asking if I'd received his first email. He'd never done anything like that before because I'd always responded immediately when he contacted me. I'd meant to wait until morning to respond to his email, but I went ahead and answered him that night.

"I got it," I wrote. "I appreciate you responding to me. I have been thinking a lot about what you wrote. I am happy that you think we might be able to work this out, and I am interested in hearing what you have to say. Should we talk by phone?"

"No," he wrote back. "We will have our 'come-to-Jesus' meeting here at the ranch. You need to come down here so we can talk face-to-face."

I thought about what Mary Pickle had told me, about how I made it too easy for this man by always going to him. I also thought about her idea that he might be some kind of serial killer hiding out.

"I agree to having this face-to-face meeting with you," I wrote back. "But I think the fair thing would be for us to meet halfway, in a public place where neither one of us can get too angry or out of control. How about we meet in Socorro, for lunch on Saturday?"

His response was swift and direct, and before I tell you what it was, I want to warn you that it will seem disturbingly brutal to a lot of you, just as it did to me. He will seem unreasonable and controlling. That is exactly what I thought, too. But I want to assure you that there was a very good reason for him behaving this way, and I will get to that in a little while. Basically, I'm asking you to resist your impulse to slam this book shut and shout, "Alisa is an idiot and this guy is a jerk," because even though that might be how it seems right now, it will all make sense in a few pages. I promise.

Now, back to the show.

"No. That is not acceptable," he wrote. "I told you, if we do this, you are going to do what I tell you to do. You're not making the suggestions or deciding where we meet. You are not in control of any of this anymore. You either come down here this weekend, or we end this. Up to you."

I was floored. Angered. And tremendously, inexplicably sexually turned on.

"I'll be there Saturday," I wrote back.

"See you then," he responded.

"I love you," I wrote.

"Good night," he wrote back.

THE COME-TO-JESUS MEETING

I drove to the ranch the next weekend. Before I left, I made sure to scrape the STOP FOX NEWS NOW bumper sticker off my car, because it occurred to me that it might be insulting to the neighbors who allowed me to park my foreign sedan at their house every time I visited the cowboy. The neighbors were fans of Fox News. They were also really nice people, people I very much liked and wanted to

consider to be my friends. They had also recently lost their son in
Iraq. He was a soldier who had died for our country, for me. I realized that while I hadn't changed my opinion of most political issues,
I no longer had this compelling need to shove my opinion down
everyone's throats all the time. I respected the rights of the neighbors to have their own opinions without me disagreeing on the back
of my car in their driveway. It seemed to me that my side was always
the one slapping bumper stickers on their cars, and that for some
reason those cars were often Subarus or Priuses. I realized that it
was almost redundant to buy a Subaru and then cover it with progressive bumper stickers. I realized that a bumper sticker had never
changed anyone's mind about anything, other than perhaps changing the minds of the other drivers about whether or not they should
like you or be polite to you in traffic. It was all preaching to the
converted. It was all a combative, monumental waste of energy.

I was tired of fighting.

I was tired of always thinking my side was right.

I was tired of the divisions.

I was tired of politics.

I was tired of being my parents' good little leftie foot soldier
when I didn't even know, deep down, whether any of what was coming out of my own mouth made any kind of sense.

It felt so good to take that damn sticker off the car. It was liberating. Truth be told, I'd put it there to impress my father. I realized
with a sickening thud in my gut that I was in my forties and yet I was
still living my life to please and impress my *father*. He'd been *that*
powerful, *that* controlling, *that* . . . domineering.

How strange.

How very strange.

The whole time I drove, I tried to imagine what these new laws
would be that the cowboy wanted to lay down for me. My mind
raced. I wondered if a part of me wasn't just repeating old patterns,
whether I had simply given up obeying my father in order to now

obey the cowboy. It worried me, but I knew, intuitively, that this was different. Something felt instinctively correct about what I was doing, even as it felt logically all wrong. I had to honor my spirit, my instinct, and not give in to the rational voice that condemned me for my emotional truth at the moment.

I assumed that the cowboy's new rules would have to do with him not being ready to commit to me yet, with him needing to date others for a while. I was bracing for that. I'd be able to handle it, I told myself, because I loved him enough to wait. Just because I felt ready to love and commit to him did not mean he necessarily moved at the same speed I did, and that was okay. We'd figure it out.

Then again, I worried, maybe he was going to tell me that he was not the kind who would ever settle down. His history certainly seemed to indicate that.

I didn't know what these new rules would be, and I wasn't even sure I'd be able to live with them. I was, however, very curious to see where this thing was heading, and whether I'd be able to go there. I'd never taken such a traditional and submissive role in relation to a man, and if nothing more, I wanted to see how such things worked themselves out.

I'd downloaded some new songs onto my iPod, and I listened to two in particular, over and over, on that drive. Both were by the group the Veronicas. One was about how amazing a guy made the singer feel in bed. The other was about how the woman knew better than to keep coming back, but she couldn't stay away. It felt just right, and very intense.

The cowboy met me at the neighbor's house as usual. I wore a dark blue pencil skirt with a yellow formfitting oxford button-down shirt and brown pumps. I'd worked very hard to look good for him, following the philosophy espoused by the Millionaire Matchmaker and every dating book under the sun that men wanted women to look like women, in dresses and skirts. (Interestingly, he also said he preferred me with less makeup than I usually wore.) All my life I'd fought such ideas as backward and repressive, but now, I realized, I actually enjoyed dressing up and feeling feminine.

The cowboy wore his usual and über-masculine ensemble. Faded, formfitting Wrangler jeans, dirty brown cowboy boots with the jeans worn over them, a clean button-down shirt tucked in at the belted waist, and a light-colored cowboy hat with expensive sunglasses. We greeted each other in a friendly enough way, but without smiling or embracing. Just a couple of hello-how-are-yous. I was on guard. He was on guard. He put my suitcase in the back of the truck, opened the door to help me in, and took his place behind the wheel, mysterious behind his sunglasses. We set off on the hour-long drive to the ranch, neither of us saying much at first. My heart thundered in fear. What was he going to tell me? What were these laws I'd have to follow if I wanted to be with this man?

The first thing he brought up, to my surprise, was the bumper sticker.

"Darlin'," he said. "I've been thinking about asking you to do something for me."

"Yes?" I asked, terrified.

"You don't have to say yes. I just wanted to throw it out there."

"Okay."

"I'm gonna ask you to do something for me," he said. "And you don't have to do it if you don't want to. And I'll not only respect your viewpoint but I'll protect anybody's right to have their viewpoint, even if it's different from mine."

That's when he asked me to remove the anti–Fox News sticker from my car if I planned to continue to park at the neighbors' place.

I gaped. "I already did," I said. "Didn't you notice? I did it this morning."

He looked at me in surprise. "No, I hadn't noticed."

The trunk had been open when he'd been at my car, I realized.

"Well, I did."

He smiled. "Interesting. Well, I appreciate it. That was a good thing to do."

"Thanks."

"I'm not trying to stifle your point of view," he said. "It's just a cultural thing. Down here, you might not agree with people, but you don't go throwing it in their face all the time."

"Okay."

"Liberals seem to always want to let everyone know how much smarter they are than the rest of us," he said. "Even when you're not."

I laughed because it was true, what he said. My side *did* think it was smarter. How else could you explain the bumper sticker I'd recently seen that said SLOWER MINDS KEEP RIGHT? My side was arrogant beyond belief. We said his kind were stupid all the time. We even referred to his side as "low-information voters" on the Thom Hartmann progressive talk radio show, the idea being that if only his side knew more, they'd be just like us. It was obnoxious. I understood that now.

"I just tried to think about it in reverse," I said. "I wouldn't want someone parking in my driveway all the time with a big old Rush Limbaugh sticker on their car."

"Neither would I," he said. "Personally, I'm not a fan of the bumper sticker at all."

I told him I'd just been thinking about that and realized that no such device had probably ever changed anyone's mind.

"Exactly," he said. "It's just a badge of membership; it's all about 'Look at me! Look at me! Look at my opinion! I'm so great!' It's all narcissism. I don't need anybody looking at me, and I don't much want to join any groups, either. I'm with Groucho Marx. I wouldn't want to belong to any group that'd have me as a member."

We drove on, in silence. I marveled at the way we had seemed to be thinking the same thought at the same time, randomly, and this reminded me again of my teen prophecy and of the strange things that happened in life that could not be coincidences. Signs. They were signs. What did this sign mean? I thought maybe it was the universe's elegant way of trying to comfort each of us, to reassure us that for all our strife and problems, and for all our supposed differences, we were truly very much alike after all.

About halfway to the ranch, he began to lay it all out for me, the come-to-Jesus stuff, the new rules.

"Basically, baby, you have two choices," he said. I watched him as he drove. "You can stay, or you can go."

"I want to stay," I said.

He looked at me as a warning to stop interrupting him. I understood and backed down. It felt good to back down. I'd never much been in the habit of relinquishing power or control to anyone, always having been too afraid of what might happen if I did. I think that deep down, I feared I would just . . . disappear, unless I fought, and controlled.

I realized very clearly now that while part of this had been my socialization in a progressive feminist family and in a feminist pop culture, a big part of it was also because I had the reactions of a child who'd never had consistency in her family, a child who'd been let down or ignored so many times that she had come to rely only upon herself to get anything done.

By *forcing* me to back down, the cowboy—and I realized this with a sense of astonishment—was actually *forcing me to trust someone other than myself.* Seen in this light, the cowboy's desire for "control" was actually quite loving. This epiphany was so powerful that I felt a deep sense of rightness in my solar plexus; an exhale, a long and soothing yes.

"If you stay, you're going to have to resolve to trust me. That means you can't question my motives, you can't spy on me, you can't go behind my back trying to catch me in lies."

"But it worked. I did catch you in a lie." I pouted.

He gave me the warning look again, and I saw his face redden a little with anger. "Stop," he said, his voice raised in irritation.

"What?"

"Stop talking. You're not talking now. I'm talking now. You're listening."

"Yes, sir," I said sarcastically, still unable to quite let go of my need to assert my supposed independence.

"Stop," he warned. He slowed the truck as though ready to turn right around and take me back. "We're not screwing around anymore, Alisa. You either do this, or you don't. And if you do it, it will be my way."

I nodded and gulped. I'd never been involved with anyone this forceful, this strong, or this intelligent. It was scary, and oddly liberating.

"The other part of this, if you want to do this, there's not going to be any back talking or second-guessing. No sarcastic smart-ass remarks, no dismissive comments that don't help the discussion. None of that *Seinfeld* shit you and your ex-husband subsisted on. That ain't gonna fly out here. You're gonna leave all that snarky shit at the door. You're going to have to stop challenging what I tell you and just listen to me."

He looked at me in such a stern and paternalistic way that I backed down again. And, again, it felt good. I was done questioning why submitting to this man felt good. I was done feeling guilty about it. I was going to do what he told me to do, and see if my instincts about it leading me to peace and happiness were correct. If they weren't, I reasoned, I could always go back to being the ball-breaking bitch I'd always been, though we all knew that wasn't exactly working out for me.

"The other option is that you don't trust me, and we just end this."

"May I speak?" I asked.

He nodded. "Go ahead."

"I don't want this to end."

"Neither do I, baby," he said, switching instantly, in the face of my submission, from stern and paternalistic to loving and firm. "But I'm not putting up with this impulsive shit anymore. You have to trust me, or not. Up to you."

"Okay," I said.

"That doesn't mean we can't talk about your feelings, and it doesn't mean that what I did wasn't wrong."

I nodded.

"I know it's hard to trust someone after they lie to you, and I'll tell you what. If you can move forward and trust me now, by sheer force of will, I will really be impressed."

"Okay."

"But it's got to be more than just trust. It's got to be the way you treat me, too. Baby, if we're going to do this, you're going to have to get a handle on your emotions and your overreactions. You can't be bouncing around out of control anymore. You're incredibly self-destructive, Alisa. You've seen it over and over again in your life. You've been self-destructive in almost every part of your life. You feel like you've always got to be in everybody's face, fighting, proving everyone and everything wrong."

"I know." He was right. I'd sabotaged myself at every turn.

"Well, I'm not self-destructive, and I'm not going to tolerate sharing my life with anyone who is. So if you want to be with me, you're going to have to stop that shit *now*."

"I'll try," I said.

"No, you won't. Trying's not good enough. You liberals seem to always think that saying a thing is just as good as doing it. You think that trying is good enough. Well, it's not. You don't try in life. You either do it, or you don't. You know right from wrong, Alisa. You know what the right thing to do is. It's not that you're ignorant. It's that you're lazy and you let your impulses rule you instead of having some goddamned self-control. So there's no excuse. The only thing that keeps you from doing the right thing is that you're too lazy to do it. You won't be trying. You'll be changing. There's no E for effort in life. It's what you get done, and what you don't get done. Because if you fuck up one more time—one more time, Alisa. If you fly off the handle one more time, we're over."

"Okay."

"Most of all, I can't have you contacting Mary Pickle anymore. You have a problem with me, bring it up with me. Leave her out of it. It's done with her."

"Okay."

"No more of this crazy shit."

"Okay."

"A few other things," he said. "When we're in the truck, I will always come around and open the door for you. You are not on your own anymore, and you will not be opening your own doors."

"But it's unnatural to me," I protested.

He shot me a look that said *Enough*, and so I apologized and said that was fine.

"Will it be every time?" I asked.

"Every time."

"I will never open my own door?"

"Not if I'm around."

"Never?"

"Never."

"Okay," I said.

"You will *never* walk on the street side of the sidewalk if we're walking together in town," he continued, seeming greatly relieved to be getting all this off his chest. I wondered how long he'd been bottling up his frustration with my modern ways.

"Why not?"

"Because the man is supposed to take that side, and I'm the man. You are not the man, so you best get that attitude taken care of right now."

"Okay," I said, thrilled. I knew that if my friends and family could see me having this conversation and giving in to these demands, they'd be shocked and probably disappointed. While it might seem strange to a lot of women who were raised to think that a man opening doors for them was simply good manners, I had been raised in an extreme socialist household, where everything was always being explained away as having to do with an oppressor and the oppressed. I had taken all of this to extremes in my own acceptance of radical feminism's most man-hating doctrines, and I had convinced myself that when a man opened a door for me, what he was really saying was that I was weak and incapable. The cowboy was forcing me to accept that my radical worldview had been incorrect, and he knew exactly how to communicate it to me in a way that would make sense to me. He understood, without my having had to tell him, that my resistance to these polite gestures was much more than it seemed to be, that it was actually the outward manifestation of an interior combativeness that was ruining my life.

In truth, I *liked* what he was saying. I especially liked that none of what he'd said so far was all that scary, as I'd feared it might be. He wasn't saying "You're the woman, so you'll do everything I say." He wasn't saying "You're the woman, so you have to ask my permission." Nothing like that. He was saying, in essence, "You're the woman, so you're going to let me take care of you and look after you." He was also saying, "I care about you and even though I myself am not perfect, I'm not going to watch you self-destruct or destroy this relationship with your old outmoded patterns of bad behavior."

This was beautiful.

I realized, miserably, that in insisting that there were no differences between men and women or the roles they should hold in society, we had thrown the proverbial baby out with the bathwater. We did not need men telling women they couldn't vote or own property—of course we didn't. But they were bigger and stronger than we were, generally, and it was nice to have them open doors and walk on the street side of the sidewalk. Why were there still so many women who were threatened by these gestures? Was it that to those women these gestures symbolized control in other areas? Why were we still thinking like that? Couldn't there be a happy medium?

"You will always go first when we walk into a room," he said. "I will hold the doors for you in buildings, just like with the truck. I will follow right behind you. I like to do this because I want to make sure you're safe, at all times. It's what I do."

"Okay."

"Never walk behind me. I don't like that. I hate when a woman walks behind her man. It's very disrespectful to *her*. There are a lot of so-called traditional men out there who think the woman should follow the man. Bullshit."

"Got it."

"When we're sitting down to a meal, I'll pull the chair out for you. Even at home, even if no one else is around," he said.

"Why?"

"Because I want to, and because I say so," he said.

"Okay."

"And in restaurants, I will always want to sit facing the door and the room. I want that because of my years as a bouncer. I need to be able to see what's going on. You'll think maybe sometimes I'm not paying attention to you because I'm always alert and looking around. I'm paying attention to you. I'm also keeping an eye on everything in our surroundings. Do you know why I do that?"

"No. Why?"

"Because I have a very powerful protective instinct, Alisa. I am all about protecting you. At all times."

"Okay."

"That protective instinct is retroactive too, so I'm warning you to be very careful what you tell me about people and how they've treated you in the past."

"What do you mean?"

"I mean I know you like to talk about how bad things were with you and your ex, or whoever, but you need to understand that I'm not going to differentiate between the past and the present. Just because I wasn't around when someone treated you like shit doesn't mean that I can't hold them accountable for that now. I will always protect you. Always. That means I'm going to protect you in the past, in the present, and in the future. Just because something happened doesn't mean we have to talk about it."

I realized then that there were probably things I would never know about this man. He had, in fact, said as much before. He wasn't going to tell me about his past relationships. He wasn't going to give me too much detail about his painful childhood, which from what I could cobble together was often extremely difficult. He wasn't much interested in talking it out. He was more interested in moving forward, in fixing what was wrong and just getting on with it. This, too, was quite liberating, after having spent so much time with people who had bought into the touchy-feely idea that we all needed to share everything about our painful pasts in order to truly understand one another. We didn't. There was value in just not bringing some things up. It didn't mean you denied them; rather, it meant that you cared enough about the other person not to burden them with it. Joyce Meyer has long pointed out that the Bible says much the same thing, its wisdom instructing people to leave their past pain in the past, to learn from it but to refuse to carry it forward with them. The cowboy knew this, had come to this conclusion himself long ago, and he was doing everything in his power to help me rise from my own past pain, to move forward. "It's never too late to be what you might have been," he was fond of saying.

We got to the camp then, and the houses, and he parked the pickup. He came around to open my door for me. I waited and let him. He held his hand out for mine and helped me down. Once my feet touched the ground, he closed the door.

I stood there, feeling very small next to him—in a good way. Protected. Six-four in his boots, broad shoulders, strong arms, powerful legs, flat belly. I was five-six, maybe five-nine in my heels. He faced me, and looked at me, and sighed as though he'd been holding a lot of anxiety inside and was finally able to relinquish it.

He removed his sunglasses and I saw his pretty blue eyes for the first time that afternoon. The expression in them was not what I'd prepared myself for after the stern email. It was compassionate, kind, loving, remorseful, but also tough.

"We can *do* this," he told me, gently, putting his hands on my shoulders. "But you have to let me care about you. You have to quit fighting me."

"Okay," I said.

He embraced me then. I wrapped my arms around him. We stood like that for a long moment, entwined, feeling each other's heartbeats, in the spring sunshine.

"I thought you were going to tell me I had to share you with other women," I whispered.

He released me and looked me in the eye. His expression was deeply concerned and mildly offended.

"*Baby*," he said, as though to say *what is wrong with you?* "I told you. I'm a one-woman man. This thing with what's-her-face was a fluke. I swear to you."

"But all that stuff about having to do things your way now," I said. "I thought that was going to be all about how I had to consent to sharing you for a while, and honestly I was okay with that."

He lowered his face closer to mine and spoke quietly, at close range. "All I meant by that was that we were done playing your little mind games, and it was time to get serious here, and do this right. From today forward, we both play straight and fair. No more lying from me. No more mistrust from you. No more sneaking phone calls. No more tantrums. No more drama."

"It's like you know exactly what I need to hear," I said. "No one has ever cared enough to set me straight. How'd you get so smart about people?"

He grinned. "Everything I know about dealing with people I learned from working with horses and dogs," he told me. "You have to learn to speak the language that the person you're talking to will understand. You can't train every horse exactly the same way. I ran across a horse one day that every technique that I used, that I'd used on a hundred other horses, didn't work. He wasn't responding the way I'd expected; it was almost like he couldn't hear me. And it got to where he was resistant. So I got off, I tied him to the fence in the corral, and I went and I sat down in the dirt and I watched him and I thought, and I thought, and I thought. And it finally occurred to me that when you're trying to teach something, whether it's to an animal or to a human being, if they're not getting it, it's not their fault, it's your fault. It's the one who's teaching's fault, which goes back to you gotta learn to speak a language that makes sense to them. So I went back and I got back on him, and I just kind of eased around. I didn't ask him to do anything, I just slowed way down, and I started to see how he responded to everything around him, watched how his ears moved, felt his body tense at certain times, and I just started going back to cueing him, but I started thinking of different ways to cue for the same behavior until I finally kind of amalgamated a language that he understood. So to reemphasize, it's never the student's fault. It's always the teacher's fault."

"Wow."

"It's like my dog Beau. You can't beat on him like you can some other dogs. Beau's gonna go and get his feelings hurt. You yell at him, or whip him, you're doing the opposite of what you want. I tell people all the time, if beating on a dog or a horse made a good animal, I'd torture them sons of bitches. But that don't make a good animal. It doesn't work like that. You don't get a good animal by abusing them. I think it's the same with people."

"Interesting."

"I know you think I'm a hard-ass," he said.

"Well, I read your email to my dad and he said it was brutal. He said I should never speak to you again."

"Baby, you tell your dad that I intentionally designed that email to be brutal."

"You did? Why?"

"To test you. To see if you'd go off the deep end again. You have triggers. I noticed that about you. You get real worked up about injustice, when you think something ain't fair, and that's when you go spinning out of control. I'm not saying it's bad to get upset about injustice. It's good. It's one of the things I like most about you, that you're sensitive to justice, but it's the way you react, the spinning out of control, the self-destructive defensiveness, that's the problem. So I wrote that email to be mysterious on purpose. You have a vivid imagination. I knew you'd think the worst, because you tend to do that. You think the worst, you get upset, and then you freak out. I told myself that if you could handle that email without freaking out, then you were growing, then we stood a chance."

"You tested me?" I asked, offended.

He grinned. "I always say, baby, in training horses and dogs, you use as little force as necessary, but as much as you have to, to get the job done."

"Are you saying that having me for a girlfriend is like training a horse?"

"I have a lot of respect for horses and dogs," he said. "So even though that might sound offensive, yes. I don't think we as people are all that different."

"But training me?"

"You have some destructive behaviors that need to be quit."

"I see."

"Do you disagree?"

"No. But people aren't dogs."

"No," he said. "That's true. If people were dogs, I guarantee you that people would be a whole lot better than they are."

"I like that," I said.

"I like you," he said, kissing me. He came up for air and added, "Why the hell do you think I'm working this hard? If I didn't like you, we wouldn't be here."

"I'm glad you like me."

"And you might as well get it through that big brain of yours that when a man actually likes a woman, and *respects* her, he's never going to ask her to share him with anyone."

"Okay."

"I can't believe you even thought that."

"You said I think the worst."

"Yeah, jumping to the worst possible conclusions. You need to stop that."

"I'll try."

He shot me a warning look.

"I mean, I will," I amended.

"Atta girl." He smiled at me.

"So there's no big scary list of rules, like, 'Alisa has to obey all my commands and do all the dishes all the time and walk around barefoot in a sundress'?"

"The only time you have to do the dishes is if I made dinner," he said. "If you make dinner, I do the dishes."

"That doesn't sound like a traditional man to me," I said.

"Some traditions ought to be updated," he said. "But others should not. You have to think for yourself and make up your own mind."

"You're not sounding like a conservative."

"This from a woman who actually knows *how* many conservatives, exactly?"

"Um, one or two," I said. "Okay, one. You."

"Dork."

"Yes, but you *like* me, so what does that make you? A dork . . . *lover.*"

He grinned at me and shook his head.

"All I'm asking is that you leave the past in the past and move forward with me with confidence and hope. No more of this insecure stuff."

"Okay."

"Why would I want anyone else? I have everything I want in you."

"Really?"

He looked at me as though I were stupid to even ask such a question. "You're beautiful, you're smart, you're articulate, you're funny, you're kind, you're passionate, you're sensual, you're successful."

"So you don't, like, want me to stop working and be a real woman slaving away all day in the kitchen?" I asked.

He looked at me in shock. "Any man who thinks that's all a woman is good for is sorry as cat shit," he said.

"That's pretty sorry."

"A real man, a strong man, is never threatened by his woman's success. He supports her in it. He's her biggest fan."

"You sound like a liberal," I said.

"You know what? Let's stop using these stupid labels, okay? They're nothing but tools to keep people divided in this country so that the people who have all the power stay in power."

"You totally sound like a liberal now," I joked.

He gave me that warning look again, like I'd crossed the snarky line he'd told me to leave alone.

"Sorry," I said.

"You're pretty when you're contrite," he said with a grin that indicated his thoughts were moving toward something less cerebral and more . . . carnal.

"Thank you."

He touched my hair. "That's the most frustrating part of all this. If you could see what I see when I look at you, you'd know that no other woman stands a chance against you."

"Really?"

"Yes. I need for you to believe that. I need for you to understand that there's no reason to look anywhere else. I found what I want."

"Okay."

"Trust me. That's what I'm asking. If you can do this, what I'm asking from you, well, I'll tell you what. I'll be pretty impressed."

"Yeah?"

"Yep. I'm already impressed, but if you can stretch what you're used to, and break out of your patterns a little bit, boy. I'll be really impressed."

"I can do that," I said.

"I'd say you've already started," he said.

"You make me better," I said. "I'm such a better person for having known you. It's not always easy, but I'm learning so much about life, about myself, just from knowing you."

He smiled, and pulled me by the hand, into the house, down the hall, toward the bedroom. We stood there, then, next to the bed, face-to-face, and he looked at me with an expression of pure, unspoken love.

"You know what it is?" he asked.

"What what is?" I asked.

"Us. This. The reason you're learning and growing. And you're not the only one, by the way. You act like you're the only one sometimes, but you've been just as good for me. But this is what it is. You're a strong person, so it's always been easy for you to run over the top of the men in your life. I think you needed to find someone just as strong as you, maybe a little stronger, to push back when you went too far."

"Yes," I said, burrowing into him.

"I like that you're strong. I don't want a doormat."

"Good."

"Because the truth of the matter is, baby, I don't let anybody run over the top of me."

"Yes, I noticed."

"But I don't want to run over anybody else, either."

"You don't?"

"No. I'm not perfect. Everybody has feet of clay, baby. I'm not saying do things my way in everything, okay? And I'm not saying it's got to be my way forever. I don't want to run you. I'm just saying that right now, for us to move forward and heal after this thing with Mary, somebody's got to take the lead and stop this thing from going down in flames. You've got issues with emotional regulation. I'm not saying what you're feeling is wrong; it's not. But the way you handle it isn't right. When you're in a burning building, you don't all try to get out the door at the same time. You need someone taking the lead and handling it calmly. You can't get anything accomplished if you're handling it in a panic, and that's what you were doing, panicking, stirring everything up and making it worse. You need someone to wrestle control away from you when you're like that, but it has to be somebody who has your best interests at heart. Which I do."

He laughed and pulled me down onto the bed with him. "Um, Miz Valdes?" he asked, pinning me down in a most delicious and inescapable way. "I don't know if you've noticed this or not, but it seems like we're pretty, um, compatible, in a lot of ways."

As he pressed himself into me, I could feel, um . . . just how *compatible* we were.

"Most compatible I've ever had," I said, sliding my hand over his . . . compatibility.

"Same here," he said. "Wouldn't hurt to test it one more time, though. Just to be sure."

And so I submitted to his methodical and very careful testing for the rest of the afternoon.

And into the evening.

We both passed, with flying colors.

WHAT'S HAPPENING HERE

The next day, the cowboy presented me with a new pair of women's lace-up ropers, in a size eight and a half—my size. Ropers are a type of ranch footwear, completely unfamiliar to me until that point except that I had seen the cowboy wear a pair of his own. They were sort of like brown leather hiking boots, but without padding at the ankles. They were kind of like those old-fashioned lace-up boots girls used to wear back when Laura Ingalls Wilder was writing books about life on the prairie.

"What are these for?" I asked, sitting on the edge of the bed preparing to put my usual black Uggs on.

"I'd like you to come help me fix some water lines today," he said. "And Uggs ain't gonna cut it. Put 'em on, please."

"Can't I just wear sneakers?" I asked.

I'm not sure why, exactly, but it felt weird to put ranch gear on. I wasn't a ranch girl, at least not yet, and I didn't think I had any business pretending to be one. Plus, I was so inept in his world that I was embarrassed and afraid to make mistakes.

"Sure," he said. "But don't ask me for help if a rattler pops up and tags you on the ankle."

"A rattlesnake?" I asked.

"Well, yeah. That's usually what 'rattler' means, darlin'."

"You think we'll actually find some?"

"Other day, I was out pushing cows, and Badger [his horse] stumbled on a whole nest of them. I like to have had a heart attack right there."

"I'll wear the ropers," I said.

"Good girl," he said.

I put the boots on. I was also wearing jeans from Chico's and a top from Old Navy that I'd thought was sort of cowgirl because of its pearly buttons. The cowboy handed me a camouflage baseball cap and told me to put it on.

"Do I have to?" I asked.

"No, but don't complain when your ears and face are all burnt to hell at the end of the day."

"I have sunscreen."

"Good. That'll help for about an hour until you start sweating."

"I'll reapply."

I followed him across the yard and road, over to the toolshed, where the ATV was parked. The dogs followed, too. The cowboy was moving fast. I was falling behind.

"Hurry it up," he said. "There's no slow walking on a ranch. Too much to do. Let's go. Move it." He clicked his tongue the way I'd heard him do to move cattle.

I hurried to his side and stood there, waiting.

"Did you just click at me like I'm a cow?" I asked.

He grinned and did it again, patting me on the behind. I laughed because he was trying to annoy me and it wasn't working.

I hopped onto the four-wheeler, scooted to the back of the seat, and waited for him to position himself between my legs. Once he was on, I wrapped my arms around him. He fired up the engine and rolled the machine out onto the dirt road leading west from the house. Ordinarily, if he were doing this on his own, he might take a horse, but because I didn't know how to ride a horse, and because, he said, his horses were "too ranchy" and the terrain too rocky for me to learn there, we took the ATV.

The dogs ran alongside us, excited to be working. The roar of the machine sent vibrations all through me, and they weren't entirely unpleasant. The sun, the wind on my face—it was wonderful. I no longer felt all that strange on the back of this thing, with the rifle in the front and his pistol on his hip. It was almost starting to feel . . . natural. No longer foreign or alien, no longer scary, just . . .

life. His life. And I liked it. A girl, I thought as we sped along miles of dirt road far from anyone else, could get used to a place like this. A writer, I thought, could get an awful lot of words out in a place like this, with no distractions. Well, few distractions. This man, well. He was quite a pleasant distraction.

It then occurred to me that the most civilized man I'd ever had the pleasure to meet lived the farthest from civilization.

I did not think this was a coincidence.

We went up a very rocky and steep and long hill. The going was very rough, and I had to hold on tightly to the cowboy or fall off. I had to trust him to guide this machine well. I let go of my need to control everything, and I willed myself to trust him. I believed it would be fine and liberating. I had never been able to do this. The old me would have panicked and insisted that I walk up instead of riding without a helmet out here. But this man, I reminded myself, knew what he was doing, even if I did not.

We made it up the hill with no problems.

At the top of the hill were a large water storage tank and a trough for the cows to drink out of. Apparently, the trough was also useful for overheating dogs to jump into and lie down in. Beau, the cowboy's sensitive dog (who also happens to be his biggest dog), jumped in, lay down, and began to howl a song of pleasure. I cracked a smile and then laughed out loud. Dogs had no guile, just as my mother had often said. They were so open with their emotions, and their emotions were so good and innocent.

The leak was here, in the pipes leading to the storage tank. The cowboy parked the ATV, and we got off. He opened the saddlebags on the ATV and began to show me the various tools he kept in there. He showed me other things, clasps and plastic pipe.

"This here's a crescent wrench," he told me. "Got it?"

"Crescent wrench," I repeated.

"These over here are pipe wrenches. There are different sizes. Bigger, smaller."

"Pipe wrenches," I repeated, running my fingers over them.

"These things? These are hose clamps. This is a nut driver. We'll be needing that. And this here is a reducer. We use this when we're matching up pieces of pipe that are different sizes. We'll probably need that today, and this torch here. You gotta heat up the pipe—it's plastic, it's called 'fast line'—get it soft, then fit it. Finally, this is a hacksaw. Got it?"

"No," I said, miserably.

He laughed. "You'll figure it out."

Then, with him as the doctor and me as the nurse, we went to the puddly spot on the ground where the pipe had broken.

"First thing you gotta learn is how to open a valve box right," he told me. "Because it's cool in there, it's a favorite hiding place for snakes."

"Great," I said, wanting to run.

"Which is why the hinge should be toward you, like this. You open it away from you, like this."

He grabbed the rope handle of the low wooden box on the ground and yanked it up and away from us, keeping a safe distance.

"Now you check inside for snakes," he said.

We peered inside. Nothing.

"Usually there aren't any," he said. "But it only takes one time."

"Right."

He instructed me now to come closer. There were cow patties everywhere, all over the ground, mixing with the wet mud and puddling water. He walked right through it all. I figured I had to do the same. I had never, to my knowledge, willingly stepped in shit in my life . . . until then. Then I held my breath, cringed, and . . . just marched into it.

"Okay," he said. Then he began to instruct me to put my foot here to hold this bit of pipe in place, or to hand him this tool or that, to hold the wrench tight while he did something over there, things like that. I did the best I could and mostly got it right. I was feeling good, using my body, enjoying the sun, doing physical manual labor, a kind of work I'd never done before.

After a while, he warned me that things were about to get a little messy because he had to open the pipe up and had no way to staunch the flow of water from the windmill down the hill until he'd gotten the new joint in to replace the damaged, leaking one.

"You're probably going to get a little wet," he said.

"Wouldn't be the first time," I said, not meaning anything lascivious by it.

He grinned up at me in a hungry sort of way, the sun on his face. He looked me up and down approvingly, the hottest man who'd ever lived, and said in a very suggestive tone, "No. No, it wouldn't."

I loved it so much when he made these little sexual innuendos. It was an incredible turn-on. No man had ever been so at ease with his sexuality to do this with me before. It spoke of a confidence, and a lust, and a playfulness that, all in concert, were utterly magical. One I really loved, that made me laugh out loud, was when I was talking about the one reason I liked Los Angeles, saying, "they have a Pinkberry," to which he replied, without missing a beat and lifting one brow ever so slightly, "So do you."

"You ready?" he asked now.

I nodded, still blushing from his earlier comment.

"One," he counted, his hands on the broken joint he was going to remove, "two . . . three!"

The water spouted four or five feet into the air, spraying us both mightily. It was cold, and the shock of it made me scream, then laugh. I was a mess. Shouldn't have worn mascara, I realized.

The cowboy wrestled with the water, which was coming out with a lot of power. He was getting sprayed pretty hard, right in the face, but he just endured it. I thought he'd curse or get angry, but he didn't. He just . . . did what needed to be done. He did it well, and quickly, his hands as nimble and capable here as they had been in the bedroom. He had to think of a couple of quick ideas when he realized the parts didn't quite fit as well as he'd hoped. Being too far from a town to just run in for another part, he rigged the ones he had in a way that was, to me at least, genius.

He called for me to hand him some more parts and tools, and I watched in amazed interest as he fixed the pipe. I'd always thought cowboys were just guys who went around on horses, terrorizing cattle, but this man was a bit of a mechanical engineer, too.

I told him as much after he'd finished, and complimented him on how smart he was.

"I couldn't ever in a million years have figured out what you just figured out," I told him.

"Oh, baby," he said modestly. "It's easy."

"Not to me it isn't."

"It will be, the more you do it."

"I'm just—I'm impressed. I had no idea this was what cowboys did."

"We spend a lot of our time chasing water, fixing water lines, mending fences. It's not real glamorous. It's not like we're out riding into the sunset all the time."

I looked at him, soaking wet, a total mess. I was likewise soaked and a mess. We stood there ankle-deep in mud. I smiled at him.

"That was fun," I said.

He grinned and stepped over to me, removing his sunglasses, and embraced me, and kissed me all over my wet face. He was dripping wet, much wetter than I was.

"You do understand, don't you?" he asked. "What's happening here?"

"Um, we fixed a water line?" I asked.

He chuckled. "Yes, we did that. But that's not what I'm talking about."

He kissed me again, and when he stopped I saw a look in his eyes that was new. He looked . . . nervous. But only a little. Just the tiniest bit self-conscious, like he was holding something in that he really wanted to say.

"What?" I asked, my heart pounding in anticipation. I thought I knew what I saw in those eyes of his. But I wanted to hear it from him.

"You *do* see what's happening here, don't you?" he asked.

"I don't know. Tell me."

He smiled shyly, so out of character for him, and blushed just a little himself, before saying, "I'd say it's pretty obvious that we're falling in love, Miz Valdes."

I felt the adrenaline surge through my body. I'd told him many times that I loved him, because I did. But he had never returned that sentiment. He wasn't exactly returning it now, but it was the closest he'd come yet.

"Oh, *are* we?" I asked, touching his cheek with my fingers.

He grabbed my grubby fingers and kissed them.

"We are," he said.

"I'm glad," I replied, kissing him, thrilled.

"Never thought I'd say this about you," he whispered in my ear, kissing my neck. "But I think you might make a handy little ranch wife someday. What do you think of *that*?"

I was too stunned to think anything at all. So I smiled, a huge smile that went on forever and ever. I did not speak, or think, or do anything but feel. And boy, I *felt*. Powerfully. And what I felt were butterflies, millions and millions of them, rising up from the mud on top of that hill, circling and bubbling inside me and all around me, from my feet to the top of my head, and taking flight in the bright blue New Mexico sky.

THERE IS NO "MY DOG" IN COUPLE

The summer wore on, and the cowboy and I continued to get along very well. So well, in fact, that an afternoon came where we were both just lounging on his bed in the late afternoon sun, reading books, and I felt his eyes on me. I looked up and saw him watching me with what appeared to be just the slightest hint of tears in his eyes.

"Hi," he said softly, with an expression on his face that made me feel like the most beautiful woman on earth.

"Hello."

He reached for my hand, and I saw his face blush just a little. Then a little more.

"What's gotten into you?" I asked him.

He tilted his head and narrowed his eyes gently. "I was just thinking."

"About?"

He squeezed my hand. "I was wondering, you know, um, well. I guess I was just, sort of, kind of—" he paused to clear his throat—"I was wondering, *Alisa*, what you might think of maybe, possibly, if you wanted to, if someday you might consider, hmm." He stopped and started again. It was odd to see him so awkward. "What I'm trying to say is, Miz Valdes, I'm wondering how you might feel about going by a different name one of these days."

"Such as?" I asked as my pulse accelerated, realizing this could go one of two ways. Either he didn't like my first name and wanted me to change it, or . . .

"Well, how do you think you might feel about going by the name, Mrs. [the cowboy's last name here]."

I stared at him. He was red in the face, totally uncomfortable and nervous.

"Is that supposed to be a proposal?" I asked.

He shrugged.

I smiled. "That is the single least committal request for commitment I think I have ever heard in my life," I said.

He frowned.

"So I'm not going to answer in any way but theoretical," I said. "Because this is all nothing but theory unless, you know." I pointed to my ring finger.

"I know."

"But, yes. I think that would have a nice ring to it. Alisa [the cowboy's last name here]. I like it."

He smiled. And then he messed up my hair. "You are such a dork," he said.

"I'm not the one proposing proposals," I said. "That's you. Making *you* the dork."

And we made love.

That's pretty much how most of the summer went, without any major problems. Well, at least not until the day I came out of the ranch house to find him dragging my dog across the yard by her collar.

"What the hell are you doing?" I cried, running to my dog and the cowboy, furious. I'd known he was sometimes rough with his dogs, rougher than I would have ever been, but I also knew that he was probably justified in his training methods for his dogs because they were working dogs. As long as he never treated my dog like that, I'd reasoned, we'd be fine. Well, now it looked like she was getting the working-dog treatment from him, and I wasn't about to stand for it.

"Get back," the cowboy told me.

"What?"

"Stop," he said. "Get back."

I was furious. "No," I said. "I will *not* get back. Let go of her."

"Stop," he repeated, looking angrily at me.

"Dude, she's my dog. Let go."

He did not. I got angrier.

"Take me home," I said. I probably didn't mean it, but at the time it felt like the only way to get his attention.

He let go of my dog, in a controlled rage. And then he looked right at me and, clear as a bell, said, "Get your shit and go."

"Excuse me?" I asked.

He did not answer. Instead, he went in the house and got his keys, went to start the pickup, and waited for me to bring my suitcase and purse. He loaded my dog into the truck.

I got in the truck, and he began the long drive back to the neighbors' to take me to my car. I tried to understand what was happening, but he was done talking to me. I had learned enough by then to know that it wouldn't do any good to try to make him talk.

I didn't understand what was going on.

"She is my dog," I said. "I respect that you train your dogs the way you see best, but with my dog, it's different."

"You don't know shit about training a dog," he said. "If you did, she wouldn't be the way she is."

That was about all he said to me before he dropped me off at my car without a good-bye. As he'd done before, he just left me there and drove away. I drove back home, fighting back the tears. I didn't want to be impulsive and email him a million times as I had done in the past when these things had happened. Things had been going so well, until this.

I emailed him, asking for his side of the situation.

He waited a day or two and then gave it to me.

There was, he told me, no "my dog" anymore. If I was going to be coming down to the ranch every weekend (which I had been doing for a good six or seven months by then) and bringing my dog with me, then there was going to have to be an understanding.

"When you guys are here, I'm the alpha," he said.

He explained to me that while this might not sit well with me, it had to be clear to my dog, Topaz, because she had begun to join him and the other dogs when he went out on cattle—and I wasn't always with them. Turns out that Topaz had almost been struck by a large rattlesnake earlier that day when they were out. He'd called to her, but she had gone instead to, well, *play* with the cute little snake thing.

The cowboy had shot the snake's head off, narrowly missing my dog in his successful effort to save her life.

"I'm sorry," I told him. "I didn't realize."

"No, you didn't," he replied. "And I didn't have time to explain it to you right then and there, because dogs only understand what is going on at that moment and I didn't have time to stop and explain it. At that moment, you caught me taking her to the pen. She was the only dog who hadn't kenneled up when she was supposed to and it was the second time that day she hadn't minded me. I wasn't dragging her like you think I was. She was leading me. She knew what she was supposed to do, but I was making sure she did it this time.

"There wasn't time to stop and explain to you what I was doing," he said. "I needed to teach Topaz something right then, and if I stopped to engage in conversation with you, it wouldn't have happened. I told you to stop, and I needed you to stop. We could have talked about it after I was done. You could have argued with me, whatever you wanted. But you wanted to engage in a fight right there, and you challenged my authority over the dog, right then and there, and all that tells me that you still don't trust me."

I responded that she was my dog.

He responded by saying that if we were actually going to eventually make a family out of our respective households, dogs and children included, that there would have to be no more "mine" and no more "yours." We were going to have to function as a unit. In matters pertaining to dogs and children, he suggested, there was going to have to be a uniformity to what he and I did and said. Dogs and children needed the adult humans in the household to at least give off an appearance of being in agreement; otherwise, there would be instability and insecurity.

"That doesn't mean we can't disagree," he said. "But we disagree in *private*. If you see me doing something and you don't agree with it, tell me afterwards. Everything doesn't have to be immediate."

I thought about this. I hadn't brought my son to meet him yet but would do so soon. He was making sense, but part of me was afraid that he would be as hard with my son as he was with dogs, and I told him so.

"I wasn't hurting Topaz," he told me. "You have to either trust me to have your best interests at heart, and hers, and your son's, or you don't. But if you question my authority and my intentions, we're doomed."

I thought about this and realized my reading of the situation had in fact been incorrect and uninformed. I did not know what had happened, and I had been very confrontational and disrespectful.

"You're free to disagree with me all you want," he said on the phone later. "And I'm more than willing to hear your side, and, when it makes sense, to change the way I'm doing things. But you have to learn to speak to me in a language that I understand."

I remembered this from what he'd told me about how he had learned to speak to me in a way I understood.

"I always do much better if you come *to* me rather than coming *at* me."

"What do you mean?" I asked.

"I mean that instead of coming at me, to do battle with me, instead of accusing me, come to me, talk to me in a civil way, don't try to run me. I never react well to that."

"I don't think most people do," I said.

"Probably not."

After that day, I really and truly understood what he meant by trust. It wasn't only that I needed to trust him not to cheat on me or lie to me. It was that I needed to trust that he was good and kind in all ways and places. I had to stop assuming the worst of him and trying to control him. It was going to be a long road for me to get to that point.

"Can we try again?" I asked him.

He said that we could.

When I came to see him the following weekend, he told me that he was going to show me what he was talking about, symbolically. I didn't understand. That's when he took me to the bedroom and told me not to say a word. Then, he began to play my body like an instrument. Ordinarily, I might give instructions—a little more this way, or that, or "just like that" or "don't stop." This time, he told me, no words. No moving him. Just let him do everything himself. And he did it almost as though he were telepathic. It was truly astonishing. Whatever I wanted him to do, he did. Without me saying a word. At the moment I needed him to do it.

When I had finished, he stared me down.

"Do you get it now?" he asked.

I said nothing.

"You underestimated me. You need to understand that I am paying attention. That I understand what you need, almost better than you do. A real man gives a woman what she needs, without having to be told. You have to trust me that I'm going to do that, but not just here, not just with sex. You have to trust me that I'm going to be thinking of you and what you need at all times. We are a unit. We are a team. That's how I see this. I stopped doing things just for me the moment I began to fall in love with you. It stopped being about me. It's about us."

"That sounds codependent," I joked.

He frowned. "Screw that," he said. "That's the problem with couples today. Everyone goes around thinking they have to be independent, that you have to be independent, even when you're in a relationship. Well, I have news for you. It's okay to need someone. It's okay to depend upon someone."

"Yeah," I said. "I think you're right."

"You just have to make sure you're depending on the *right* someone."

Boy, was he right about that.

THE DAY I ALMOST GOT THE COWBOY KILLED

A day came, not too long after that, when I almost got the cowboy killed through my liberal "bunny hugger" ways, and by insisting that he listen to me when I told him what to do.

I visited the cowboy at the ranch. He took me out on the four-wheeler, to run the Catahoulas. At some point, we came upon a wild longhorn bull.

The bull belonged to the neighboring ranch, but because the older man who owned that place had sort of given up on taking care of his cattle or keeping water around for them, and because, as the cowboy says, "the only fence that will stop a determined longhorn is an eight-foot cinder-block wall," the bull had wandered over onto our side.

The animal weighed about eighteen hundred pounds, according to the cowboy, and had caused problems in the past—charging the dogs and the cowboy. Like all the longhorns on the neighbor's ranch, this one was "wild as a deer" for having never been handled or managed by people at all.

The cowboy wanted to "handle the situation" and push the bull back to his side, but because I was there with him and because I felt sorry for the bull ("his eyes are so pretty; he seems so scared of the dogs—I mean, all the poor guy wants is a drink of water!"), the cowboy let it go. I could tell he wasn't happy, but he was willing to accommodate me. I felt triumphant, like I was finally getting through to the cowboy, making him more "humane," as my city friends and I liked to say.

The next day, I stayed in the house writing while the cowboy went out on the four-wheeler with the dogs again. A couple of hours later he came back to the house, and he wasn't happy.

"That's the last time I let you tell me how to manage anything out here," he said as he went to get some gauze, bandages, and antiseptic.

"What's going on?" I asked as he went back to the front door. He told me to wash my hands. Then he told me he needed me to hold Effie, his female dog, while he cleaned her wound.

"What?" I asked, horrified. I followed him outside.

"That goddamned bull sliced her right up the middle," said the cowboy. I saw the beautiful girl dog, bleeding like crazy from her chest and belly. "He unzipped her."

I sat in a patio chair. The cowboy put Effie on my lap. She was trembling, licking her chops, wincing and flinching as he poured antiseptic on her wound.

As he worked on the dog, he told me what else had happened out there. The bull had thrown another of the dogs, Taz, up in the air like a rag doll. Then he'd hooked the four-wheeler, with the cowboy on it, and knocked it onto its side. The cowboy had taken cover behind it and tried to get the rifle to fire as the bull charged him. The rifle had jammed.

The cowboy could have been killed by the bull. The bull I'd felt so sorry for the day before, the same enormous animal I'd convinced the cowboy to leave alone.

Once Effie's wound was cleaned, the cowboy determined it might have been a deeper gash than we could handle here. He wrapped her up tightly in bandages. Then he loaded me and the dog into the ranch pickup, and off we went to town, two hours' drive, to the veterinarian. We left Effie there. She wouldn't be home for a week, and it would cost a boatload of money.

As we drove back to the ranch, the cowboy worked hard to remember why he liked me. I watched the land roll by outside, and I realized how arrogant I had been. I realized that no one in the city understands how things ought to be done on a ranch. I realized that what seemed to me to be brutality on the cowboy's part toward the bull was nothing but prevention of a worse brutality.

I apologized and promised that I would trust him from now on. I'd trust him to know his place (the country) and how to handle it, and I'd remember my place (the city) and when to get out of the way.

I realized, with a shock of sorrow for Effie, that real rural life, and real animals, weren't a Disney movie, and that city girls like me didn't have a damn clue. More than anything, though, I realized that I didn't know how to trust a man to live his own life. I had a need to control him and the way he did things, a need to make him just like me. It was not only wrong; it was dangerous.

I realized, that day, that submitting to this man would mean trusting him to make the best decisions for himself, and sometimes for me. It would mean, sometimes, holding my own feelings at bay, biting my tongue, and just getting out of the way. It wasn't just about longhorns and ranches. It was about realizing I didn't know everything. It was about understanding that the values I had long taken for granted as being "right" might actually be wrong in a different context. I'd accused this man, and people like him, of being rigid and cruel, but I had never, until that moment, realized that my touchy-feely "compassion" and demands for equality at any cost could have cruel and deadly results, too. That day, my life changed. I changed. And I haven't looked back.

MY SON MEETS THE COWBOY

Things calmed down a lot after that. I began to control my emotions more and to bite my tongue more often. I let things go, things that would have set me off before. I just learned to coast, to live, to relax, to let go of the need to always win.

Interestingly, I also began to lose weight. I wasn't trying to lose weight, necessarily. It was almost as though the moment I began to find balance and peace in one area of my life, it transferred over into all the other areas as well. Eight months after having met the cowboy, I was thirty pounds lighter and I'd dropped four dress sizes.

And after a while of things going well, I decided it might be time for the two most important people in my life to meet each other.

When I first began to talk to the cowboy about my son, I pretty much toed the liberal line that said something like, *Yeah, my kid's got problems. It was because he's "special"—either because he's "gifted" or because he (maybe) has an autism spectrum disorder or social difficulties.*

This sort of thinking dominated the liberal circles from which I drew my friends, was heartily accepted (and fretted over) by my family, and was prevalent in the public schools that my son had attended.

The cowboy, however, had other ideas. After meeting my son for the first time, when I took the boy down to the ranch in the early fall of 2011, and after watching us interact up close, the cowboy came to a simple conclusion. "There's nothing wrong with that boy," he told me. "His only problem is you, and I assume all the other so-called grown-ups in his life. You all need to stop making excuses for him and hold the bar higher."

I was deeply offended by this. My son was special, I assured him. If Alexander didn't pay attention in class, it was because he couldn't, I said. Not because he wouldn't. It was because as a gifted kid with social deficits, he simply had difficulties. If he couldn't make a bed properly, it was because his gross motor skills were delayed due to his asynchronous development—I'd read that in a book! I'd heard it from school counselors and teachers. It had to be true!

"What a bunch of bullshit," said the cowboy after my son had gone to sleep in the guest room. "One of the problems with America today is that we want to make excuses for everybody, and call everything a disorder. The only problem your kid has is a lack of structure and discipline, and the fact that all of you keep making excuses for his bad behavior."

Furthermore, he said, my son not only saw through all of my

excuse making for him (excuse making parroted and underscored by his Albuquerque public school); he'd come to internalize this expectation of failure and had simultaneously begun to look for the easy route in most things. "If you don't expect much of him, he'll never expect much of himself, and he'll probably come to resent you, too. You're setting him up for a life of failure."

The cowboy told me that as long as Alexander was at the ranch, there would be no excuse making for his coming up short. The cowboy was unwavering in his insistence that Alexander would not be treated as "special" there, that he would be expected to pick up after himself, and to be respectful, to tuck his shirt in, to set the table, to mind his manners and wash dishes, etcetera.

Oh. And to make his bed.

Morning came, and Alex did not make his bed. This was because he never made his bed at home, either. He struggled with making his bed, and I figured it was as the school had said, that my son had gross motor skill delays. The cowboy had other ideas.

Instead of wringing his hands and searching the yellow pages for a gross motor skill development specialist, the cowboy marched my son back into the guest room and said, "Please make the bed, Alexander. I'll wait here until you're done."

Then the cowboy just . . . stood there. All six-two of him. Six-four in his boots. My son was aghast. None of us had ever been so firm with him. Alex seemed to weigh his options. Normally, with me, for instance, he would have resisted and talked back. A close look at the cowboy's stern face dissuaded him from pursuing that route, however. Alexander turned toward the bed and did what he could, piling the sheets and blankets sloppily on top of the mattress and halfheartedly smoothing them down. The bed was made as badly as a bed ever has been.

I stood in the hall, watching through the doorway, afraid that the cowboy would cause permanent damage to my son's delicate self-esteem.

"Are you done?" asked the cowboy in a calm but firm voice. My son nodded and tried to scoot past him. The cowboy stood in his way to stop him, pointed to the bed, and said, "Come back here, son." Then the cowboy took all the covers off of the bed, piled them on the floor, looked my child dead in the eye, and said, without anger, "Do it again, but this time I want it to look the way it looked when you got here."

My son was mortified. "But I just made it!" he cried.

"You just made it *badly*. That's not making a bed, Alexander. That's faking it."

My man and my son exchanged a long look; then the cowboy narrowed his eyes a little and said, "I get the sense you go through life faking a lot of things, son. Looking for shortcuts because you can."

My son's eyes registered surprise, and the shock that someone had noticed his trick. I certainly never had. I realized in that moment how wrongheaded I'd been about my kid, and how right the cowboy was.

The cowboy grinned and put his hand on my son's shoulder. "Well, you can't do that here. Make it right. You and I both know you can. If I have to, I'll stand here all day until you get it right."

My son was as stunned as I was. I'd never been that hard on him, never demanded anything from him really, and I didn't know how he'd handle it. Alex looked to me to rescue him, but I came and stood at the cowboy's side and said that what he said, went. It was a traditional attitude, the one I was taking, but this was also because the cowboy had told me that the only way I would be allowed to bring my son to his place would be if we agreed to always put on a unified front with him. If I disagreed with the way the cowboy handled my son, he'd told me, I would have to wait to talk to him about it when the boy wasn't around, and vice versa. If he disagreed with me, he would wait until my son could not hear us discussing it, and then we would figure out how to move forward.

Alex miserably began the task of making the bed again, and my heart began to break. He had trouble with motor skills. The school had told me so. This was hard for him, I thought, and I hated to see him struggle.

And yet . . .

After four or five tries, Alexander finally got it right. The cowboy stood by each time, and every time Alexander failed, he took the covers off and insisted the boy do it again.

"Don't try," said the cowboy. "Around here, there's no trying. You succeed."

My son griped and whined and moaned about it. But he made that darn bed, and he made it well. The cowboy looked at the perfectly made bed and shifted his gaze to my eyes in an *I told you so* expression. I was stunned.

Later, as my son and I drove home from the ranch on our own, Alexander complained about how the cowboy wasn't "fun" like his dad. I grew worried that they wouldn't get along, but then I remembered that the role of a parent, or a father figure, isn't to be liked by the child, or to be the child's friend. It's to help that child grow into a responsible adult. My son's father and I had spent entirely too much of our energy trying to get our son to "like" us, instead of making him a responsible, confident, capable, and productive human being.

Seeing my son make a bed well that day opened my eyes. We probably were making excuses for him. Obviously, he was capable. He'd just never felt the need to live up to anything higher than the lousy expectations we had for him.

"That kid will rise as high as you set the bar for him," the cowboy told me on the phone after I'd returned home. "There's not a goddamned thing wrong with him, physically or otherwise. The problem with America today is that we want to say everything is a disorder. Well, I have news for ya. I bet you most of what parents and teachers think is a disorder is nothing but sloppy, selfish parenting. Most kids just need a boot in the ass."

I clarified that he meant this metaphorically, that he would never hit my son.

"Of course I'll never hit him," he told me. "Unless he gets to be bigger than you, and he hurts you, physically. Then you're damn right I'm gonna hurt him. And if I can't do it, I'll find someone who can."

"You can't do that," I said.

He laughed. "Darlin', I care about that kid. But I care about you first. And no one hurts you. Not even that kid. I'm not saying he will ever do it, but I'm saying, you have a boy there who might break six-three, six-four as a man. Pretty soon he'll be bigger than you and stronger than you, and if you don't get a handle on it now, you're going to be in trouble. Adolescence is right around the corner, baby. We need to get a handle on that boy now, before it's too late."

"He's not that bad, is he?" I asked.

"You don't see how much he knows," he said. "That kid plays you. He's a lot smarter than you realize."

"You think?"

"Yep. You need to change the way you deal with him, and quick. When a kid has serious issues, it's usually never the kid's fault. It's almost always bad parenting. I know you're doing the best you can. But I'm telling you, something about the liberal ethos just ends up making excuses for a kid who's perfectly capable of being a great kid. It's not good for him."

Soon thereafter, the cowboy came to visit us in the city. The lessons continued.

An after-dinner walk the three of us took around my neighborhood comes to mind, when my kid began to whine in high-pitched frustration because he couldn't get a knot out of the laces of his sneaker.

"Mom!" my son cried. "I can't!"

Per habit and custom, I scurried over to do it for my easily frustrated progeny. For ten years I'd been doing just about everything for my boy, because, you know, that's what good moms did. Or at least that's what I thought they should do. (This might be a good time to note, again, that my father, raised in Havana, was not required to lift a finger to do any sort of chore, ever, having had women and nannies for that sort of thing.)

Then I heard the cowboy clear his throat.

I looked up and found the cowboy, in his hat and boots, subtly shaking his head at me, as though to say, *Don't.* His eyes showed mild annoyance.

I stopped. Thought about why he might do that. I remembered what he'd said, several times already, about single moms tending to emasculate their sons through good intentions. His exact words, as I recall, were offensive to me at the time, as we discussed the fact that my son was being bullied at school. He'd told me, "His problem, dear, is that he's been raised mostly by a woman."

Suddenly, I understood what he'd meant. He had not meant to offend me. He'd been descriptive of a reality that I only saw now, through his eyes.

I realized with a drop of my heart how ridiculous it must look to this capable man, seeing me rush to help my son (who is five feet tall already, weighs ninety pounds, and has the same size foot I do) tie his shoe.

I moved away. My son looked at me, heartbroken and confused. "But, Mom!"

"I think you need to do this yourself," I told my son, my eyes darting to the cowboy. Why hadn't I thought of this? What was wrong with me?

"But I can't!" my boy whined.

The cowboy stepped toward him, calm and firm, and said the words my son most needed to hear and yet which I, always doing everything for him, had failed to impart: "Yes, you can."

And guess what? My son did it. It took five extra minutes of standing in the hot sun, and I had to endure tears and frustration as my kid doubted himself and complained. But, given no other alternative, my son figured it out.

Soon my boy was up on his feet again, racing down the street, leaving me and the cowboy to talk.

"I guess I look like a pretty lame mom to you," I said with an embarrassed grin.

The cowboy wrapped his arm around me and kissed me on the cheek.

"No, darlin'," he said with a light in his eyes. "You look like a great mom to me. It's hard to be both a mom and a dad to a kid. But you gotta remember, give a man a fish, he'll eat that fish. Teach a man to fish, he'll eat for the rest of his life. Sometimes single moms get so used to doing everything by themselves, they forget they don't have to." He gave me a significant look.

I felt the tears come. No man had ever bothered to think about what was going to be the best thing for my son in the long run, and no man had ever been strong enough to stand at my side and suggest I do things differently. No man had ever really, truly helped me raise my son to be a man.

Together, we watched my kid "running" down the street. He half-skipped, on his tippy-toes, with his hands perched out in front of him like a T. rex's.

The cowboy's face registered manly concern once again.

"What now?" I asked.

"Next order of business," he said with a sigh, "get him to start running . . . um . . . more 'efficiently.'"

So I began to demand more of my son. It was exhausting. Being a good parent is never the easy route. You must repeat yourself, you must be consistent, and you must never waver.

Fast-forward four months. At the cowboy's suggestion, I had moved my son and myself to the small town of Belén, south of Albuquerque, into a town house owned by my mother that was sitting empty. It was just a two-bedroom house, but the independence would be good for both of us, he reasoned. And it was.

What's more, the small town had a private Catholic school that the cowboy suggested I enroll my son in. A child like my son, he reasoned, needed structure and discipline, and a Catholic school might be just the ticket for that.

Fast-forward two months, and we got the first straight-A report card from Alexander we've ever gotten. What's more, his new teacher at the parochial school had zero complaints about his behavior. In fact, she took me aside and told me how special and wonderful my son was and how she would not be surprised to see him end up at Notre Dame or MIT someday. She said he was making friends and doing very well.

This had never happened, not in his ten years of life.

My son began to be . . . happier. There were many changes to my parenting style that the cowboy helped me to develop, too many to list in this book (but perhaps enough to fill another that I'd like to call *The Cowboy's Guide to Raising Boys*). In short, my son is a new child today, as I write this, because of this man in our lives.

I have no doubt that the bulk of the positive changes have been due in large part to the cowboy putting his boot down on both of us, metaphorically. He stopped me from being one of those parents who makes excuses for the "bad" behavior they themselves bring out in their children by being too concerned about their kids "liking" them. And he stopped my son from thinking all grown-ups were idiots who didn't think he could do anything for himself.

"Now, let's do something fun with Alexander," said the cowboy upon seeing the report card. "We need to reward him for his hard work. We should show him that there *is* fun in life, but you have to earn it."

Amen.

LASAGNA AND LIMITS

Around this same time I decided it would be a good idea to introduce the cowboy to my parents. I told my mother about him.

Let me take a second here to fill you in on what happened between my mother and me from the time I was sixteen and sent by social services away from her, to the moment that I told her about my cowboy. I will give you the abbreviated version, because the full version is another book unto itself and not one that I am at liberty to write.

My mom had a hard time after I left New Orleans. She got very sick with thyroid cancer and faced her mortality. That was a pivotal moment for her, and it was then that she found God again. She had been raised Catholic but had left the faith when she got to college and even more so when she was married to my atheist father. Finding God again was very good for my mother, and it was sincere. She grew as a person, and she got her act together. She worked for many years as a legal secretary. She reached out to me and apologized, and we forged a new friendship and relationship when I was in my twenties. She went back to school to get her master's degree in creative writing. When my son was born, she moved back to New Mexico to be near us. She has been a good grandmother and a good mom. She has supported me emotionally and financially in recent years, and at the moment I write this, she is the person who is paying my son's tuition at Catholic school. Her spiritual transformation was impressive and inspiring to me and my son. God touched her, and changed her, and she was able to put her past pain behind her and move forward in love. I am blessed now to count her among my best friends, even after all the difficulties we went through together. She is an intelligent, talented, good-hearted person who, like so many of us, has had periods in her life that were spent wrestling her demons. I do not hold any of it against her. We have both grown, forgiven, learned, moved forward. It's a beautiful thing, and one that I think exemplifies the incredible thing that is family. Friends, you can drop. Spouses, even, can be dropped. But family? Blood is forever. You have to figure out how to make it work, or at least how to love someone without understanding them or accepting them sometimes. So that's it. That's the reason you get for my mom suddenly being the kind of mom and grandma who is involved and caring, where the last you heard about her was the painful stuff from high school. People change. I guess that's the point. That, and I love my mom.

So there you go.

She was now living in a new house in Santa Fe, purchased with money she'd inherited when her mother, my wonderful grandma Kat, passed away. She said she was happy I'd found someone but did not seem all that happy to learn that he was a conservative. My mother was convinced, and told me as much, that conservatives were destroying the world.

I'd thought for some reason that my mother would like or at least approve of the cowboy. For one thing, he was physically stunning, and my mother, a beautiful woman herself, had always had an appreciation for good-looking men. She'd had a thing for the actor Tom Selleck at one time, and in his youth people had told the cowboy he resembled that guy. I don't see it, but he insists. Point is, he's the kind of guy my mom would probably think was handsome—and, yes, I just now realized how totally creepy that sounds. Let's forget I said it and just try to move on to something else.

Another reason I thought my mom might not be too offended by the fact that I'd fallen for a real-live cowboy was that she was the granddaughter of a literal ranch-owning cowboy. Her own father had grown up on the family ranch in Mountainair, New Mexico, and she'd spent weekends there when she was growing up. I thought, in a way, that she, more than my father, might approve.

So the cowboy and I drove up to Santa Fe, to my mother's pretty little three-bedroom adobe town house, one evening. My father met us there, driving up on his own from his house in Albuquerque. To their credit, both my parents wanted to be happy for me that I was in love and had found a man I couldn't stop raving about. If nothing else, perhaps it offered a glimmer of hope that I'd stop relying so much on them for emotional support. But they were both cautious because neither one trusted people of the cowboy's "type," each for their own complicated reasons and unspoken prejudices.

My mother had made lasagna and salad but to my surprise seemed a bit wilted and depressed that afternoon, in her long skirt and baggy, oversize sweater. This was a woman who had such pride in her beauty that she rarely left the house without makeup, but she hadn't put too much effort into her appearance that night. I was worried about her. She'd been very sad since her own mother died, and I wasn't sure she'd quite adjusted to the unwelcome idea that she, once a free-spirited child of the generation whose motto was "never trust anyone over thirty," was now nearly seventy and the matriarch of our family. So long accustomed to playing the role of wayward and rebellious daughter, my mother was now expected to be the sound and sensible mother and grandmother who was expected to prepare and serve meals to her daughter's fiftysomething boyfriend. It must have been disconcerting. For the record, my mother has exactly two bumper stickers on her old Ford Taurus. One reads WHERE HAVE ALL THE HIPPIES GONE? and the other reads I AM DANCING TO THE BEAT OF MY OWN ACCORDION. I'm fairly certain she was not ready to be flung into this role. She gamely took it on anyway. And I knew she did this because she loved me.

I wore a beige skirt with a brown floral top that is prettier than I just made it sound. I had on heels. My hair was shiny and bouncy and my makeup was perfect. I wore pearls. The cowboy wore dress Wranglers and a very smoothly starched baby blue button-down shirt. My dad wore a sports coat, which I found to be a nod of consideration and decorum. It was almost like a normal family. No, wait. It was. In spite of everything we had all been through, in spite of all the various ways each of us had gone off in our own impulsive and reckless directions on this journey through life, we were normal, and we were loved, and we loved one another, and we were here.

Everyone was polite because in such situations no one wants to come into the thing being rude. It was as awkward as you might imagine. I wanted to please everyone, to win everyone's approval. I wanted them all to get along. I was trying very hard to figure out how to integrate these two very different worlds that made up my life now. I probably tried just a bit too hard, smiled just a bit too strenuously. I wanted to be there, but I also couldn't wait for the night to end because it was just about killing me from stress.

Finally, we sat at the table. My mother and father, long divorced but civil to each other, sat on one side. The cowboy and I sat on the other. My father began to dominate the conversation, as he often does, and probably without realizing he was doing it. His narcissistic tendencies are well honed after years of being a professor with a captive audience, and he will often turn any conversation back to himself and to Cuba. He started to do this then, and as I had always done my entire life, I endured and even encouraged it. This was a way I had learned long ago to get his attention and his love, to worship him and his story as much as he did. I was an enabler.

The cowboy, however, wasn't having it. He listened for a bit to my father's monologue, and when the practiced story began to follow the time-honored "I'm a poor and tragic orphan boy from Cuba and no one ever loved me" path, the cowboy simply interrupted and began to talk about . . . himself. The cowboy. Almost as though to mirror what my father was doing.

Everyone else at the table froze. Every family, I realized, has its own unspoken rules of conduct, and the cowboy was breaking one of the cardinal rules of our clan. He was not indulging my father's narcissism. He was, in fact, almost aggressively preventing its expression altogether.

I had the strangest feeling then. Pity for my dad. It was inappropriate, I suppose. I felt incredibly sorry for my father. I felt protective of my dad and his ego. It hurt me to watch my father trying to get a word in edgewise, trying to continue to awe everyone with his tragic personal mythology. He was frustrated, of course, because this approach of his had worked on almost everyone he'd ever met, for decades. It was the one magic trick in the box that always got the crowd to its feet. I was even a little bit offended for him, and tried, I am sorry to say, to find a way to turn the conversation back to my dad's pity party.

The cowboy did not allow this to happen, however, turning instead to my mother and asking her questions about when she was a kid.

My mom, who had been sighing, slouching, and staring with a blank sort of sadness off into space for much of my father's soliloquy, perked up just a little and began to answer the cowboy's questions. But soon enough she was revealing her own little pitiful dance, by being overly self-deprecating and aggressively negative.

"Did you ride horses as a kid?" he asked her.

"Well, as much as they'd let me," answered my mother in typical negativity. "Horses don't seem to like me much, kind of like people. I've never been much good with living things. Just ask my daughter. Even she never liked me much."

That sort of thing.

Adhering once more to the unspoken rules of the family, I jumped right in to save my mom again, as I had always done. "Of course I like you! I love you! You're amazing!" I cried, as I'd always done. I had always tried to make her feel good, always tried to reflect back to her just as I did with my father, unconditional love and support.

"Oh, that's not true, Mom!" I said cheerfully. "You're really good with dogs, right? Tell him about your dog growing up, and how close you were."

But to my surprise, the cowboy summarily cut my mother off

too, as soon as she started the woe-is-me talk about how worthless she was and how lucky everyone else was.

"Alisa's been so lucky with her writing," my mom said at one point. "All my life I wanted to be a writer, and here Alisa up and does it and just keeps cranking these books out. It's like winning the lottery."

The cowboy didn't like this at all. "Funny how the people who don't have much discipline always think the ones who do are lucky," he said.

He interrupted her then and talked. And talked. He talked about all sorts of things—his work as a truck driver in the oil fields; his job training truck drivers; his days playing football; his favorite books; and me. He talked about me quite a bit. Bragged about me, talked about how much I'd touched his life and the ways in which I'd begun to change him. He just . . . talked.

To my horror, he talked over both of my parents until it was time to go.

On the drive back to my little house in Belén from Santa Fe, I told him that my mother had taken me aside as we were leaving to tell me that she was worried about me being involved with a man who so dominated conversation.

He chuckled.

"Do you understand why I did that?" he asked me.

I didn't. Not exactly. I knew it wasn't how he usually acted, but I was unsure as to why. So I waited for him to explain. This is when he told me that, being a quick read of people as always, he had realized that both of my parents were manipulating me to feed their insatiable and narcissistic egos. They had not been interested at all in hearing about my life, he said, and they hadn't been particularly interested in asking him about his. Both of them, he said, were alike in that they were self-absorbed and felt sorry for themselves and had trained me to do everything in my power to boost their egos constantly, at great cost to my own sense of self-worth.

"They both expect you to be their main emotional support," he said. "And you do it. I couldn't let it happen. You tap-dance like crazy, trying to get them to like you, but they don't see it. It wasn't fun to watch that happen to you."

I thought about this. I felt tears come.

"I told you, baby," he said. "I'm very protective of you. Your parents are nice enough people, I'm sure, but there's a whole routine you all do when you're together. Your dad brags about himself and expects everyone to find him fascinating but doesn't pay attention at all when you talk about what you're doing. Then your mom sits there getting mad that she's not being included in the conversation, but she never actually tried to join in. She waits to be invited, which I take to be a form of extreme narcissism, even though all of you seem to think she's got low self-esteem. I'd say it's just the opposite. And you're usually the one doing the inviting. You spend your whole time and all your energy serving their egocentric needs, running yourself ragged making sure everyone is getting what they need—except for you. Nobody at that table seemed to care one way or the other what you thought, baby. Nobody in that family listens to you unless you force them to, and I'd bet that's why you have led a life of always being in people's faces. You feel like you have to assert yourself or disappear."

I began to cry. Here I'd thought he was being mean to my parents, but in truth he was actually protecting me from the way they had often disregarded my feelings without realizing it, the way they had put themselves first. Most of all, he noticed the way my father dominated the dynamic when my mother was around, and it helped him to understand how I had come to seek solace in the doctrine of radical feminism. The combination of family and feminism as the antidote to those personal issues was the root of many of my problems, this song and dance with my parents, and I was horrified to realize it had continued *even until that day*. So much of the fighting I'd been doing with the world at large—and with the cowboy himself—was owing to the way my family interacted and the way I had turned to radical beliefs to solve the contradictions inside myself.

"I don't have a lot of patience for people who complain about how hard the world is on them," he said. "Especially if they don't do anything to fix it. I like your dad. I admire him. He's accomplished a lot and he's overcome a lot. And I like your mom. She's a complicated woman. But I love you, and I will always be protective of you."

There are moments in your life, shining moments of dawning awareness, that come very infrequently and stay with you forever. This was one of those moments for me. It was the first time in my life anyone had understood so quickly and with such compassion for me just exactly what it was that I was up against in my family. The cowboy had seen it, recognized it, and read it for what it was, and he'd handled the situation.

From that day forward, both of my parents seemed to treat me and my relationship with the cowboy with a newfound respect. It wasn't what I'd expected at all. I'd expected to be punished, shut out of their lives, as I'd always been if I had challenged their behavior, their disregard for me. But in the cowboy, it seemed, they realized in some way that they'd met a man they could not control, a man with healthy boundaries, boundaries that he widened enough to accommodate me, too.

SUBMITTING

The cowboy and I had many conversations over the summer and into the fall about the roles of men and women in relationships. We talked at length about the idea of submission, domination, leadership, following. I began to talk about the idea for this book that you are reading, and the cowboy balked. He was clear about expressing that he does not believe all women should submit to all men, and he didn't exactly want people thinking he was some kind of domineering a-hole. He was also clear in saying that he doesn't think I should submit to him all the time.

"Different people have different strengths," he said. "Whatever that person's strength, that's where the leadership comes in."

He and I agreed that in most relationships, the roles of leader and follower would be interchangeable, depending on the situation. If we went to a horse sale at the Roswell Horse Barn, for example, he'd be the leader because I had no idea what the hell was going on there. If we went to a meeting with a famous screenwriter in Hollywood, about adapting my first novel for a feature film, as we did, I would be the leader. In both cases, the other member of the partnership would be there to support the leader.

None of this meant, however, that a couple needed to keep a running tally of who was doing more leading or more following. It did not have to be equal, or fifty-fifty. It had to be whatever configuration made sense for that particular couple.

Interestingly, as I became more excited about the idea of taking a traditional female role in relation to the cowboy, he became more wary of it. He was not the one telling me to submit, after all. It was I, wanting to submit. He was the one out of the two of us who, when I began to talk about the idea for writing this memoir, cautioned me against counseling women to go against their own best interests.

"Until we as a culture can teach men to be real men, there's no use in any woman submitting to most of the sorry-ass men out there," he said. "You can't advocate women taking a more traditional role if men aren't doing what they need to be doing."

And what was it, you ask, that men should be doing? They should be, we agreed, protecting women—and never abusing them. There was absolutely no time when it was appropriate for any woman to submit to a man who abused her, be it physically, verbally, emotionally, sexually, or otherwise.

"A woman should only submit to a man who is worthy of her," the cowboy said.

Amen.

I have no doubt, as I sit here to write this, that I will be on the receiving end of a lot of grief once this book comes out. I have no doubt that I will be seen as the enemy by many in the women's movement. I will be seen as espousing something that many people fear will set women back a couple hundred years. I also know enough by now, having been a newspaper reporter for a decade and a novelist for that same amount of time, to understand that some people will want to fight, no matter what you say to them. I used to be one of those people. I know that there are some people for whom I will always be the bad guy, no matter how I explain myself.

Nonetheless, I do feel a need to explain myself here.

I'm aware that the word *submit* is charged with emotion, both negative and positive. I am a writer. I understand the power of words.

I have intentionally chosen this word for its multitude of meanings, all of them relevant to my relationship with the cowboy and to the changes he's brought to my life.

As a transitive verb, *submit* means to give something over for consideration and analysis—as in "I submit this book to my editor." In finding real love, I've had to submit my spirit, my behaviors, my *self*, to the cowboy; he, one of the strongest, smartest, most compassionate people I've ever known, has helped me to grow as a result.

As a transitive verb, *submit* can also mean to offer an opinion, as in "I submit to the judge that the evidence is clear." In loving the cowboy, I've learned to submit my opinion (in other words, disagree) in a healthy way, for the first time in my life.

As a transitive verb, the word *submit* also means to yield to an authority; *yield*, not obey. I've had to learn to do *that* too, especially on the ranch, where I know nothing and where my controlling nature could be fatal, as it nearly was the time I asked the cowboy to spare the life of a bull that later nearly killed him; as a formerly domineering woman, letting someone else be in charge was hard. Is hard. Continues to be hard. But so valuable. It took meeting a man as strong as me to teach me the value of placing your trust in another person.

At any rate, sometime in early November, I had lunch with my father. I told him about how well Alexander was doing and about the changes I'd made in my own professional life, thanks to the guidance and leadership of the cowboy. I told him that I was thinking of writing a memoir and that it might challenge many of the ideas he and my mother had raised me with. I hoped that wouldn't hurt him, I said, but I had been sabotaging myself in my personal and professional life for decades now, and it was time, I told him, for a new approach to womanhood and to my position in the world.

My father listened, still skeptical, I thought. But when I got home, he surprised me by calling to tell me that he'd been researching the idea of femininity and masculinity "vis-à-vis the Cuban Revolution" and that he'd been pleased to find that many of the top women in the movement . . . agreed with me. Including Vilma Espín, whom he quoted as saying that American feminism would not be adopted in Cuba because it was so fundamentally flawed and unnatural. For my father, a Marxist scholar of the Cuban Revolution, this was tantamount to a tacit approval of my relationship with the cowboy.

I was shocked.

Around that same time, I began to notice a lot of people responding differently to me. This was because I was finally putting up proper boundaries with the world, and within myself.

In social media, where I'd once been completely unfiltered, airing my dirtiest of laundry, making extremely stupid and controversial statements, I'd reined myself in and was more thoughtful. I no longer thought it was okay to post anything and everything. I was smarter. As a result, my fans began to return—ones I'd scared off. Several of them commented openly to me about how I seemed happier, more balanced. My book sales began to slowly creep up again.

Among my friends, every single one of them noted how much happier I seemed. They assumed it was just love. When I told them that it was also me embracing a traditional woman's role in many aspects of my relationship, they seemed skeptical at first but eventually came to accept me. Interestingly, many of my friends, empowered by my own transformation, began to confess to me that they, too, shared some of my misgivings about the direction romantic relationships had taken in the wake of the 1970s. They'd never heard it articulated before, they said, but now that I laid it out there, what I said made sense to them.

I talked to them about one of the most liberating and fundamental tenets of difference feminism, which is that women's entire psychology and strength are different from men's because we experience the world through our female bodies. If reproduction is the driving force in life, then women experience their own essence in a very different way than men do. Strength and power for women derive not from the male model of aggression and taking, which is symbolic of the male role in reproduction, but rather from the female role, which is to submit, to give, to open up, to allow inside. Women's strength lies in those very actions that radical feminism taught us were weakness, because radical feminism was incapable of moving beyond the confines of the same patriarchal paradigm they railed against. In difference feminism, women's strength is repeated, like fractals, at every level of their being, our greater capacity for empathy, for instance, being just another manifestation of the physical act of allowing a man to enter us. Submission, intelligent submission, was our power. Aggression, force, entering another—that was the strength of men.

In my professional life, part of submitting was that I went back through all the mistakes I'd made by being a ball-breaking bitch, and all the people I'd hurt when I had acted out in emotionally un-stable ways, and I apologized to them. For what, you ask? For doing things like taking to social media to do battle with a business part-ner, humiliating her instead of coming to her calmly and compas-sionately with my concerns one-on-one. There were endless examples of times I'd confronted authority in a destructive and com-bative way that was not necessary. Emails that were cruel and nasty. Fights and more fights. I came clean with them all, and I was deeply sincere in telling them I was sorry. They all, to a person, reacted gracefully, kindly, and supportively. I could not have done any of this if I hadn't met the cowboy and learned, through his incredible loving strength, to let go of the need to control everyone, to fight all the time. The results went far beyond just atoning for my sins. My new attitude drew to me a group of incredibly good, supportive, and wonderful agents, managers, and others, the kind of top-notch peo-ple who might in the past have been far too wise to work with some-one as crazy as I had been.

Submitting, it turned out, wasn't just for romance. It applied in friendships. It applied in the workplace. It made you a better listener, a better communicator, a better . . . woman.

I began to keep a blog (www.learningtosubmit.com) where I chronicled my adventures in teaching myself traditional womanly arts such as cooking, knitting, sewing. A whole new group of readers found me there, folks in the agricultural community, the conserva-tive community, women who like strong men. The support and love I found there was unlike anything I'd encountered before. It made me think of the cowboy's constant refrain: "I give what I get, dear."

So did everyone, it seemed.

In learning to submit, I learned not just to trust, but also to love, in a healthy way, for the first time in my life. And the world, taking note, sent love back to me.

Finally, my family—my once radical hippie academic family, my parents, who'd both held prejudices about conservatives for their own reasons—noticed, too. Thanksgiving came, and I invited everyone to my house for dinner. The cowboy, my cousin Mark, my mom, and my dad. My son was also with me that year for the holiday.

At dinner, my father (unsurprisingly) sat at the head of the table, and the cowboy sat directly to his left. My son sat to my father's right. I watched as my father watched the cowboy interacting with my son. My father's eyes said it all. He was impressed with the cowboy's firm yet compassionate way with my son. He was impressed with the way my son seemed to want to please the cowboy and did his best around him. I could see in my father's eyes that he was as amazed to see my son acting like a "normal" kid as I had been the first time the cowboy made my child tie his own shoes.

My mother watched, too. She was not as impressed by the interaction between the cowboy and my son at the dinner table, however, as she seemed to be by the way the cowboy got up to clear the table, and how the cowboy and my son did the dishes, at the cowboy's command. My own father sat at the table without offering to help clean up. I think that until then she had assumed that the cowboy's conservatism or traditionalism would automatically mean a disregard for housework or a notion that women should always do the cleaning.

As my son and the cowboy interacted, and the cowboy brought out the best in my child, I saw my father's face soften. After the dishes were done, the cowboy went to sit on the sofa in my living room, and I saw my father, the avowed Marxist, come to sit next to him. I busied myself cleaning the table off nearby but eavesdropped anyway.

My father placed his hand on the cowboy's shoulder and said his name in a dramatic way.

"I know we didn't get off to the best start," he said to my boyfriend. "And I might have underestimated you and even been wrong about you. But I want to tell you, that after seeing you here with my daughter and my grandson tonight, and after seeing the changes in their lives since you came into them—I just wanted to tell you that I do believe you are the best thing that has ever happened to my daughter or my grandson, in a very long time."

I smiled to myself, because what my father had just said was true. I also understood, quite clearly, that he had come around to liking the cowboy not because I got in there and tried to control the situation and convince him, but rather because I just let the cowboy be the cowboy, and my father came to see him on his own.

It was then that I understood how profoundly my life had been changed, for knowing this one intriguing, difficult, demanding, and extremely protective and loving man. I knew then that even if this relationship of ours didn't last forever, and even if I didn't ride off into the sunset with this man as his wife someday, and I had no illusions about that, really, the cowboy's impact on my family would last forever. First and foremost, my son would always know, now, that he was capable of more. Second, everyone in this family would know that there was nothing at all wrong with this child we had all made excuses for, for so long, and we'd expect more of him, too. Third, I would never again be out of control with my public persona or emotions, now that I had a handle on what had plagued me, and, hopefully, would never self-destruct professionally again as I had done before on more than one occasion. Fourth, I understood now, and truly believed, the cowboy's notion that "people will treat you just about as well as you let them."

But most of all, I understood very well in that moment that I would always be a better person for having known the cowboy, this enigmatic traditional rural man I once thought had nothing to offer me but who, to my great surprise, gave me a new way of living. I would always be grateful for having loved him, for him having loved me, and for him having helped me learn, after so many years of needless, exhausting battle with the world, society, and my own sex, to let go, to relax, to be happy . . . to submit, or trust, as a woman.

ABOUT THE AUTHOR

Alisa Valdes is a *New York Times* and *USA Today* bestselling author of commercial women's fiction and young adult novels including *The Dirty Girls Social Club*. She has a master's in journalism from Columbia University, is a Pulitzer-nominated, award-winning former staff writer for the *The Boston Globe* and the *Los Angeles Times*, was named the top essayist in the nation by SUNMAG, and is an Emmy-winning former TV reporter for WHDH-TV. Alisa has written and sold pilot scripts to Nickelodeon, NBC, and Lifetime television as well as a forthcoming feature film. A single mom, Alisa lives in New Mexico, dividing her time between her house in the city and her boyfriend's cattle ranch in the country.